FRAGMENTS of HAWAIIAN HISTORY

As recorded by

JOHN PAPA Ii

Translated by

MARY KAWENA PUKUI

EDITED BY DOROTHY B. BARRÈRE

PUBLISHED BY THE BISHOP MUSEUM PRESS, 1959

Bishop Museum Press
1525 Bernice Street
Honolulu, Hawai'i 96817

© 1959 by Bernice Pauahi Bishop Museum
Second printing 1963
Third printing 1973
Revised edition 1983 as Special Publication 70
Second revised edition 1993
Sixth printing 1995
*Originally published as a miscellaneous publication of
B.P. Bishop Museum*

*All rights reserved
No part of this book may be used or reproduced without
written permission from the publisher
Printed in the United States of America*

ISBN 0-910240-31-0

In memory
of Irene
Kahalelaukoa Ii

John Papa Ii

PREFACE

John Papa Ii, one of the leading citizens of the Hawaiian kingdom during the nineteenth century, was born at Waipio, Oahu, on August 3, 1800. His mother was Wanaoa and his father, Malamaekeeke. At the age of ten John was brought to Honolulu and placed under the supervision of his uncle, Papa, who was a *kahu,* or attendant, of Kamehameha. John Ii was placed by Papa in the household of Liholiho.

Upon the arrival of the missionaries in Hawaii in 1820, John Ii, among others, was sent by Liholiho, by then Kamehameha II, to study under the Reverend Hiram Bingham. As time passed, John Ii divided his time between the ruling Kamehamehas and the missionaries, particularly Reverend Bingham. John soon became an assistant to Bingham and a teacher at the latter's school. King Kamehameha II desired that John Ii spend much time with the missionaries so that the king could observe the effects of the new Christian teachings.

By 1841, John Ii was general superintendent of Oahu schools and was an influential member of the court of Kamehameha III. In 1842, with Dr. G. P. Judd and Timothy Haalilio, John Ii was appointed by the king to be a member of the new Treasury Board. This Board was empowered to set up a system of regular and systematic account keeping, something which had not been attempted before.

In 1845, as a member of the Privy Council, he was appointed with four other men to the Board of Land Commissioners. In 1852, as a member of the House of Nobles, he was selected to represent that body in drafting the Constitution of 1852. Judge William Lee represented the House of Representatives and Dr. G. P. Judd represented the king. John Ii's service in the House of Nobles was from 1841 to 1854 and from 1858 to 1868. He served as a member of the House of Representatives during the session of 1855.

In addition to his duties in the two legislative houses of the kingdom and his service on various governmental commissions, John Ii served on the bench. His first term as an associate justice of the Supreme Court of Hawaii extended from 1846 to 1852. He was reappointed for a second term and served from 1852 until he resigned in 1864.

The last years of John Ii's life were spent in Ewa, Oahu, and in the service of the Christian ministry. At nearly seventy years of age, after a life devoted to the furtherance and development of Christianity in Hawaii and the development of a democratic form of government, John Ii died in May 1870.

These, then, are the bare facts of John Ii's life. Politically, his lifetime spanned many years of the Kamehameha Dynasty, beginning with the autocratic rule of Kamehameha I, extending through the transition period of rule by king and chiefs, and continuing into the rule by constitutional monarchy. John Ii, born non-Christian, saw the kingdom turn from the ancient kapu system and the worship of many pagan gods to Christianity, brought to the islands by the early missionaries. With these many profound political and religious changes taking place, we must turn to John Ii's contemporaries to find the true worth of the man.

His fellow teachers in the early missionary schools give many glimpses of his character. The Reverend H. H. Parker says, "My earliest impressions of John Ii date back to the midsummer of 1846 or 1847, when I met him at the country residence of Kamehameha III in Nuuanu Valley, the occasion being La Hoihoiea, or Restoration Day. In a suit of dark broadcloth he stood in an open square or field, a brilliant yellow feather cape over his shoulders, and in his hand a beautifully polished spear. Alone, erect, nearly six feet in height, full chested and muscular, he presented a splendid figure. Opposite him on the mauka or inland side stood a group of expert spearmen wearing yellow feather tippets and armed with spears tipped with a kind of soft, bushy material. At a signal the weapons began to fly at the human target. Ii at first parried with his single lance but presently, as the shots became faster, seized a passing spear aimed at him and parried with both weapons until the play ended amid the prolonged cheers of a great crowd of witnesses. It was years afterward that I came to know and love the man. He was clean and unselfish, and on questions involving moral issues, the community always knew where to find him. He was possessed of ample means as things counted in his day and many looked to him for help which they were sure to get in one way or another. He lived in an old fashioned cottage where the Judiciary building now stands. His home was named 'Mililani,' which means exalted or lifted heavenward. Hospitality was a marked feature of his character."

The Reverend Richard Armstrong had this to say about John Ii, "John Ii, a man of high intelligence, sterling integrity and great moral worth."

Reminiscences of Judge John Ii as printed in the Star-Bulletin Centenary Issue of 1920 contains the following, "No finer example of the refining and uplifting influence of Christian civilization is to be found in the annals of missionary endeavor in Hawaii than in the life of John Ii, teacher, preacher and judge, who, from the time of his conversion as a young man to his death [at] nearly 70 years of age devoted himself to the betterment of his people."

Mary A. Richards in her "Chiefs' Childrens' School" says, "Through the perspective of a century, John Ii stands as one of the most remarkable Hawaiians of his time." John Ii and his wife Sarai were the always dependable advisers in the conduct of this school, directed by Amos Starr and Juliette Montague Cooke. In all the years Mr. and Mrs. Cooke were associated with John Ii their admiration for him never changed.

ZADOC W. BROWN

FOREWORD

Hawaii was left with a unique and invaluable record when John Ii wrote of his childhood and youth while the ancient regime was still in force, telling of the events he witnessed during the early years of the great transition which followed the crumbling of the ancient order.

Owing to the hereditary position of his family, Ii was trained from earliest childhood for a life of service in the court of the high chiefs, with the understanding that he would enter the court to serve the chief of his choice. From the age of ten, Ii served as Liholiho's companion and personal attendant, and was close to Liholiho during the period when the heir was instructed in the conduct of government and in ancient religious rites. After Liholiho left on his fatal visit to England, thirteen years later, Ii continued to serve the rulers of Hawaii.

He was in constant contact with the political, religious, and social concerns of the court until he retired from the service to his chiefs in 1864, just six years before his death. Thus he was able to write authoritatively on matters of the greatest concern to the Hawaiians of those days, and his writings offer an abundance of details about events and customs which have been tantalizingly obscure heretofore. His writings and those of David Malo and Kelou Kamakau —both of whom also lived under the kapu system—provide a sound basis for reconstructing a picture of early Hawaiian life. Samuel M. Kamakau and other, occasional, contributors who lived within memory of the original Hawaiian life also supply considerable information. However, not all of the source materials have been translated, and only a portion of them has been published. Of these Hawaiian writers, Ii alone presents personal experiences, thereby revealing the Hawaiian pattern of culture as it actually functioned.

Ii was prompted to write about happenings in his time when he was asked to write a biography of Victoria Kamamalu, whose childhood guardian he was, for *Kuokoa*, following her death in 1866. He wrote, "These things remind me of that loved one." Upon the death of Kamamalu's father, Mathew Kekuanaoa, in 1868, John Ii began another series of articles for *Kuokoa* with "An expression of affection for Kaimihaku," or Kekuanaoa. This series, which started on December 5, 1868, ran until Ii's own death in 1870. He was stimulated by Samuel M. Kamakau's newspaper articles about the history of the times. He obviously followed Kamakau's accounts and his own writings amplify some incidents related by Kamakau. This explains the brevity of some portions of Ii's "historical incidents." The corrections he made in the retelling of several incidents were based on first-hand knowledge, whereas Kamakau, fifteen years his junior, lacked such personal knowledge.

Although John Ii adopted foreign ways and became a staunch Christian, he retained a profound love and respect for the culture of his ancestors. The discipline and training of ancient life, with its emphasis on devotion to the chiefs and one's family, is the keynote of the "Fragments of Hawaiian History."

Many years ago Mary Kawena Pukui foresightedly made a literal translation of all of Ii's articles which appeared in the Hawaiian newspaper *Kuokoa* from 1866 to 1870. For the present work, Dorothy B. Barrère went over this translation with Mrs. Pukui, following the original Hawaiian text to clear up obscure points and to clearly interpret Ii's own renditions. The work was originally conceived to provide material for anthropological study by specialists. Much of the original Hawaiian text, important for terminology and description, was incorporated, and all glottal closures were shown in quotations and in proper and geographic names to preserve their correct pronunciations. Mrs. Barrère documented this material by painstaking research covering a span of three years for genealogical and historical material in order to supplement Ii's work with the correct English terminology for relationships and to supply dates which he did not include or in which he was in error. A manuscript in this form is on file in Bishop Museum for the use of students. In this form it can aid in interpretation of Hawaiian writings of the early period, and is a model for future literal translations.

For the published account Mrs. Barrère selected the material for inclusion, and searched out lesser known drawings and photographs to illustrate the text. Original sketches by Dampier, Choris, Webber, and Arago are shown, as are copies of Webber's sketches. Hitherto unpublished illustrations include the work of Webber, D. Howard Hitchcock, and A. Francis Judd. The maps and heiaus were drawn by Paul Rockwood and Gerald Ober, Bishop Museum artists.

Eloise Christian, Museum editor, advised Mrs. Barrère in the final draft for publication, and her experience and knowledge have resulted in an organized and polished presentation of Ii's observations and experiences rearranged for the modern reader but retaining Ii's own Hawaiian mannerisms of style and his interpretations of the events of Hawaiian history which he recorded. Joseph Feher, Artist-Historian on the Museum staff, designed the format, Gerald Ober designed the dust jacket.

For making accessible in printed form these records of John Ii, Bishop Museum is indebted for financial support to his grandson Francis Ii Brown and to his three great-grandsons, George Ii Brown, Kenneth F. Brown, and Zadoc W. Brown, and to their mother Mrs. Julia W. Brown.

KENNETH P. EMORY

CONTENTS

CHAPTER

I	Kamehameha	3
II	The Luluka family	17
III	Kapu loulu rites and medical practices	33
IV	Early 1800's in Honolulu	49
V	Activities in court circles	63
VI	Foreign influences	79
VII	Places and persons on Oahu	89
VIII	Kamehameha's return to Hawaii	103
IX	Kamehameha's court at Kamakahonu	117
X	Life in Kona	127
XI	Fragments of history, 1819-1832	141
XII	Kamamalu and Kekuanaoa	161
Glossary		179
Index		185

CHAPTER I

KAMEHAMEHA

Kamehameha was born at Kapakai, in Kokoiki, Kohala, Hawaii, and the chief Naeole carried the infant away as soon as he was delivered from his mother. Later, Alapai, ruler of Hawaii and great uncle of Kamehameha, and his wife Keaka took charge of him. Some years later Alapai and his chiefs went to Waiolama in Hilo, where Keoua Kupuapaikalani, the father of Kamehameha, was taken sick and died. Before Keoua died he sent for Kalaniopuu, his older half brother and the chief of Kau, to come and see him. Keoua told Kalaniopuu that he would prosper through Kamehameha's great strength and asked him to take care of the youth, who would have no other father to care for him. Keoua warned Kalaniopuu, saying, "Take heed, for Alapai has no regard for you or for me, whom he has reared." After this conversation, Keoua allowed his brother to go, and Kalaniopuu left that night for Puaaloa.

As Kalaniopuu neared Kalanakamaa, he heard the death wails for Keoua and hastened on toward Kalepolepo, where he had left his warriors. There they were attacked by Alapai's men, who had followed Kalaniopuu from Hilo. First the warriors from the lowland gained, then those from the upland, until night fell and the battle was postponed until the next day. Kalaniopuu continued his journey and at midnight reached Puaaloa, where he arranged for the coming battle. The next day all went as he had planned. His forward armies led the enemy into the forest of Paieie, where there was only a narrow trail, branchy on either side and full of undergrowth. There his men in ambush rose up against the enemy warriors, and his rear armies closed in behind them. When Alapai's men realized that they were surrounded, they fell in ignominious death.

When news reached Alapai that his warriors had been destroyed, he sent another company of warriors to meet Kalaniopuu at Mokaulele on the outer road, which was an ancient road, known from the time of remote antiquity. Again, Alapai's men were destroyed and Kalaniopuu was the victor. He returned then to Kau, the land of his birth.

Here let us recall what Keoua had predicted before his death.

After the purification ceremony for the dead Keoua, Alapai, now in ill health, returned to Kawaihae, for he recalled the warm sands of this land where he had lived and loved, the "land of the whispering sea." His son Keaweopala and the other chiefs were there with him because of his illness, as were his wife Keaka and her *kaikunane* cousin Luluka, who took care of Kamehameha. So also was Kekuiapoiwa II, Kamehameha's mother.

Before the death of Alapai, he expressed his will to his son Keaweopala, saying, "My son, you once told me that I would see your bravery. I was anxious to see proof of it; but instead, I saw your cowardice and flight in the war of the commoners in Kohala, hence the land is not for us. It goes to Kamehameha, the child of the chiefs, for they went to all the wars with the sons of my sister Kekuiapoiwa. This youth shall have the land, but take heed lest his uncle Kalaniopuu take him away, and you have the care of him no more." Then Alapai died.

Kalaniopuu, hearing of the death of Alapai, went to Waiea, South Kona. When news of his arrival reached Kawaihae, Keaweopala marched with a procession to Kona and remained at Kauluwai in upper Kealakekua, where he encamped with his multitude in warlike display. Kalaniopuu heard of this and moved on to either Honaunau or Keei. The ensuing battle, fought at Kepulu in the upland of Kahauloa at Napoopoo, was won by Keaweopala. All of the victims of the battle were borne up to Kauluwai, where Keaweopala was staying with the young Kamehameha. When all of the dead had been transported, Keaweopala sacrificed the bodies. He did not leave this work to Kamehameha, the person to whom the kingdom properly belonged, hence Kamehameha's mother commanded Kamehameha to go to Kalaniopuu and give him the right to offer human sacrifices. Kalaniopuu had not had the right to do this before. This privilege came through Keakealaniwahine.

After the sun had set, Kamehameha followed his mother's command, keeping in mind all she had told him. He went into the presence of Kalaniopuu, who sat him upon his lap and wailed over him. When Kalaniopuu had finished, he asked, "What purpose brings my lord (*kuʻu haku*) down here at night?"

Kamehameha replied, "I have brought this message to you: 'Above and below, inland and sea; that is my purpose in coming here,' "—figuratively saying

A canoe such as Kamehameha sailed in the time of Kalaniopuu. Original sketch by John Webber in Hocken Library, University of Otago.

that the kingdom was to be Kalaniopuu's and, with it, the privilege of offering human sacrifice.

Kalaniopuu asked, "Has your mother heard of this?" After Kamehameha replied that she had, Kalaniopuu turned and said to all of the chiefs, "This is a valuable guest."

"What is his value?" asked the chiefs.

"He is telling me to beat the drum and offer the human sacrifice."

"Then he is valuable indeed," replied the chiefs.

Thus we see how Kamehameha left (*waiho ana*) the kingdom he had received from Alapai, who favored him, to his uncle Kalaniopuu. Kalaniopuu was the elder brother of Kamehameha's father, Keoua, through their mother Kamakaimoku. There were many things to show that Kamehameha was a ruling chief, though he was not yet ready to rule. He was too young, being about 19 or 20 years old, and the custom then was just as it is now. But, strange to say, he was regarded as a ruler from the time of his birth.

A few days after Kamehameha placed the kingdom in his uncle's charge, the opposing sides again met in combat. After a short battle, Keaweopala fell into the hands of Kalaniopuu's army, and this brought peace to the kingdom. Kalaniopuu then returned to Kau, but he left Kamehameha with his mother, Kekuiapoiwa II, and his guardians, Keaka and Luluka, at Puu in Holualoa, a place inhabited in Alapai's time and before. It was in the Holualoa lands of Kona that the chiefs dwelt in olden times, from the time of Keakamahana, the great kapu chiefess of Hawaii, and earlier. Where the large stone wall is located above Keolonahihi was Keakealaniwahine's dwelling place, for her parents, Keakamahana and Iwikauikaua, resided there. These were lands occupied by the chiefs because the surfing there was good, and the food abundant in ancient times. There Kamehameha learned to surf and to glide with a canoe over the waves, guarded by the *kaikunane* of Keaka, in accordance with her commands. Because he was well trained, Kamehameha excelled in these arts and in sailing canoes.

When Kalaniopuu next arrived from Kau, it was to take Kamehameha away with him, perhaps because Kamehameha's mother had died. This was in accordance with Keoua's request before his death. When they left, they were accompanied by Kalaimamahu, son of Keoua and Kamakaeheikuli and half brother of Kamehameha. Upon their arrival in Kau, Kalaniopuu placed Kamehameha with his wife, the chiefess Kaneikapolei, who put Kamehameha in the hands of her *kaikunane* relatives, Inaina *ma*. He was there for some time and was familiar with the life of the court by the time he became associated with his older cousin, Kiwalao, the son of Kalaniopuu and Kalola.

It was the custom of the chiefs to have sports such as racing, *maika* throwing, diving feet first, hiding the *noʻa*, boxing, surfing, sledding, sham fighting, and many others. These increased when the kingdom was at peace, as it was when Kalaniopuu first became king.

It was customary to hold frequent sham battles at the court to train the men in the art of war. The contestants, armed with spears of hau wood, were divided into two groups. As the men were divided, so were the chiefs. Kiwalao headed one side and Kamehameha the other. Kamehameha's side was always victorious, for he was an expert in dodging spears, and the other side became much annoyed.

Kamehameha ate sparingly at times, so he was healthy, and his body properly developed. Because his physique was perfect and his features well formed and admirable, the women took a great fancy to him, as they did also to his younger brother Kalaimamahu. They were the handsomest men of those days, and the chiefesses gave them many gifts. Thus beautiful physiques and handsome features earned them a livelihood. This led to trouble with their uncle Kalaniopuu, for they were taken by Kaneikapolei, wife of Kalaniopuu. This happened twice, the first time with Kalaimamahu and the second time with Kamehameha. It was probably in this way that Kaoleioku was conceived. Their uncle was "peeved" and would not allow his nephews to see his face. Keaweamauhili, who stepped in as mediator, told his half brother Kalaniopuu to stop resenting his nephews because everyone knew that a woman was like an easily opened calabash, or a container with a removable lid. Upon these words, Kalaniopuu's anger ceased, and he sent for his nephews to come and see him.

After Kamehameha and Kalaimamahu went to Kau to be with Kalaniopuu, Keaka, Kamehameha's *kahu hanai*, sent her nephew Kamahauluae there. He was the son of her *kaikunane*, Luluka, and Keaka a Mulehu of Maui. It was because Keaka and Luluka were filled with affection that tore at their hearts for these royal wards of theirs that they sent the boy Kamahauluae to Kamehameha with some of Kamehameha's personal belongings (*na ukana pili i ke kino*). The boy was told to stay with his cousin, Ululani, the wife of Keawe a Heulu, who resided with Kalaniopuu in Kau. Keaka instructed the boy in what he must do when he reached there and in the proper signs to give before landing on his return so that they would know whether or not Kamehameha was well.

When Kamahauluae reached Kau, he located the place where he had been told to land and took the canoe ashore there, where a house was ready for him and his companions. That day he raised his banner near the place for surfing, a pastime much enjoyed at that time. He knew that his beloved chief, Kamehameha, was very fond of surfing and that this would probably be a good way to have the chief recognize him immediately. He was right. When Kamehameha arrived at the surfing place, he recognized the banner and went to the boy at once. In greeting him (*a honi ana i ka ihu*) Kamehameha said, "So you have come to land?"

"Yes," replied Kamahauluae.

"When did you leave home?"

"Only yesterday."

"How are Kalopelekai and her companion (Keaka and Luluka)?"

7

"They are well and send their regards to you."

"Are you to return?"

"Your guardians said that I am to go home after I have learned how you are faring."

"Yes, that is well. I am going surfing now and shall return. Have you a malo of mine?"

"Yes, I came prepared with such personal articles of yours."

When Kamehameha had finished surfing he returned to find his container of bathing water and a fresh malo ready. Kamehameha remained there day after day, and the two met daily. Because Kamehameha did not return home for many days, his attendants were puzzled and told Kaneikapolei about it. She, in turn, told Kalaniopuu, who asked about Kamehameha's habits and the place at which he was staying. Then he sent for Keawe a Heulu, and while they conversed Keawe a Heulu told him of Kamahauluae, the cousin of his wife Ululani. So Kalaniopuu understood, and he left his nephew with Keawe a Heulu. Thus did the affection and respect between them remain, down to Keohokalole, the mother of Kalakaua.

Kamahauluae was very anxious to see his two granduncles who lived up at Keaa, and he told his chief of this desire. He went there and remained with them for three or four days, listening to what they had to say. Someone had come to them with a gift offering and some *maunu* "bait" to bring about Kamehameha's death by sorcery. Each time they had tried to light a fire with their rubbing sticks, it had refused to burn, for just as the fire would be about to light, an owl some distance away would flap its wings and put it out.

Kamahauluae's granduncles said, "This happened repeatedly, until we stopped trying. We were puzzled over it and sought to find out, by divination, the will of the gods. We saw a vision of your chief and knew then that the gods did not approve of our work, hence we asked for some hair of the man who had brought the 'bait,' and we still have it here. We did not hear of your arrival. We are of the opinion that many people are united in wishing evil to your chief. When you go back, ask him if he has a boil. He is being safeguarded from sorcery, and those who sought to bring about his death are going to perish in the future." It is believed that this was why Inaina *ma* died in the battle against Kahekili at Kakanilua, Maui. Such indeed are the lies that are current today.

After a few days Kamahauluae returned to the lowland to tell the chief what he had heard from his granduncles. He found that the chief did have a boil. Their sorcery had been successful to this extent, but not powerful enough to kill him.

When he knew how his chief fared, Kamahauluae felt that he had reason to go home. He told the chief of his wish to leave and tell Kamehameha's former guardians all he had learned, and it seems that the chief was pleased to let him go. As they bade farewell, Kamehameha said,

'Ike aku ia Kalopelekai,   When Kalopelekai is seen,
Ku la o ka la'i eha i Kona.   The four-fold calm appears in Kona.

At these words of his beloved chief, Kamahauluae turned back to listen while he recited the praise of his *kahu wahine*, Keaka.

Upon his arrival in Kona, Kamahauluae allowed the canoe to rest near the landing, as Keaka had told him to do, to show that their beloved chief was well and that his own quest had been successful. Several other signs were given so that she might know these things before he landed.

He told his elders all he had done, and they were pleased with his report. He also told them how their beloved chief had recited the praise of "Kalopelekai in the sunlight," at which Keaka said, "Let the name chant be his." Thus it became a name chant for Kamehameha.

As a result of Kamahauluae's report, Keaka and Luluka sent all the children of their family who dwelt with them to join their ward Kamehameha. These children were Kamalo, Wawae, Papa, and Kamahauluae himself.

Some time after Kamahauluae's visit to Kau, Kiwalao, the son of Kalaniopuu, disagreed with his father over something and determined to leave him and go to Maui to join his mother Kalola and other *makua* relatives. Kamehameha accompanied him as far as Kohala and then said, "Let us go back to take care of our *makuakane*."

Kiwalao replied, "Go back yourself and take care of him, while I go to be with my *makua* on Maui."

It was said that the chief Kiwalao frequently sailed to Maui, and so it was that his back was tattooed like that of Kahekili, king of Maui and brother of Kiwalao's mother, Kalola.

After Kiwalao had gone to Maui, Kamehameha and his companions returned to Kau to care for Kalaniopuu, following him everywhere he went. Sometimes Kalaniopuu would ask Kamehameha to offer a prayer, but when it came time for the *'amama*, or concluding portion, he would join in, and they would say it together. A chiefess, who died in 1869, was named Amamalua by her parents to preserve the tale of the double *'amama*. Perhaps the giving of this name was to increase the number of Kamehameha's children [supporters] in the kingdom of Hawaii.

Here let us talk a little of Kekuhaupio, Kamehameha's companion during training for spear fighting. Kalaniopuu had sent for Kekuhaupio, who was living in South Kona, because he had heard of Kekuhaupio's prowess in sham battles. His fame had preceded him, and when he arrived, the chiefs took a great liking to him. It was known that Kamehameha was the chief he served and that the instructor who had trained them both in spear dodging was an expert. Kekuhaupio was a warrior from head to foot and was excelled only by Kamehameha. When they made the *'ailolo* offering at the end of their training, Kekuhaupio's pig was spoiled when it was cooked, whereas Kamehameha's was perfect. Thus did their instructor predict over Kekuhaupio's pig: "You shall be a great warrior in all the battles you fight, but when your chief Kamehameha becomes the ruler you will meet your death in a sham battle. Your chief shall remain a warrior until he falls asleep on the mat. These are the omens that I see in your offerings."

This prophecy came true, for Kekuhaupio was eventually struck by a spear of kukui wood and died, hence the name of the father of H. K. Kapakuhaili (Kalama, wife of Kamehameha III), Naihekukui, or kukui spears.

When Kalaniopuu sailed to Maui to war against Kahekili two persons gained fame, Kamehameha and Kekuhaupio. In a battle at Kalaeokailio—when the allied armies of Maui, Oahu, and Kauai gathered and attacked—the army of Kalaniopuu was quickly routed. It was a bitter defeat, and the warriors of Hawaii, including Kamehameha, fled to where their canoes were floating. When the chiefs of Hawaii boarded the canoes, Kekuhaupio was still ashore, dodging the many spears thrown at him by the warriors of Maui, Oahu, and Kauai. Hearing a harsh voice say, "Your attendant is dead," Kamehameha leaped ashore at once, unobserved by his uncle Kalaniopuu. When Kamehameha arrived at the battlefield, he saw that Kekuhaupio was not dead, but was resting, while two of his companions dodged the many spears thrown at them. The spears were then concentrated upon Kamehameha, and they piled up behind him as he advanced, dodging them all.

When Kalaniopuu missed Kamehameha and asked for him, he was told that he had gone to the battle site and was fighting there, that the tide of battle had turned, and that he fought beside his attendant, Kekuhaupio. Because of this report, the order was given for the canoes to go ashore again. The battle lasted until night, when the warriors of both sides went to sleep, with a field of sugar cane between them. Thus ended the fighting for the time being.

At a later battle, fought at Kakanilua, Kekuhaupio did not participate. Kahekili's company of "bristling dogs" pressed hard against Kalaniopuu's forces until they became exhausted, having no reinforcements. Their dead lay in heaps, and only one warrior at Honuanele escaped. He reported to Kalaniopuu that "Our warriors are all dead, only I remain."

When Kekuhaupio heard of the defeat, he prepared for battle. He began at Kamaalaea, on the ridge of Puuhele, for there were tall *'ilima* bushes along a very narrow trail and he felt that it would be a good spot from which to fight. Hence the name given to him by the women, who spoke jokingly: "Hewahewa koa o ka moku 'ilima (The deranged warrior of the *'ilima* thickets)." There he fought against the warriors of Maui. He proved himself a fearless fighter as the spears rose up before him. Because of the narrow trail the enemy could advance only one at a time. While he ate his meal the spears kept coming, so his steward did a clever thing: Kekuhaupio would take a mouthful of food and then hand the calabash back to his steward. When a spear passed him or the steward, he would take another mouthful and then another. After the noonday sun was high in the sky, Kahekili heard of the fight and sent Oulu, a man who was an expert in slinging stones. When the latter drew near enough to sling his stones, Kekuhaupio sent a plea to his god, saying, "O Lono, let the slingstone be yours." After the second stone he called "O Oulu, let me have that stone." Thus did the stones fail to find their mark. Oulu went back to tell Kahekili the following: "That is not a human being and I don't know what he is. Our stones missed their mark. The first stone passed and with the second one he cried, 'O Oulu, let the stone be mine.' It is uncanny."

Kalola, the mother of Kiwalao, was there with her brother Kahekili; and while they were conversing with Oulu a voice proclaiming the *kapu moe*, or prostrating kapu, was heard. "The chief Kiwalao must be approaching," said Kahekili. "Remove my head covering (a wig) quickly." Then Kahekili saw that Keawe a Heulu was in front with the kapu stick and that behind Kiwalao were Kahekili's younger cousins, Kamanawa and Kameeiamoku, one with a feather cape and kahili, and the other with the spittoon and mat, so he said to his sister, "Wait before you remove my wig, for it is a retainer who comes first. When our 'young one,' Kiwalao, comes up, that will be the proper time to remove it."

As Kiwalao advanced, all of the warriors prostrated themselves, putting an end to the fighting. Thus was the prostrating kapu observed among relatives.

Then Kiwalao met Kahekili, and an order was given to stop the fighting. This was agreed to by Kahekili, the uncle of the chief. A proclamation was sent back by Kiwalao, the chief of the prostrating kapu, to report the cessation of war. When this word was received by Kalaniopuu he went up to see his brother-in-law, Kahekili. Kalaniopuu's forces remained on Maui for some time and peace existed on both sides, with nothing to disturb it. Finally those of Hawaii became anxious to go home, and it is said that they asked permission to do so.

When all were ready to leave, the sands were covered with the canoes of the Hawaii warriors from Kahului to Paia. After a last farewell to the kamaaina of the land, Kalaniopuu boarded his canoe and left Kahekili *ma*. When Kalaniopuu and his "children" returned to Hawaii, they visited the land before going home to Kau.

Kalaniopuu greatly enjoyed the hula in his old age. When a gathering assembled for the hula and the spectators were waiting to see what kind of dance it would be, he would come forth and stand before the dancers to watch them. With his hands outstretched, he would say to the drummers back of the dancers, "More excitement! More excitement!" Those who did not recognize Kalaniopuu grumbled, saying, "The hula is enjoyable except for the interference of that old man."

At last Kalaniopuu was laid low with sickness and died at Waioahukini, in Kailikii, a place on the other side of Pakini in Kau, Hawaii. Then Kame-

A gathering for the hula, a drawing by Louis Choris. Reproduced from a lithograph in *"Voyage pittoresque autour du monde."*

hameha set aside the place where his uncle had died. It was said that Kalaniopuu left no commands. It was probably so.

Following the days of mourning for Kalaniopuu, the chiefs of Kau suggested a division of districts, giving three to Kamehameha and three to Kiwalao. Kamehameha was to have Hamakua, Kohala, and Kona, and Kiwalao was to have Kau, Puna, and Hilo. The chiefs of Kau asked Kamehameha for South Kona also, where they could go and enjoy tranquility. When Kamehameha agreed, it was decided to deposit Kalaniopuu's corpse at Hale o Keawe in Honaunau, South Kona.

Kamehameha was agreeable to everything that was said in Kau, feeling a deep respect for his older cousin Kiwalao. After everything was settled, Kamehameha departed for his own land at Halawa, Kohala. However, the chiefs of Kau changed their minds and wanted the remains of Kalaniopuu to go to Pa o Umi in Kailua, North Kona, so that more Kona lands would belong to them, and more calm places in which to live. This disturbed the chiefs of Kona, and so Kekuhaupio, who had been to Kau and had heard what was said, hastened to Kohala to bring Kamehameha to Keei before the arrival of the Kau chiefs in Kona. He left to hurry on his journey, for part of Keei belonged to him and to some of the other chiefs.

When the company from Kau reached Kapalilua in Kona with the corpse of Kalaniopuu, they heard that Kamehameha had arrived at Keei. That was probably the reason why the corpse was not taken to Kailua but to Honaunau, as they had originally agreed. If this is true, then it was the beginning of the error, and of the unworthy ideas, of that side.

After the Kau chiefs had been at Honaunau a while, Kamehameha and his canoe paddlers arrived in his single canoe, named *Noiku*. They landed back of Akahipapa, a lava flat extending into the sea. No sooner had his foot touched land than those on shore were ready to hurl spears of hau wood at him, a custom observed upon the landing of a high chief. This they did, and those on land watched with admiration asKamehameha thrust them aside. A person remained near the chief with a container of water for his bath; and after the spear throwers had finished and had seated themselves, Kamehameha bathed and donned a dry malo. He went up to see his cousin Kiwalao, and when they met food was made ready. Thus they met graciously. As Kamehameha went there to see Kiwalao, so did his cousin visit him at Keei, spending the night time and again. It was said that Kamehameha served his cousin as steward during these visits. As Kiwalao was in no hurry to return to Honaunau, his uncle, Keaweamauhili, came for him. He left at Keaweamauhili's insistence, which caused Kiwalao to remark to Kamehameha that his uncle seemed to be disturbed over their friendly association. "Because of this, trouble may brew between us," he said. It happened so.

The lands of the chiefs of Kau were divided within their own district, each being given a portion and each asking for what he wanted. For this reason, a skilled war leader whose name I have forgotten said to Keoua Kuahuula, son of Kalaniopuu and half brother of Kiwalao, "Perhaps you should go to the chief and ask that these lands be given us. Let Waiakea and Keaau be the container from whence our food is to come and Olaa the lid." Keoua did so, but the other Kau chiefs objected to this and spoke disparagingly to him. When Keoua returned, his advisor asked, "How was your venture?" When Keoua told him all that had been said, the man remarked seriously, "A break in a gourd container can be mended by patching, but a break in the land cannot be mended that way."

That night, overseers sent a proclamation to all the men of the chiefs to go to the upland of Honaunau for some taro. That same night the great warrior taught Keoua all the things that he was to do on the morrow on the sands of Hauiki in Mokuohai. When day came, all the men had gone to the upland, having started while it was still dark because of the long distance they had to travel to-and-fro. This gave Keoua and his companions a chance to do their work. After eating, they went to the beach to bathe or dive (*lele kawa*). They went along the shore diving until they reached Hauiki in Mokuohai. There coconut trees were hewn down, houses burned, and men killed. After this act of war, they turned about and went home. The work was then taken up by others, for the news had reached the chiefs of both sides. They prepared for war and the war canoes were made ready.

Kiwalao was the first to arrive on the battlefield, with the men who were to fight with him. Kamehameha was getting ready, and was preceded to the battlefield by Keeaumoku Papaiahiahi, his uncle. Kalaimamahu, Kamehameha's younger brother, was in charge on Kamehameha's side. They went to the place where they were to encamp, for the purpose of asking the will of the gods. While they were encamped there, a report came that Keeaumoku had been taken captive by his opponents and was to be stabbed. Kiwalao, who was standing close by, said, "Be careful of the *niho palaoa* on Keeaumoku's neck," and at these words Keeaumoku thought, "The chief has no regard for the life of a *hulu makua* (an older relative)." This news of Keeaumoku's peril caused Kamehameha to hasten to the battlefield. Kaahumanu, later the wife of Kamehameha, and daughter of Keeaumoku, was borne thither on the back of Pahia, a man who was an expert in stone throwing. When they drew near to Kiwalao, Pahia let Kaahumanu down and took some stones into his hand which he flung with such force that Kiwalao fell when they struck his temple. Kiwalao landed on Keeaumoku, who took him by the throat and slashed it with a *lei o mano,* or shark-tooth knife, killing him.

Though Kamehameha gained the victory in this battle at Mokuohai, the words of the man who had instructed Keoua Kuahuula came true: "A break in a gourd container can be mended but a break in the land cannot." So Keoua Kuahuula was routed and fled to Kau, where he planned his wars against Kamehameha. However, it was not long ere his "eggs" were exposed to view, and

Kamehameha sacrificed him at the heiau of Puukohola. Those who never control their desire for wealth and honors never escape penalty. Keoua's efforts to smite with a *pohuehue* vine—figuratively, to rouse others to anger—were almost wasted. Had he gone to Kamehameha to repent his fault he would not have died at all.

Keopuolani, sacred wife of Kamehameha, gave birth to Liholiho in the year 1798 in Hilo. Kamehameha had left Oahu after his victory at Nuuanu and returned to Hawaii because Namakeha had started a rebellion in Hilo. Chief Namakeha was taken captive in this Hilo battle called Puana, the same battle in which Henry Opukahaia almost died, so he said.

Kamehameha placed Liholiho in the hands of his trusted server Hanapi, who took the child to rear him in the lands of Kalaoa in Hilo Paliku. After five or six months, Liliha Kekuiapoiwa, mother of Keopuolani and grandmother of Liholiho, had him removed from Hanapi's care because she felt his diet was not right. Liliha told her *kaikunane*, Kamehameha, about seeing with her own eyes the carelessness of the wet nurse. Kamehameha then sent Kaahumanu to get the child. Kaahumanu went by canoe, landing at Kahalii, and returned with the baby.

[Between the death of Kiwalao at the battle of Mokuohai in 1782 and the sacrifice of Keoua Kuahuula at Puukohola there were some ten years of almost continuous warfare among the chiefs of Hawaii, Maui, and Oahu.

During this period, Kahekili, the hereditary ruling chief of Maui, conquered Kahahana, then ruler of Oahu, and became ruler over that island, as well as over Molokai and Lanai, already under the control of Oahu chiefs. Then came an attack on Maui by Kamehameha, culminating in his victory at the battle of Iao, where he killed or took captive many of the chiefs of that island. He was forced to return to Hawaii with all his fighting forces, however, to renew his warfare with Keoua Kuahuula; and he left no conquering army in control on Maui. Thereupon, Kahekili and his half brother Kaeo, ruler of Kauai by virtue of his marriage to Kamakahelei, hereditary ruling chiefess of that island, joined forces and re-established themselves on Maui, leaving Oahu in the charge of Kalanikupule, Kahekili's son, who had escaped from Maui after the battle of Iao.

Keoua Kuahuula's death left Kamehameha in complete mastery of Hawaii, and he began his preparations for the conquest of the other islands. After the death of Kahekili in 1794 he set forth with his first great *peleleu* fleet of war canoes. He stopped for provisions at Maui and Molokai where there was no need for battle, since their chiefs were on Oahu. When he reached Oahu he gave battle to Kalanikupule, utterly defeating his forces at the battle of Nuuanu early in 1795. Kamehameha thereby became ruler of Hawaii, Maui, Molokai, Lanai, and Oahu.

During all this time Kauai remained at peace, with Kaumualii, the son of Kaeo and Kamakahelei, the acknowledged heir. A year or so after the battle of Nuuanu, Kamehameha set out from Oahu to invade Kauai, only to be driven back by a storm. Soon after, he returned to Hawaii to quell a rebellion there by the chief Namakeha. After the suppression of this revolt and the death of Namakeha, Kamehameha remained on Hawaii for six years, preparing a war fleet for the invasion of Kauai, which this fleet was destined never to reach. Soon after it had arrived on Oahu, late in 1803 or early in 1804, a terrible pestilence, called the *okuʻu* [cholera?] broke out, decimating the armies of Kamehameha. It was not until 1810, when Kaumualii, in order to avoid inevitable conquest by war, ceded his kingdom of Kauai and Niihau to Kamehameha. Thus were the islands united, from one end to the other, fulfilling the ambitions of Kamehameha I.]

CHAPTER II

THE LULUKA FAMILY

The person whose writing this is, John Papa Ii, first appeared amongst the chiefs when but a small child, at Kawehewehe in Waikiki, Oahu. His uncle, Papa Ii, and most of their people were there at that time, for that was their first residence when the company arrived from Lahaina at the time of the coming of Kamehameha with his great *peleleu* fleet of canoes intended for the invasion of Kauai.

Kamehameha's houses were at Puaaliilii, makai of the old road, and extended as far as the west side of the sands of Apuakehau. Within it was Helumoa, where Kaahumanu *ma* went to while away the time. The king built a stone house there, enclosed by a fence; and Kamalo, Wawae, and their relatives were in charge of the royal residence. Kamalo and Wawae were the children of Luluka and Keaka, the childhood guardians of Kamehameha.

This place had long been a residence of chiefs. It is said that it had been Kekuapoi's home, through her husband Kahahana, since the time of Kahekili. Haalou, a *makuahine* of Kamehameha, lived there with her younger daughter Kekuapoi while en route from Hawaii to Kauai to consult Kapoukahi, a seer of Kauai, for means whereby Kamehameha would gain victory over Keoua Kuahuula. Kapoukahi was an expert in selecting heiau sites, and his advice led to the restoration of the heiau Mailekini and the building of the heiau of Puukohola in Kawaihae on Hawaii.

Perhaps it was then that Kekuaokalani, Kamehameha's nephew, who had been sent by Kamehameha from Molokai to Kahekili on Oahu for some reason, met Kekuapoi and saw what a beautiful woman she was. It is said that Kekuapoi insisted on going to Hawaii with her mother, who feared that she would take away Kamehameha, the husband of Haalou's granddaughter, Kaahumanu. Haalou joined forces with the chief Kuihelani to discourage her daughter and to tell her how very good the granddaughter was. They spoke in a beguiling manner to Kekuapoi, and she did not accompany them.

The family of Luluka, to which Papa Ii belonged, had encountered trouble in Hilo, perhaps before or after the battle of Puana. There was no threat of death, but their right to care for the king's personal property and food was taken away by Uluhaha. The trouble arose during the time Kamehameha was having an affair with Kanahoahoa.

One evening the king was to meet with the gods in the house of Hiiaka, after a meeting in the house of the male gods, where Kalaipahoa, whose correct name was Kaneikaulanaula, had been taken. But after the ceremony there was over, Kamehameha went to spend the night with Kanahoahoa, with the knowledge of the god and the attendant who carried it. The attendant took the god to the king's sleeping house where Kaahumanu and her sister, Kaheiheimalie, were awaiting Kamehameha's return. They asked the attendant of the god where the chief was, and he replied, "They two are at Olo, only at Olo." This reply of his was used in a hula chant the chiefesses composed:

O Kaneikaulana'ula ke aloha la,	We are sorry for Kaneikaulanaula,
I ka lele wale mai no 'a'ohe kahu la,	He flies unattended,
Aia i Olo, i Olo wale laua la,	For they two are at Olo, only at Olo,
I ke alo o Kapo, wahine a Puanui la,	In the presence of Kapo, wife of Puanui,
Nui ko aloha, maka hi'o iaia la.	Great is your love, it keeps your eyes on her.

When the king returned later that night, the chiefesses were chanting and dancing to the words they had composed. Perhaps he had given them the incentive for the composition by arousing their anger, which was like the sea sweeping over the embankments of the ponds of their hearts. He asked them at once what they were doing and to explain the underlying meaning of the words they had composed, but they would not reveal it. Because of his insistent questioning, the two chiefesses finally pointed to a sleeping boy, who had not heard what had been said before. The boy, Kalapauahiole, was the bearer of the king's spittoon and was a relative of the chiefs, of the family of Luluka. Kamehameha's wrath rose as the sea that washes up to the beach morning-glory vines growing on the dry sand. Only because of the excellent report on all the possessions in the family's care made by Hoomakau, father of Kaopua, and others to the king and to Uluhaha were the things held by Papa and his people spared.

O companions, let us look at the complications of the olden times. The king was the one who did wrong, but fault was put on an innocent person. Perhaps the king's conscience within him knew that what he had done was wrong and that he should repent, thus shortening the matter and letting it end. Perhaps it was like the saying, "Fire never says it has enough," or like the rich man, who never says, "I have all I want." So are the suppressed desires within us; they keep surging until they force themselves into the open.

Luluka and his contemporary relatives were descendants of Luahine, the younger brother of Palena and Paia. These three had the same father and mother. These were the chiefs who saved the life of chief Kuaana in Kawaihae when the ruling chiefess, Keakealaniwahine, ordered him drowned. They persuaded her to have Kuaana set adrift on a raft of beach morning-glory vines instead. When the raft was out of her sight, they came to his aid, and Kuaana was able to land on Maui.

Luahine's descendants were connected to the lineage of Haloa—figuratively, ruling chiefs—through Keakealanikane, father of Keakamahana and grandfather of Keakealaniwahine. They were close blood relatives of Kauaua a Mahi, Alapainui, Keawepoepoe, and Keeaumoku Papaiahiahi, all of whom were of the same ancestry.

Luluka had descendants too numerous to count, all called Luluka. As Luluka, the family name of Luahine and Palena, was found only in the presence of the chiefs, they were all recognized in the courts.

Luluka mated first with Keaka a Mulehu, a chiefess of Maui, and to them was born Kamahauluae. Later Luluka mated with Keaka and had Holomaialuhe, Kamalo, and Wawae, all by that wife. He also mated with Keakaakipoo, and to them were born Papa Ii; Ilipeahi, a girl; and other children.

Kamahauluae returned to Kau during the reign of Kalaniopuu to be with his chief, Kamehameha; and he took with him all of his *kaikaina*, the sons of Luluka. This Kamahauluae mated with Wanaoa and had Haalou, Keimolaaupalau a Keeaumoku, and Maoloha, a man who was killed by strangling at Pawaa about the year 1807.

Wanaoa mated again with Kanepililua and had Kamaloo, and afterwards she and Kuaena had this son, John Papa Ii, the youngest.

The boy Ii's father answered to two names, Kuaena and Malamaekeeke. He was related to Nahiolea and was a *kaikunane* of Kamakahukilani, the mother of Kalanimoku, Wahinepio, and Boki. Perhaps that was why he accompanied Boki on his journey to search for sandalwood. As Boki said before he left, Kuaena was not reared on the food of the Luluka family but on that of Boki's family, and so he forsook us. By this we see that there was wisdom and a sense of justice even in the unenlightened. Knowing right from wrong has existed from ancient times.

Kalaaumaloo, the father of Wanaoa, Ii's mother, was a blood relative of Luluka and Keaka, the childhood guardians of Kamehameha. Kalaaumaloo mated

19

with Poaeaewahine, a descendant of Imaikalani, the blind chief who was skilled in fencing with spears in the time of Umi, the chief famous for warring.

John Papa Ii was born in Kumelewai, Waipio, in Ewa, Oahu, on the third day of August (Hilinehu in the Hawaiian calendar) in 1800, on the land of Papa Ii, whose namesake he was. Papa was the owner of the pond of Hanaloa and two other pieces of property, all of which he had received from Kamehameha, as did others who lived on that *ahupuaʻa*, or land division, after the battle of Nuuanu. He gave the property to his *kaikuahine*, who was the mother of the aforementioned boy. Her names were Wanaoa, Pahulemu, and Kalaikane.

Wanaoa and Pahulemu were descriptive names. Among the servants Wanaoa was likened to trees with branches going in every direction, forcing them to keep their distance because of her rank. The name Pahulemu (Shove-from-the-rear) was derived from a lack of skill in surfing, which required the aid of the skilled. The learner would lie down on the board to ride in on the surf, while the skilled one held onto the back end (*lemu*) of the board when the surf rose. When the surf drew near, the instructor gave the board a shove (*pahu*) and the surfer rode nicely toward the shore. This was the meaning of that name, O companions.

When Ii was a small boy he went from Kumelewai to Honolulu with the attendants who cared for him. Before they left, the attendants prepared some mullet from the ponds containing taro mounds so that the boy would have food when he became hungry on the road. The fish were salted, wrapped in taro leaves, and taken on a carrying pole. There were two places on the way where they would rest and eat, one at Kahuawai in Kalauao and the other at Napeha in Halawa. At Kahuawai, when the taro-leaf bundles were opened, the fish were stiff with salt and bent like the tusks of a hog. So they called this "a land with two points."

As the party drew near Napeha on their return from Honolulu, the boy became tense with weariness. He wanted to be carried on the back of one of the attendants who already had bundles to carry containing clothing and food. Because the boy would not stop crying they went slowly. Behind the boy came two haole men from Honolulu who were on their way to their lands at Waimalu. When one of the two attendants, either Mela or Kiwalao, saw the men he remarked, "Here come the haoles, who do not like children who cry too much."

The men heard him and asked in the native speech, "What was that? What are you saying about us?"

"Haoles are good, but the boy is not—he cries too much," was the answer.

The boy was fearful of foreigners, a fear that was usual with country children. The men asked, "Is this boy yours?" and the attendants told them who his parents were and the name of his namesake. When the men said, "If he is a boy who cries without stopping we shall take him," the crying stopped at once.

O companions, these words of theirs were to deceive the boy. So do ignorant parents and guardians talk constantly to their children; but it is because

Copy of a sketch by John Webber, showing a typical household of Ii's youth. In Bishop Museum.

the children are stubborn, just as this boy was until he realized how troublesome he was being.

From the time he was little, Ii was taught by his father, Kuaena, the rules of good behavior, in preparation for his position in the royal court, where he was destined to go at the age of ten. They brought him up carefully, instructing him in all things, and saw to it that he was quick and capable, as they wished him to be when he went to live in the presence of the chiefs.

Once when the parents of the boy brought up the subject of his going to the court, they warned him of the things he might encounter in the place where his older brother Maoloha had died for committing a misdeed. "Therefore make yourself wise," said they. The young boy said, "How strange for you to take me to the royal court to stay where my older brother died. Perhaps the same fate will befall me there."

His mother answered, "Yes, that may be true, if you do not heed all we have taught you. Your brother died because he did not observe all we had taught him. Your uncles who are now in the royal court do not go about as they please, but heed the instructions they received from their elders. So do we teach you. Because we have nothing to give to those in whose house we live, your father and I have agreed not to keep you to ourselves though you were born to us, a son from our loins. We know that you are capable of taking care of yourself if you heed our teachings. These you practiced before us, therefore I am letting Papa, my *kaikunane*, place you with any chief he chooses. To him, you must be obedient. Thus did your uncles become seekers of the welfare of their chiefs' homes from the time they were poor until they became prosperous. They bore with patience the poverty and the many troubles that rested upon them. So must you, if you heed our teachings and those of my *kaikunane* for whom you are named."

The boy knew by the words of his mother that she was determined to make him a member of the court. He made no more comments, feeling it best to comply.

A few days after the above conversation, a niece of Wanaoa Kalaikane came from Kukuilolo, in Waialua. Her parents had named her Kalaikane for Ii's mother, as they were close relatives of hers. Kalaikane of Kukuilolo was a descendant of Keawekuikekaai [son of Keakealanikane and Kaleimakalii, an ancestress of the Lulukas], whose kapu, it was said, required the men to sit, whereas the women were allowed to walk. She found a husband in that land and she had two sons and a daughter. One of her sons was Papa [who was later known as Daniel Papa Ii]. Her second son was named Kekoena (The-Remainder) after some food or fish that had been left over at some time. These names applied to Wanaoa's *kaikunane*. The name of her daughter, Kaleimakalii, was believed to be for the *lei* (beloved child) Maoloha, who had died.

Kalaikane and Wanaoa talked of their children. The lady of Kukuilolo told of the farming ability of her oldest son Papa, and so on. The other expressed admiration for the things her companion told her and agreed that it would mean support when Papa's mother and grandmother were old. So they talked, on and on, for they knew how smart were some of the relatives' children. Their discussion stemmed from the growing hope their children would serve in the royal court, where they were all eligible to serve. Kalaikane of Kukuilolo was the first to express a desire to have her son serve there.

Near the end of that year, it was suspected that a nephew of Papa named Kalakua had worn the malo of the king. Kalakua fetched and carried the king's possessions such as his kahili, mat, or spittoon wherever he went; and at one time the loin cloths they wore were of a similar pattern. When they returned to the king's house, Kalakua was taken at once and kept in solitude while they tried to verify their suspicion that he had worn the king's malo.

It was at this time that the king, chiefs, and court members left Honolulu and sailed by canoe to Waianae. Liholiho, the heir to the kingdom, went overland with Papa and others from Honolulu and spent the night at Kumelewai in Ewa. Before the company arrived for the night, Ii was sent with a message to the dwellers of the land to be ready with fish, dogs, vegetable food, and clothing that would be of help to the travelers. Thus were all things supplied from upper Waipio to the sea. There was enough for the traveling company of the young chief, who was spending the night there. This did Ii do for the young chief and his companion Papa.

The travelers stopped only one night and spent the following night on the other side of Pohakea. The elders and the children who went with them slept above Kunia, on this side of Pohakea. The coming of the retinue was announced in Waianae; and it was told that the family, elders and children together, would be set on fire for the wrong committed by Kalakua. Though he alone was thought to have committed the misdeed, the whole family was held guilty. The company, somewhat in the nature of prisoners, spent a night at Lualualei near the fish pond on the plain. The next day they reached the southern side of Kanepuniu, and there they encamped for eight days to await an announcement concerning the death and burning of the wrongdoers. Finally, a proclamation from the king was given by Kaulainamoku, stating that there would be no deaths, for Kalakua had not worn the king's malo. Thus was the Luluka family spared a cruel fate. A child born in the family later was named Lualualei.

The king's company left Waianae and returned to Honolulu as peacefully as they had set forth. A few days later Wanaoa brought her son Ii to Honolulu. That must have been the fourth time he appeared there. Kaoaopa was their place, and there he lived with the whole family.

After their return to Ewa, a *kaikua'ana* of the boy thought of going to Waialee, Koolauloa, also a land of his elders. The boy asked to go along, and the request was granted. In this way he first saw the other side of the island. On the way he met the other Papa Ii, who was farming at Kukuilolo. They visited a little while there and went to see all of the things they had heard of earlier. They did not remain long, but continued to Waialee on the same day on which they had left Ewa. Waialee was a delightful land, well-provisioned. There was a pond there, surrounded by taro patches, and there were good fishing places inside the reef.

At Waialee a few days later, when the strangeness had begun to wear off, the boy took his calabash and salt dish and sat outside of the door of the house. There he ate, for he respected the gods and was somewhat religious. While he ate, he seemed to relish his salt as he would meat, judging by the large scoops of poi he took. His *kaikuahine* was watching from inside the house and, seeing his great relish, asked, "What kind of 'meat' have you?"

"Just salt," answered the boy.

"Oh, my poor 'brother,'" she said. Then she came out of the house and went to the beach. She returned shortly with four *manini* and two *'opule* fishes. She scaled the *'opule*, stripped off the skins of the *manini*, and laid a sufficient number of fishes before him. Thus the boy knew that his *kaikuahine* was concerned over him. He was to remember all of the things she did for him while he remained there. Not long after, he and his *kaikua'ana* returned to Ewa and told their parents about their visit.

We have already mentioned the boy Ii's religious nature; but we should speak a little more fully about it, for it was a usual trait with him from the time he was a small child, too small to wear a malo. He was often taken by his father and male attendants to the altar on the mornings of Kane [the twenty-seventh day of the Hawaiian month], and so he was a constant observer of the god.

Sometimes his mother sent him net fishing at Puuopae, one of their pieces of land. The fish ponds there were under the care of his father's *kaikuahine* and her husband. A number of boys always followed him, and they carried the fishes on the return trip. When they neared the houses, they all stopped to rest and open the bundles; and Ii selected suitable fishes for the male and female gods and divided the remainder for himself and his friends. Then each boy went to his own home. The first time he returned from net fishing the remaining fishes were counted in the presence of his mother and she requested that some be set apart for the male and female gods. "They are already separated," said the boy. "My companions have had their share, and this is ours." This caused his mother to say, "My son, these fine deeds that you have done here with us will benefit your work in the place we have told you about. You are going into the court with my *kaikunane*, Papa. If you continue as you are now doing, all will be well. Take care of all of the left-over food and everything else placed in your charge. When you are asked for them say, 'Here they are.' In so doing you will be recognized as my child and that of my *kaikunane*."

An original pencil drawing by William Dampier of fish ponds at Pearl River. In Bishop Museum.

Because of his religious nature, the boy was sent frequently with the priests in the early dawn of Kane to relieve any trouble at the pond of Hanaloa, to make the offerings, and to present the gifts they had brought to the appropriate offering place. Such a place was called an *aoa*, a place where offerings were made to the gods for whatever concerned the ponds.

Kuʻula shrines were for inshore and deep-sea fishing, for the fishing grounds of the *aku* or *ʻahi* fish perhaps.

The offerings on the *aoa* shrine were a black pig once or twice a year, a bunch of raw taro, a bunch of bananas, several times four mullet, enough for those who were aiding in the work, and some *kohekohe,* a grass found in taro patches. In the early dawn of Kane, all things were made ready and the imu prepared with the three or four stones and the kindling of dried pili grass left there beforehand. To light the fire, the kindling was placed under the stick that was rubbed (*ʻaunaki*) before it was worked with the stick held in the hand (*ʻaulima*). The latter was about four or five inches long and as thick as the finger that one uses to dip up poi, the index finger. The two ends were sharpened to a point to help in rubbing it into the *ʻaunaki*, which was held down by a foot or a hand while a companion did the rubbing. The stick was pressed with the palm of one hand overlapping the other when rubbing. Then the kahuna uttered a prayer he had memorized to the *ʻaumakua o ka po*, the gods of dim antiquity, and the *ʻaumakua o ke ao*, the gods of traditional times.

These things relating to worship were not regarded by the boy as worthless, for he had seen them done by his parents from the time he was little. He was obedient to his parents in the worthwhile and the worthless things they taught him, so he was well versed in this kind of worship. To his mind, these gods were like the true God. Later, we shall see more of the real nature of the boy.

Iʻi's aunt on his father's side, Kaneiakama, came from Waianae with her husband Paakonia. They visited the family's houses to rest a while before continuing on to Honolulu to their landlord. These people, who were bracelet-makers and residents of that land of the foamy sea, were well known. They were of chiefly stock and were privileged to place their bundles with those of the chiefs. Their landlord, Pahoa, was in charge of Kaahumanu's extensive lands, granted her by her husband Kamehameha; and there were very few *ahupuaʻa* in which she did not have a portion, for she was a great favorite of the king. Kaahumanu was fond of Kaneiakama and admired her skill in composing chants. Because of this, perhaps, the land at Waianae was given to Kaneiakama and her husband.

After two days at Ewa the aunt and her husband continued their journey to Honolulu, to return again in about three or four weeks. At this time they made themselves well acquainted with the boy. They were relatives of an older generation, and his parents had explained to the boy his relationship to this aunt who was a stranger to him. She gave her name to the boy by calling him as follows: "O Kaneiakama, here is your aunt, *hoahanau* of your father. Answer to this call."

The boy replied, "Eo (I answer)."

"Yes, that's it," said his aunt.

They taught him many things and his aunt developed a deep interest in him. When she asked, "Would you like to come to Waianae?" he assented at once.

After the aunt and her husband had gone he dwelt on the invitation to Waianae and his wish to accept. When his mother did not refuse permission, he and his male attendant prepared to go. As a playmate with weak eyes insisted on going along, there were three on that first journey to visit Ii's aunt.

There were three such journeys, one by way of Pohakea, one through Kolekoke, and one by a route below Puu o Kapolei. On the first two trips they went to Pahoauka, where his aunt and her husband lived.

The aunt and her husband had been at home for several months before the boy and his two companions made the first visit. A few days after their arrival, when the morning meal was over, Ii and his playmate went to the bank of a ditch and peered in from some rocks which were in full view of everyone. As they were perched there watching the water of the ditch flow down to the taro patches, a boy named Kahina, a stranger to them, appeared and shoved Ii's companion into the ditch, then ran away. The boy who was shoved into the ditch was hurt and his mouth was swollen. He cried, but Ii comforted him and told him to forbear, promising that if the bad boy came to their place they would give him a beating. These words made the injured boy stop crying, and Ii left his friend and went in to tell his aunt of the incident. The mischievous boy was summoned, and when he was identified by Ii the aunt said, "This is a mischievous boy. Do not play with him." However, this experience made Ii want to go home, though he appreciated the hospitality of his aunt and uncle.

When the boys returned home laden with their possessions, they greeted Ii's parents with a pressing of the nose (*honi i ka ihu*), with them a gesture that was like a holy kiss. They told the parents of all the benefits derived from their stay at Waianae, also mentioning the injury inflicted by Kahina and their plan to punish him if he should visit their place with his parents. The mother said, "You must not do that. Ho‘omanawanui ka maika‘i loa (To be tolerant is best). This is the right procedure, for it is what you must be in the royal court in the future. Therefore, you must think of that man and this man, that boy and this boy, that chief and this chief, that you may act rightly. Thus does the uncle for whom you are named. He serves all of the chiefs in the court, where you are going to live." Her words made the boy realize that this was the right thing for him to do.

Thus the boy's parents frequently discussed subjects pertaining to the nature of man, "from head to feet and from inside to outside, his goings and comings, his life at home, his observations of commands, both right and wrong, looking at them both, selecting the good and setting aside the bad, choosing between things that bring life and setting apart those that bring death, and so on." "These will make you wise," said they.

His parents taught him without punishing him. They cared for him tenderly, knowing by his deeds that their son was good.

When the family went to Kipapa from Kumelewai by way of upper Waipio to make ditches for the farms, his mother trained him in the observance of the *kapu noho*. She placed on his back a bundle containing a wonderful malo made of feathers from *mamo* and *'apapane* birds attached to a fine net, with rows of human teeth at the end; this he had seen when his mother put it out to sun. Slipping his arms into the loops of the bundle, she taught him to cry "E noho e! (Squat down!)." They continued along the road without meeting anyone, for most of the others had preceded them.

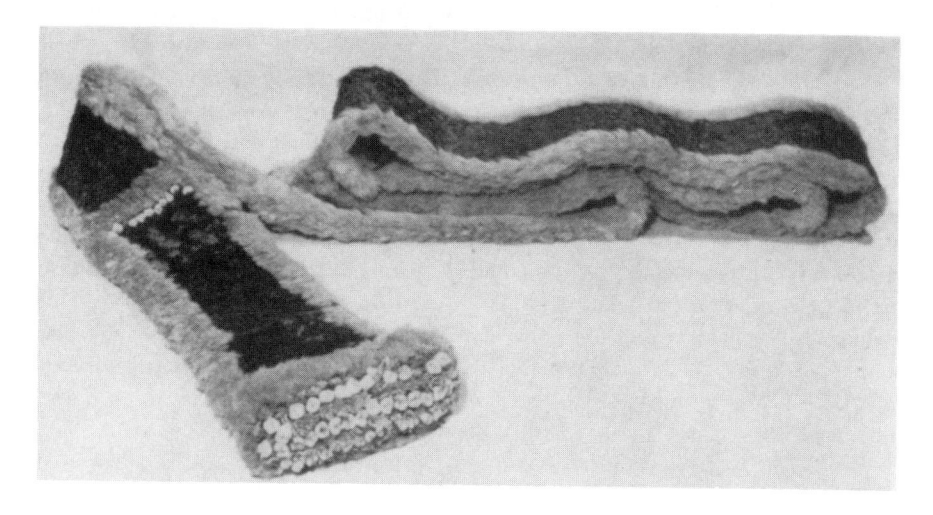

The "wonderful malo of bird feathers" in Bishop Museum, perhaps the one Ii carried.

The proclamation of this kapu was an exceedingly common practice in the court, and one which flustered many a newcomer who did not know that he must squat quickly and slip off his tapa wrap (*kapa*) or shoulder covering (*kihei*). It was the only way for all to safeguard themselves while passing along the road. If a person was wearing a lei on neck or head, he must remove it and throw it away when the cry to squat down (*noho*) was heard, otherwise the penalty would be death. Should one be fully clothed from top to bottom, he was saved only by prostrating himself.

Ii was eight or nine years old when he was again seized by a desire to go to visit his aunt Kaneiakama, and he was given permission to do so. He had heard that his aunt was at Nanakuli, so he and his attendant departed by way of Puu o Kapolei to Waimanalo and on to Nanakuli. There he found his aunt and her husband who were in charge of the fishing.

During his visit Ii observed how the children of Nanakuli produced a long quavering sound while chanting. This was performed while the children sat on the branches of breadfruit trees. They sat apart from each other on branches from the base to the top, chanting. When the boy listened carefully to the long, drawn out sound, he could distinguish the words that they were chanting. He asked his aunt to let him join the children, and he quickly saw how the quavery sound was produced. He noted that one of the boys held up two fingers on his right hand and tapped his throat in order to make the quaver. Ii learned the chant at once. This is the chant that they were using:

Kau koli'i ka la i luna o Maunaloa,	The sun sends a streak of light on Maunaloa,
E ke ao e lele koa,	The clouds go scurrying by,
Halulu i ka mauna	There is a rumble on the mountain top
Kikaha ke kuahiwi o Kona he la'i,	That echoes from the mountain of Kona, the calm.
Ku papu Hilo i ka ua.	Hilo stands directly in the rain.
Paliloa Hamakua,	Hamakua's cliffs are tall,
'Ope'ope Kohala i ka makani,	Kohala is buffeted by the wind,
Huki Kauiki pa i ka lani, etc. [sic]	Kauiki reaches and touches the sky, etc.

This was memorized by all and was chanted in perfect unison, and the boy noticed how pleasing it was. Thus did Ii enjoy himself with the children of Nanakuli, and he continued to spend his spare time with them.

During their stay at Nanakuli they learned of the burning of the houses in Waimanalo. The overseer in charge of the burning told them that it was so ordered by the royal court because the people there had given shelter to the chiefess, Kuwahine, who ran away from her husband Kalanimoku after associating wrongfully with someone. Kuwahine was a daughter of the Kaikioewa who reared Kamehameha III in his infancy. She had run away because she had been beaten for her offense and for other reasons, too, perhaps. She had remained hidden for about four or five days before she was found. Here we see the sadness that befell the people through the fault of the chiefs. The punishment fell on others, though they were not to blame.

When the boy heard these things discussed, he became disturbed over the possibility that his parents' home might be affected. Though Kaneiakama assured the boy that no such deed was committed there, he asked her to let him go home. He found his family without trouble, as usual.

When Ii first saw Kaoaopa in Honolulu, he saw the model ship (*moku ho'oholoholo*) which the heir to the kingdom, Liholiho, sailed to-and-fro in a sea pool. It looked exactly like a real man-of-war with twelve guns mounted on it. It was a sight to attract attention.

There were two who managed the sailing, Puupuu on one side and Niauloa on the other. They were skilled in setting up the sails and in plying the steering paddle. When the tide was full and high and a fine breeze blew the sailing began from the starting point at what was later Ainahou. The ship sailed directly to the other side, then back. Sometimes a suitable wick was made ready for the firing of the guns, which made a noise like those fired on a man-of-war; and at anchor, the little ship was treated like a man-of-war.

When John Adams Kuakini, a chief who enjoyed sailing such little ships to the day of his death, obtained a similar craft, he asked the beloved young chief Liholiho for some of the guns. Six were given to him.

These small ships were much visited. The first such ships were made so that the king's heir would know about some of the arts of foreigners. Without this teaching, the people would have remained ignorant of such things.

It was, perhaps, the nature of a country boy to take a fancy to things and hope to possess them. Just as he took a fancy to the small ship, so he felt toward the first horse he saw. But these things could not be owned by all boys.

Back home, in the country, the boy looked at the fine tobacco pipes his father carved and asked, "Can one obtain a horse with these things you are carving?"

"Perhaps so, but a horse cannot be had with ordinary tobacco pipes. A pipe with carvings suggestive of the foam of the sea may be a means of getting one, because of its unusual appearance. If two such pipes were made perhaps a horse could be obtained."

In vain, they discussed the problem for several days. Because he could not get a real horse, the boy made one out of a banana tree stalk. He took two sticks, drove them into the end of the stalk, and tied them where they met. The end of one hung down like the nose of a horse. The second stick was about a *haʻilima*, the length from the finger tips to the elbow, beyond where the first stick was fastened. The first stick was tied fast to the stalk with a rope, then the second joined onto it to form the head of the horse. Underneath, where the sticks joined, were the reins, which ran to the nape of the boy's neck. The boy sat astride the horse, leaped about, and made sibilant sounds with his lips as though to a real horse. He galloped in front of his playmates and stopped before his parents. His father asked, "Is this a horse?"

The boy answered, "It is, and it is a good one, too."

His parents and playmates laughed, but his playmates imitated his horse.

When Ii's father was ready to go to Kailua in Koolaupoko to hew *noni* trees for the red dye used for coloring malos, the boy begged for his mother's permission to go too. They traveled by canoe to Honolulu, and the next day went up to Nuuanu as far as Kaniakapueo, where some people from their own neigh-

Nuuanu Pali as it appeared to Ii. Reproduced from "Narrative of the United States Exploring Expedition," volume 3.

borhood in Ewa awaited them. When they reached the place, the boy saw them first, for he had run ahead. He said to his father, "There are Kaimihau and his companions! Where have they come from?"

"From overland, this morning," replied his father.

"My, how fast they traveled!" said the son.

Joining the others and forming one company, they continued up to Nahuina in Kahapaakai and through Kukuipuka, above Luakaha. Kukuipuka was an arched kukui tree, its trunk standing on the left side of the trail as one went up. When young and tall, its top, or perhaps a big branch, had been trained by bending it over to touch the ground on the right side of the trail. The arch, about 8 or 9 feet high, was wide and well-formed. To Ii, it was a wonderful sight.

The party continued, climbing to Nuuanu Pali, and then down. The boy was not actually led, but his father clung to his hand until they reached a safe place, away from the sheer drop of the cliff. Finally they reached the houses where they were to stay, located near a hillock and a group of hills. These were at Kailua, whence some of his father's people hailed. When they had all of the *noni* they wanted, they returned to their residence in Ewa. They found the people at home well, as usual.

Next, his father's task took them all down to Kapuna in Waikele, a good place for dyeing tapa. There, patches of taro were grown, draw nets made, and houses built. The fishing was done in the sea of Honouliuli. Because the people of the place did not like Waikele's farm overseer, and for other reasons too, perhaps, they would say, "We are of Honouliuli." If the farm overseer went to Honouliuli, they would say, "We belong to Waikele." It was true that their homes were in Waikele, but all of their fishing was done in Honouliuli. It was laziness and dislike of the overseer that made them point one way and then another.

CHAPTER III

KAPU LOULU RITES AND MEDICAL PRACTICES

In addition to Liholiho, Kamehameha I had two other sons, Kinau by Peleuli and Kekuaiwa [also known as Lunalilo or Kamehameha] by Kaheiheimalie, who were considered as possible heirs in that order.

In late 1803 or early 1804, while he was living with the chiefs at Halaulani, Waipio, Ewa, the king became ill. At this time, Kinau, his people, and one of the chiefs—either Keliimaikai or Kalaimamahu—were residing at Waimalu and the following comment by Kinau's men reached the king: "When will the moon which has been shining so long set, so that we may have control of the government?" These words caused Kamehameha to think deeply. When he recovered under the treatment of Papa, his medical kahuna, he returned to Honolulu, having boarded the canoe at Miki in Waikele. This was shortly before the ʻokuʻu epidemic.

Keopuolani, mother of the young chief Liholiho, was taken seriously ill then, just as the period of the *kapu loulu* drew near. The king remained with the young chief for ten days at Laeahi (Leahi, or Diamond Head) for the ceremonies, at which time all the chiefs, including Keeaumoku, father of Kaahumanu, separated from their women and gathered in the heiau [Papaenaena] there to seek peace and prosperity for the kingdom. The king was not feeling very well in those days, and it was decided that the best thing for him was to sleep where they were. The house in which they dwelt was called the Hale Pahu, for that was

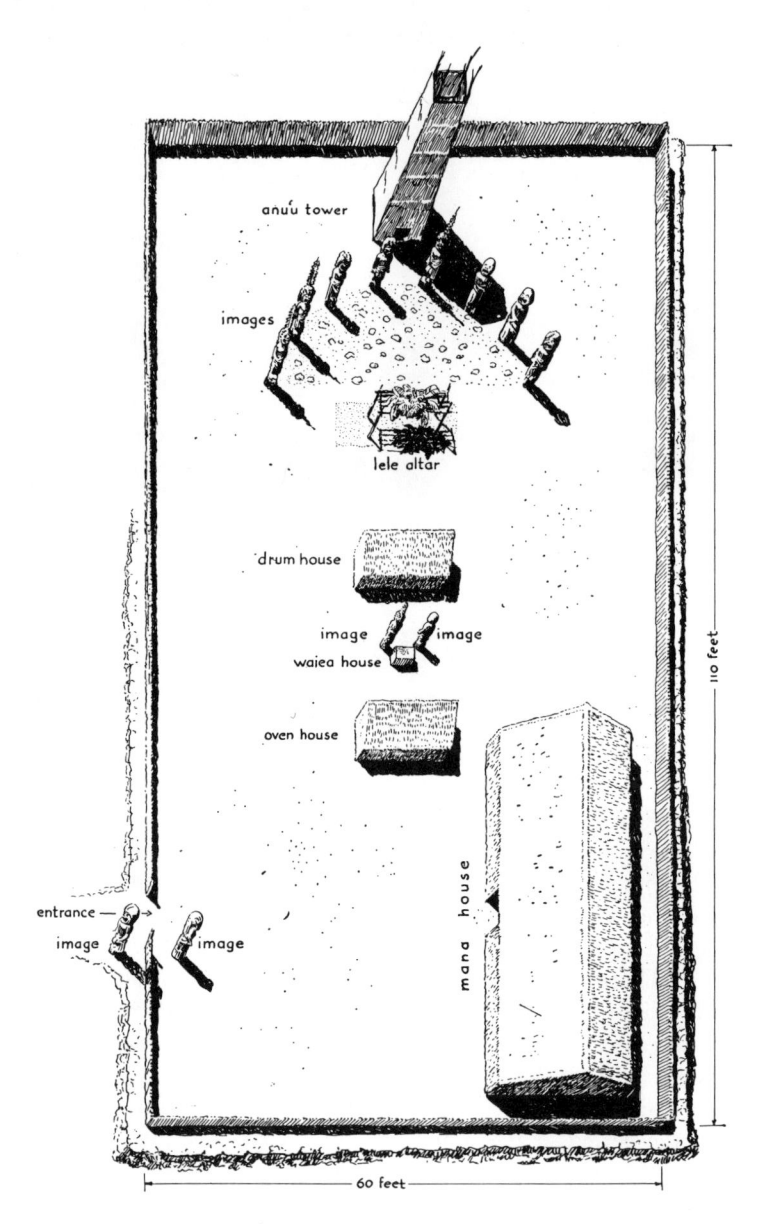

*A luakini heiau as depicted in the text.
Drawing by Paul Rockwood.*

where the drums of the gods were kept. These drums, which were sounded every morning at dawn, were kept in the gods' houses by their keepers, who did the drumming. It was also said that the drums were sounded in the Hale Pahu when the king did not utter the 'amama prayer.

The Hale Pahu was closed from top to bottom on the side and back walls, whereas the front had only posts, like a lanai. It faced the 'anu'u tower and the row of idols in front of the 'anu'u. Between them was the lele altar. Three of the houses were thatched with leaves of the loulu palm (lau lauli'i). The largest house, called the Hale Mana, was long, like a halau. Its front and door faced the entrance of this luakini heiau. The third house was the Hale Umu, or Oven House, which stood on the left side of the Hale Mana, extending forward of it a little, with front and door directly toward the back of the Hale Pahu. The fourth house, called the Hale Waiea, was a small one between the Hale Umu and the Hale Pahu. It was twice the length of the distance from fingertip to elbow in length, its height and breadth being half that measure. Two images stood before it on either side of the opening, and the king and kahuna conducted their 'aha services at the right side of the opening, in the dark of the night before the birds began to twitter.

While they were at Leahi, two swift messengers, Lalaione and Kaiwiopele, who were the fleetest of all the runners, perhaps, were sent to tell the king that the chiefess Keopuolani had fainted and was about to go the way of all the earth. At this time, three men who had been caught eating coconuts with the chiefesses were seized because coconuts were prohibited to women in general and it was kapu for men to eat with women. When the three men who had eaten freely with the women were taken, their hands were bound by the keepers of the gods. They were taken away from the presence of their haku, Keopuolani, imprisoned, and condemned to die.

On the day of the kauila nui ceremony, the chiefs assembled with the king and the three potential heirs to the kingdom, as well as the kahunas, the gods, and their keepers. The kahunas uttered the prayers with many words, similar to meles. The 'aha service the night before had been maika'i (successful), so the fires could be lighted and the pigs and the lawbreakers killed for sacrifices. These were to be laid together on the lele altar after the king had uttered the 'amama prayer. So were the pigs of the chiefs and kahunas to be offered to the gods, and they were all held in readiness by the keepers of the heiau property. After the fires were lighted, the sacrificial pigs and the men were put to death. The skins of the men were scorched like those of the sacrificial pigs and laid together in a special place before the kahunas, the king, and all the others who had assembled there to worship the god idol, the group of idols, and the line of idols. Pictures of such heiaus were made when the first foreign ships came to these islands, such as Captain Cook's ships and others that followed.

Keikipuipui heiau in Kona, as seen by Jacques Arago. Engraving in Freycinet's Atlas of "Voyage pittoresque autour du monde."

Kamehameha was lying down, and the two sons, Kinau and Lunalilo, sat on either side of him. It was thought that one of them was to utter the *'amama* prayer, but the king did not wish it so. The young chief Liholiho sat at some distance from him, on the lap of Keeaumoku, who was instructing him in how to utter the *'amama*. This indicated that the other two would be denied this right, despite sitting so close to their father. The people and some of the chiefs behind them offered words of encouragement, for the kingdom and the kingship were highly prized. The kahunas paused in their work of praying, waiting for the *'amama* to be said. Then the voice of the king was heard to ask, "Where is the young chief?"

"He is sitting on Keeaumoku's lap," someone replied.

The king said, "Have him utter the *'amama* to the gods."

So the young chief rose from Keeaumoku's lap, walked forward to the spot where the sacrificial pigs and dead men were heaped up together with the coconuts and bananas and said,

E Ku, Kuka'ilimoku,	O Ku, Kukailimoku,
Ku ke ala 'awa,	Ku of the bitter path,
Lononuiakea,	Lononuiakea,
Kane me Kanaloa,	Kane and Kanaloa,
Eia na mohai a pau	Here are all the offerings
Imua o 'oukou.	Before you.
E molia aku	Curse
I na kipi o waho a o loko ho'i	The rebels without and within
I ke ka'ili 'aina.	Who wish to seize the land.
E ola Kamehameha	Grant life to Kamehameha
A me na'li'i a pau,	And to all the chiefs,
Ka hu a maka'ainana,	To the people in general, the common people,
A me ke aupuni mai o a o,	And the kingdom, from one end to the other,
A ia'u no ho'i.	And to me also.
Lele wale aku la ...	It is said ... [literally, it has flown]
Ua pau.	It is finished.

The young chief turned to go back and the happiness of the spectators and the king was great. Keeaumoku was the happiest of all because he spoke so well. As to the other two sons, they "sat at Kulou in the circle made by Kukanaloa *ma*," as did the chiefs and the people who favored them. They sat with bowed heads and were dampened by tears. Not a sound came from them.

Thus the words of his followers caused the loss of the kingdom to the chief Kinau and led to dissension among the chiefs of that time. Such was the result of following the wild talk of men and ignoring the will of the elders, whose teachings advocated good behavior and security for the people. Such was the course of the other boy among them, Liholiho. Otherwise, Kinau would have long before been chosen heir, for he was the son born in the troublous times of war. It is said that Keoua Kuahuula and Moo had taken him from Kau and that he had become an in-law to these chiefs when he was young, at the time of the first battle of Laupahoehoe.

Before the gathering was dismissed, the young chief returned from uttering the *'amama* and sat upon Keeaumoku's lap again. Then two men went by, each with two coconut leaves plaited with coconut fibers, entering the space in the middle of the *'anu'u* tower. One offered his prayers at the right corner of the *'anu'u;* his companion, at the left. The first, holding one of his plaited objects in his right hand, called out,

Iaia e penei ka 'aha,	Thus goes the *'aha*,
He 'aha na Ku, na Lono, Kane, Kanaloa.	The *'aha* for Ku, for Lono, Kane, and Kanaloa.
Molia i ke kipi ka'ili 'aina,	Curse the rebel who tries to take the land,
I ke kuhi lima e ke 'o'ia,	Who reaches out his hand to seize,
O ka 'oukou ia e molia ai.	By you are they to be cursed.

Then he tied the plaited object to the outside corner of the *'anu'u*, while his companion did likewise. The first man then repeated the prayer and tied his leaf to the back corner on his side, and the second man did the same. They stood together up on the *'anu'u* to await the response from below, then they moved as though dancing. While the drum sounded, voices recited,

Maki'iki'i, e Maki'ilohelohe,	Makiikii, Makiilohelohe,
Aia i 'ele e ka mauna,	Darkness is on the mountain,
Oia i 'ele e ka moana;	Darkness is over the ocean;
Ma kai 'ouli, ma kai akea,	At sea is an omen, in the wide sea,
Ki'eki'e ka hoku, ha'aha'a ka malama;	The stars are high, the moon is low;
E ka 'ohiki, e ka 'ohiki, pae.	O sand crab, o sand crab, come ashore.

Figuratively, this means, "Let that which is unknown become known." After the sounding of the drums and the response, the two sat down.

While the keepers of the gods sounded the drums, their pig was cooked; and so were all of those in the other imus. They were bundled and laid on the pebbled area within the enclosure, which had images standing both inside and outside of it, where stood the kahuna in charge. After he had offered dedicatory prayer over the pigs, he took the right legs of the king's pigs and waved them for emphasis, as prescribed by the ritual, perhaps.

When these things were brought before the king and the chiefs, they prepared the food that they themselves were to eat, as well as that to give away. Whole pigs were given only to those who were eligible; others received leg, chest, or other meat. The dispossessed ones received a share from the king, including things brought from elsewhere and heaped before him. Each chief divided among his own people the things he received from the king and from his own possessions brought from elsewhere. Hence the expression, "Na'li'i po'e kauwa (The chiefs who are servants)." The term *pu'ali* was different, meaning one who had no servant or servants. It applied to an adopted man or boy.

There was much more pertaining to the *kapu loulu.* There were four major divisions to this *loulu* worship [the *kauila nui* ceremonies, the fetching of the *haku 'ohi'a* and the *kuili* and *hono* rites]. The fifth division was in the Hale o

Papa, perhaps named for the wife of Wakea. The ceremony there was the ending, or freeing, of the kapu. Then each person returned to his own home, except the keepers of the gods, men who did not associate with women. There were many regulations, any infraction of which could cause death during the period of the *kapu loulu*. Perhaps it would be well to explain briefly the five divisions in this worship that all may see the ignorance and confusion of the Hawaiian rites, so like the confusion in Israel in the days of Jeroboam.

If the *'aha* was the Hulahula, it belonged to the Moo Ku order, whose kahunas were of the class called Kanalu. Hewahewa and his fellow kahunas were of this order. If Hoowilimoo was the *'aha*, it belonged to the Moo Lono order. These *'aha* were used in the *luakini* heiau, whose *paehumu* enclosure and house beams and posts were all made of *'ohi'a* wood. The *'aha* Hulahula ceremony itself was at the beginning of the *loulu* worship and if it was *maika'i* then only half the number of pigs were killed the next day. They were apportioned to the *lele* altar, the *akua hulu* (feather gods), the priests, and the king. During this ceremony, most of the men remained outside of the enclosure, where an idol stood on the right side of the entrance. An image also stood on the right inside of the enclosure entrance. Should the service of the two at the Hale Waiea be conducted perfectly, the kahuna asked the king at the end of his praying what he thought of it. When the king answered that it was *maika'i* and the prayers successfully performed, those on the outside hearing the king's reply responded by repeating "Lele wale ka 'aha e (the *'aha* is successful; literally, has flown away)," so that all those nearby who took part in the *loulu* ceremonies would know that the service had been perfect. The cooking of the pigs in the imu was the work for the coming day.

In the next few days the men of the district, or island perhaps, readied the *luakini* with the building of all the houses previously mentioned. Those who were to gather small lama trees got ready and, taking a pig with them, went with the kahuna in charge of the work, all shouting aloud, like hurrahing. The first tree to be cut down was tied with *'oloa* tapa, and afterwards other trees with their leaves left on were cut down. This was after the kahuna had offered his prayers for the cutting of the tree and the killing of the pig. At the close of his prayer a pig was cooked. When the trees were all heaped up, those who came for them ate of the pig with the kahuna. Any remaining food was buried at the base of the first tree that had been cut down. After everything was ready, the kahuna uttered his final prayer, and they turned to go back. On their way down, one spoke first and then all the others shouted, thus:

E Kuamu, e Kuamu—Mu!	O silent ones, silent ones, hold your silence!
E Kuawa, e Kuawa—Wa!	O loud voiced ones, loud voiced ones, shout aloud!
Wa i ka ua lanakila uwa—Uwa!	Shout aloud of victory! Shout!

So they went along shouting thus to the unthatched buildings, where the workers were assembled. After the houses were thatched, in a single day or perhaps in two days, the *kauila nui* ceremony took place. During these days, those

Examples of feather images in (top) Dominion Museum, Wellington, and Bishop Museum and (bottom) in British and Berlin Ethnographic museums.

who were living under kapu mingled with those who were thatching the houses, and all of them participated in that ceremony. When all the men had been arranged, the kahuna who had gathered the lama trees erected them in the spaces between the men in rows, until it looked as though they were in a beautiful forest in the shade of the trees.

Then appeared the feather gods carried by their *kahu*. With them was Kahoalii, a man who impersonated a god of that name, and the person who carried the *kapuo* stick, to whom questions of all kinds were addressed by the kahunas. The bearer of the *kapuo* stick was the first in line. Then came Kahoalii; then, the feather gods. The last god in the line was called the *akua panauea* (slow god) because he moved along so slowly. There were only two real men in the line, Kahoalii, who did not wear a real malo but only a small white strip in front as a concealment, and the person who carried the *kapuo* stick.

Before the gods began their procession, the kahuna of the lama trees stood up and smote some hala clusters, five or six of them perhaps. As they broke up, pieces flew among the men who sat in the *kauila* ceremony as though on canoes. The people who were watching the ceremonies laughed at the ducking of heads to dodge the flying pieces. It was like a game, something they could laugh at with impunity.

According to the rules of this rite of the procession of gods, the *kapuo* stick bearer, who was directly in front of the line at the center of the kahunas standing there, made a left turn and marched to their right. The line of gods followed and turned where he had until the last one [except for the *akua panauea*] reached the spot from which the *kapuo* stick bearer had started. Then he turned again and came back to the left, as the rest remained standing. Again they each turned at the same spot and returned, finishing the procession. On their return, Kahoalii hurried to catch up with the *kapuo* stick bearer and the *akua panauea* on the latter's left. The *akua panauea*, because of his slowness, had just reached the spot from which to turn left the first time. Having reached this spot, the *kapuo* stick bearer and Kahoalii stopped. Each of those following behind drew up to his proper place. Then they all turned left again. The *akua panauea* moved slowly in front of them and returned to his place at the end of the line. His slowness was prescribed, for that was the nature of this god, perhaps.

As the gods stood there in a row before the kahunas, the kahunas asked questions in unison of the person who carried the *kapuo* stick, like this:

> The great news is told of what?
> The great news is borne of such-and-such, a canoe hauled for so-and-so.
> The great news is told of what?
> The great news is borne of such-and-such, a canoe hauled for so-and-so.
> The great news is told of what?
> The great news is borne of *Noiku*, the canoe hauled for Kamehameha.
> The great news is told of what?
> The great news is borne of *Humuuloa*, the canoe hauled for Iolani [Liholiho].

Perhaps if the custom were practiced to this day, questions like this would be asked concerning Kamehameha III, Kamehameha IV, and so on. It is thought that the person who was questioned was an assistant to the high priest of the Moo Ku order. The manner in which the answers were made and the way the line of gods made their circuit were subjects of great praise.

When this ceremony was over, the one who offered the prayer for life stood up, and this is what he said, "E ku kaikaina, hiki, hiki a ola (Stand ready, younger brothers, to receive life)." Then everyone stood up together. Those who sat among the leafy lama trees shouted in unison until all was over. Then all the men were dismissed to go to their own homes without bothering those who remained under the kapu. What a strange atmosphere!

The following night, before going for the *haku 'ohi'a* [the *'ohi'a* log from which to carve the principal image], the sacred adz was consecrated. This adz was called an *'olopu* and had been handed down from ancient times. If the night was without rain, thunder, lightning or other signs of storm, all was well. The king, the kahunas, and the feather gods and their keepers went upland with adzes to the place where the *'ohi'a* trees grew. The one whose duty it was to select a suitable tree for the *haku 'ohi'a* went ahead. Having noted how to reach it, the kahunas, the king, the bearer of the *'olopu* adz, and one who carried a pig healthy from its birth went together. As they went the kahuna uttered the customary prayer, thus:

Ka ke ala, mauele ka,	Cut a path, clear the brush,
Ka i luna ke ala, mauele ka,	Cut an upward path, clear the brush,
Ka i lalo ke ala, mauele ka,	Cut a downward path, clear the brush,
Ka i uka ke ala, mauele ka, etc. [sic]	Cut an inland path, clear the brush...

The kahuna touched with this *'olopu* adz the tree selected for the cutting, and the pig was put to death. The tree was hewn down with another adz, and an imu was lighted for the pigs offered for the tree and for the gods. All the kahunas responded with memorized prayers in the form of chants, for this was as much a part of their work as it was that of composers of chants. After the kahuna had offered a prayer, the pigs were cooked, the drums of the gods were beaten, and all the other foods brought with them to the forest were made ready. At the end of the feast, the remnants were buried at the stump of the cut tree. If there was a man who had broken a law, his body was buried with the other things at the tree stump. Such a man was called a *kanaka no mau ha'alelea* (man left behind) because he was eliminated from the procession.

The men made ready all the logs, which were stripped of their bark, and bore them down to the lowland and to the grounds of the heiau. They walked in pairs, in front of and after each log. So it went, from beginning to end of the procession. If the carriers had many large logs, they also had many small ones. As the procession began to go down, one led in the shouting, and all the others followed suit, thus:

E Kuamu e Kuamu, Mu!	O silent ones, silent ones, hold your silence!
E Kuawa e Kuawa, Wa!	O loud voiced ones, loud voiced ones, shout aloud!
Wa i ka ua lanakila uwa! Uwa!	Shout aloud of victory! Shout!

They kept up the shouting until they came to the outer grounds of the heiau, a fearful and terrifying procession. It was not wise for anyone to pass by while the procession was returning, lest he die. Death was the penalty for an infraction of the rules for any of these ceremonies. When they arrived all of the logs were set upright there, and everyone returned to his own house.

Like the laws governing the fetching of the ʻohiʻa logs, so were those of the *kuili* rites prescribed. Fuel was made ready, kukui-nut candles were lighted in the Hale Mana, in which the priests offered their *kuili* prayers, and the three or four pigs cooked at dawn each day for the kahunas were carried to this house. The *kuili* prayers began after the evening meal, about seven or eight o'clock by modern calculation, and continued until six in the morning. The king and chiefs were present to listen to the recitations of the kahunas. The saying, "na kahuna kuʻi lena ʻai puaʻa (yellow-molared, pork-eating kahunas)," came from this ceremony, because only the kahunas ate pork until the nights of the *kuili* were over.

As the *kauila* ceremonies and the *haku ʻohiʻa* and *kuili* rites [of the ʻaha Hulahula] had been *maikaʻi,* the Hoowilimoo ʻaha ceremony mentioned previously was performed.

That same night, perhaps before the Hoowilimoo ceremony, the laws governing the *kapapa ulua* were observed. This was a fearful activity; and the children and loved ones were closely guarded, for those who took part were ready to kill anyone, man, woman, or child. Canoes were readied with victims, or if there were none caught, then with various kinds of fishes, such as the *ulua* and squid. All the offerings of that night were taken by the *kahuna kapapa ulua* to the *loulu* rites. As he passed, everybody was very quiet, and no one moved until he entered the proper place to leave what he had brought with him. Then he left, continuously uttering his prayers. It was during this rite that warriors of an opposing side were offered. They were brought on a hook (*maunu ʻia*) before the gods and put to death. When the *kahuna kapapa ulua* returned peacefully, it was said that all was *maikaʻi.* If the day remained *maikaʻi* until night, the kingdom would be at peace. Such was the nature of the *kapu loulu.*

After the Hoowilimoo rites were over, the ritual of the dreaded *hono* ceremony was observed. This began the following day or on the second day. On that day, all the chiefs and men went bathing to rid themselves of the odor and grease of the pigs that they had eaten shortly before and, perhaps, in order to be purified. There were three or four pigs to be cooked that day for those who were to take part in the ceremony.

After bathing, the participants in the *hono* were seated. The few who participated did so only in the expectation of receiving some pork from the three or four pigs cooked especially for the ceremony. The men sat crosslegged in rows in line with each of the images that stood from one end to the other before the ʻanuʻu tower, each man erect, one behind the other. Both elbows rested on the upper part of the thighs, the left wrist under the right one. The participants waited to be told to "put up the hands, up above." Whoever wished to could raise both his hands, but that was optional. Those who raised only the right hand rested the left one on the right knee, assuming as humble a posture as he saw fit. It was forbidden to shift one's position or move more than his arm while the kahuna of the *hono* uttered his prayers, which lasted a whole hour. When one of the company felt his upraised arms growing tired, he lowered them slowly to rest upon his thighs. But none dared to raise his head, lest he die.

In this ceremony, a person who kept both his hands upraised until the time was up made a decided impression. One who held the thumb of his upraised right hand erect was called a "catcher of flies" (*poʻi nalo*). When the ceremony was over, it was common to hear someone who had participated boast over the steadiness of his upraised arms and his immobility, even when some thing he dreaded, such as a lizard or a rat, climbed onto his body. Perhaps such boasting was no different than it is today.

On the day chosen to finish the observance of the *kapu loulu* the kahuna whose duty it was made ready. There were two or three female images that stood on the places chosen for such. These were covered with tapa dyed with turmeric. Two of the images were called Kalamainuu (Kihawahine), a lizard goddess, and Haumea, also known as Kamehaikana when she entered a breadfruit tree in her supernatural form. It was said that her husband Makea was killed and his corpse placed on a breadfruit tree, which she entered. Makea was not the real name of the person who died, it was Punaaikoae.

In the tradition of Punaaikoae it is said that these women, Walinuu, the first wife of Punaaikoae, Kalamainuu (Kihawahine), and Haumea, fought in their human forms over this man who was their husband, perhaps because of jealousy. In the fight Kalamainuu lost the sight of one eye and Walinuu's nose was broken. This was shown in their images that were set up at the Hale o Papa. When they were borne before the audience, they were just as they had been described in the tradition.

After this, the kahuna of the Hale o Papa uttered the appropriate prayer in the presence of the assembly to end the *kapu loulu*. Before he started a fire, the sacrificial dogs and pigs were killed. The assembled people kept quiet as the women at the head of the kingdom brought forth several malos of *ninikea*, a fine white tapa. A suckling pig was borne squealing in the arms of the *kahuna kaʻi malo*. The kahuna held the pig and one end of the malo, while the other end was held in the right hand of the chiefess whose malo and pig they were. It was she who uttered the ʻ*amama* before the assembly and chiefs. At the end of her ʻ*amama* each returned to the place where she had been sitting before, just as Keakealaniwahine had done. After the dogs were cooked and the feast eaten the kahuna of the Hale o Papa stood up to pray, and when he had finished, the king stood up and pronounced his *'amama*. The same kahuna replied in this way:

He mu waia,	Let the disgraceful one be silent,
He mu.	Be silent.
He mu ka 'ai ku, ka 'aia,	Let the wicked, careless eater be silent,
He mu na lawehala,	Let the wrongdoers be silent,
He mu.	Be silent.

After the kahuna uttered a line, the assembly of people repeated it in unison. This continued until the rite was over. The remainder of the feast and offerings were laid on the *lele* altar with *popo'ulu* or *iholena* bananas, varieties that were permitted to the goddesses, and hence were appropriate for the altar of the Hale o Papa. Thus ended the rites of that benighted period.

After two or three days, another kapu period was imposed in the Hale o Papa which lasted two nights and a day. Pigs were sacrificed, but not as many as for the preceding period. After this *kapu ho'omahanahana* [kapu for the "warmth of life"] the places in the *luakini* heiau were closed up.

This *kapu loulu* brought peace for the duration of the reign of the king, so those of that time declared. Should the king die, war would follow, they said. However, the descendants of the idolators must understand that all things are from the presence of the Almighty, who created all things.

Perhaps two years after Liholiho was chosen as heir, a proclamation was sent to the people of Kumelewai to get materials for thatching heiau houses, and Ii's attendant had to go to his parcel of land, where his tax was to be collected. So the boy left his parents for love of his attendant. His parents gave their permission, for they knew his attendant took good care of the boy whenever they went anywhere.

All the people who went on the journey arrived in the upland of Kalihi, near the diving pool of Waiakoae, for they thought that that would be the nearest place to obtain dry ti leaves, timber, thatching sticks, and *'ie* fibers for tying on the thatch. Here the boy joined the children of the region in bathing and diving while the men, including his attendant, went inland for all the supplies needed. At this place there were many expert canoe makers, whose children were among Ii's playmates. The first time that they met with Kamehameha's canoe makers, his attendant explained who the boy was, a usual procedure.

When the heiau houses were to be thatched, the attendant and the boy went to Honolulu. There he was seen by his namesake, Papa, who asked, "Is that little boy Papa?" and inquired with whom he had come. The boy was called to sit in his presence and they conversed quietly, face to face. So it went until the houses were completed.

Papa was the owner of the houses for the worship of the gods of healing, Lonopuha and Kaneikoleamoku and others. Such houses were built for the gods following training in feeling for and diagnosing diseases, in studying the location by making an outline of the body with pebbles, in selecting the medicine to use, and in the treating of the ailment after diagnosis. As Papa was most skilled in this art, he acted as Kamehameha's medical kahuna whenever the king was sick. Whatever nature of disease the chiefs had, Papa excelled in treating them.

Kuauau, another kahuna, treated the people. Like his father, Kama, he was skilled in his work. It was said that his methods of preparing medicines and treating people were entirely different from those of Papa. Papa's methods were greatly feared because a patient fainted often, though he recovered completely afterward. The skill of Papa, Kailio, and Kama was famous.

The method of training promising members of the court as medical kahunas is believed to have developed because of the great death rate among chiefs and commoners in the year 1806, perhaps owing to the terrible *'oku'u* disease, when the epidemic spread among all of the chiefs and commoners of these islands. We believe it to have been the time when Henry Opukahaia and his companion left Kealakekua, Hawaii, and sailed to the United States where he learned of the true God. In that year, the person whose writing this is left the bosom of his mother to eat in the men's house, or *hale mua*. Perhaps you can understand how it was, his worshiping in ignorance. Though he understands and is familiar with the unenlightened rites of that period, he does not turn to the left or to the right from the Bible or from the power of the Holy Spirit.

Peleula was covered with healing heiaus, where offerings were made and methods of healing were taught. The locations of all diseases they had sought and found in man were marked by the placing of pebbles. This helped them to recognize the nature of the disease. Feeling with the hands indicated whether the disease would be fatal or was curable if treated then. They learned the proper remedy, the methods of treatment, the results to expect, and the island where a disease was first discovered. For instance: "It appeared on the island of Niihau (or Kauai, or another island); such-and-such was the place; such-and-such is the pig to offer; such-and-such is the clothing; such-and-such is the disease; and such-and-such is the remedy."

This went on until all the islands were mentioned, with the diseases and medicines, the kinds of pigs, and the clothing suitable for offerings. All of these things composed and arranged for memorizing were learned by all the students of the art of healing. These were among the things they recited to the medical instructors, including the names of the *'aumakua* gods of healing from remote times. This was done in front of the heiaus we have mentioned, and if the recitation was perfect, it was believed that such a person would attain skill in treating various diseases. A live pig, squealing on the way, was brought to the kahuna as a gift from the patient. If there were many kinds of diseases in a patient, the methods of treatment were many and it was understood that the expense would be great.

Perhaps some may question how this or that disease originated on any particular island. This is an important tale, which began in the time of Milu. No one knows what year it was that Milu lived in the land of Waipio, in Hamakua, Hawaii. It was said that some men came from Kahiki with their wives, but which Kahiki it was no one knows. They were all like gods, it was said. They first arrived on Niihau, then continued on to all of the islands. They came to the southern part of Hawaii, to Puna, to Hilo, and then to Kukuihaele in Hamakua, above Waipio Valley. On every island where they went, fatal diseases spread among the chiefs and commoners, and it was believed that this was their doing. It was said that these were the same people who lived in Kukuihaele in the time of Liloa or earlier, but this was not ascertained. The names of some of these people are Kaalaenui a Hina, Kahuilaokalani, and Kaneikaulanaula. When Milu, the chief whom they had long sought to destroy, was dead, they departed from Kukuihaele. They journeyed on the windward side of Maui as far as Wailua, where two of these mysterious beings, Pua and Kapo, remained. The company continued to Maunaloa, at Kaluakoi, Molokai, and took possession of the woods there, and there they remained. It was said that they went into the trees of that mountain woodland.

Kamakanuiahailono came later. Whereas the others brought destruction, he brought healing. Here let us speak briefly of the land of Kukuihaele where Kamakanuiahailono made his abode and which was believed to be the land of medical kahunas. So it seemed, and the descendants of the medical kahunas continued to live there, down to Kama and his son, Kuauau, all the days of Kamehameha's life, if I am not mistaken.

As we have seen before, the diseases and medicines and remedies were arranged according to all the islands down to Hawaii. The symptoms mentioned were chills, fever, dull headache, a pain that shut off the breathing, and so on. If the disease was the *papaku* (extreme constipation), or the *eho* (ulcerous sore), or the *haikala* (a severe disease accompanied by cramps), then *waiiki*, a mixture of green gourd juice and kukui sap, was the very best medicine to use. Some kahunas did not know the proper treatment, and many persons sickened and died quickly in the time of Boki *ma*.

As those we have talked about before were famed for their skill, so were Boki and Kalamaku and their treatment of serious diseases with *waiiki*. Their fame dated from the time they treated Kekuanaoa. It was said that he had one of these diseases in his youth and that it was believed he would die unless treated, but that with treatment he would live to have his second hair color, gray. Perhaps this was said for his own good. When they began to treat him, he fainted two or three times, but with succeeding treatments he ceased to faint. Thus they were nearer to their cure, and so it continued. He was hardly ever sick after that until death took him.

So it was with Kaoo. He too was famous for his treatments, and his method was similar to theirs. He described the ailment of the person whose writing this is in his youth. It was the *hokale* (a mastoid infection), and the remedy was to be a series of treatments. He said that if the body matured, no remedy would help. Death would result if he was not given the *waiiki* treatment in his youth. All of the assistants made preparations, for within two weeks he was to be given the *waiiki*. But when some people heard that he was to be so treated, they were afraid lest he faint away into death. Therefore the treatment was not given, and now the things Kaoo said have come to pass, and the writer is much troubled and suffers.

We may well ask the question, "Who is able to treat diseases now?" It is uncertain, for actual treatment is now mixed with superstition and spiritualism and mere lies. The medical kahunas whom we described did thus: The matter was presented to the gods in the evening, and the next day the method of treatment was studied. If the case was a good one, the god was consulted to find out whether the treatment would be successful. Such were the ways of the times, but now they return like dogs and pigs into ignorance and do not consider the Will of God. Why should that be, now that we have come to the time of light, when those of heaven dwell with us?

Let us talk a little of Kalanimoku's sickness. He knew that he was going to suffer with *'opu'ohao* (dropsy) if he was not treated in time, and he consulted Kaoo *ma*. It was agreed that the *waiiki* was the only suitable treatment for that type of disease. Kalanimoku agreed to undergo treatment by them, for his brother Boki was away with king Liholiho in England then. Before he was given the *waiiki*, Kalanimoku told Moluhi and the others what to do when he fainted, and that they were not to be afraid or worried over his frequent fainting before the discharge came. "After the discharge, I shall recover," he said. He fainted two or three times, but his bowels did not act and the discharge did not come. It was Moluhi who prevented the full treatment from being given. When Kalanimoku came out of the faint, he asked whether they had done as he had said. When they replied, Kalanimoku said, "I shall not be rid of this disease because you were all afraid." It was as he said.

Perhaps we should tell how Boki knew that Hookio, the son of Kaluhiapawa and a skilled orator, would die. This was after Boki and the others returned from England. Boki felt him, and said, "You are seriously ill and there is no remedy to help you. You are going to die."

At this, words came from Hookio's mouth, "You have discovered the nature of my disease and that I am going to die. I, too, see that you are very seriously ill." The sickness that he saw in Boki was shame over his wish to rebel against Kaahumanu. The words of each were fulfilled.

CHAPTER IV

EARLY 1800'S IN HONOLULU

Once Kinopu gave a tribute of fish to Kamehameha's son, Kinau, at Moehonua's fish pond in Kalia. While Kinau and his wife Kahakuhaakoi (Wahinepio) were going to Waikiki from Honolulu, the sea came into the pond and fishes of every kind entered the sluice gate. Kinopu ordered the keepers of the pond to lower fish nets, and the result was a catch so large that a great heap of fish lay spoiling upon the bank of the pond.

The news of the huge catch reached Kamehameha, who was then with Kalanimoku, war leader and officer of the king's guard. The king said nothing at the time, but sat with bowed head and downcast eyes, apparently disapproving of such reckless waste. Had they caught enough for a meal, perhaps forty or twenty, nothing would have been said. However, Kalanimoku, apparently knowing why the king kept his head bowed, commanded Kinopu to release most of the fish. Kinopu's act became common knowledge, and the report caught up with the two travelers, Kinau and Kahakuhaakoi. When Kalaimamahu, Kamehameha's half brother, heard what his nephew Kinau had done, his anger was kindled against him.

Like Kinau, Kalaimamahu was disappointed in his expectations. At the time of the battle of Mokuohai he had been the war leader on Kamehameha's side, and they had lived together in their beardless youth and were involved together in the affair with Kaneikapolei. Perhaps disagreement came between them later. The king took Kalaimamahu's first wife, Kaheiheimalie (Kalakua), from him. Then Kalaimamahu lived with their niece, Kahakuhaakoi, and to them was born Kahalaia. After that, Kahakuhaakoi was taken by Kinau, and Kekauonohi was born. Having no wife then, Kalaimamahu took to wife Kekela, who was to die in June 1865.

It is said that Kekela left Kalaimamahu in annoyance and retired to his lands in Laie, Koolauloa, to stay. She remained away so long that it troubled him. So he arose and went to Laie. They remained there enjoying themselves until they were said to be like kamaainas. Finally, Kalaimamahu was taken sick there. When the news was borne to the king, he ordered some chiefs and servants to meet the people on the other side of the Koolau Range. In that company was Kalaimamahu's beloved nephew Kinau. On its return, the company ascended to the rock Kahoowaha, on the way up to Kaipu o Lono. Kalaimamahu, lying on a stretcher, saw Kinau coming up behind him and chanted in *kepakepa* style, thus:

Keiki 'ino ho'olawehala,	Bad boy, who causes trouble,
Hala i Kahuaiki a pae ke keiki.	Kahuaiki has been passed, the boy lands.
I hewa kaua ia 'oe e ke keiki.	You have caused us woe, my boy.

These words uttered by the uncle to his nephew showed how feelings of affection welled up in him at the sight of Kinau. He felt that they were both condemned, he for standing by the son borne to his brother in his youth. All of their friends remembered this and that it had cost them the privilege of holding government positions, their punishment for not supporting the kingdom and the king. The chant Kalaimamahu uttered as the company ascended the cliff of Kaipu o Lono in Nuuanu was quickly memorized by those who heard it, and became something to recall.

After Kalaimamahu reached the lowland of Honolulu, he lived only a few weeks. His land in Koolauloa was inherited by his daughter and, later, by his grandson, Lunalilo.

When Kamehameha took Kaheiheimalie away from him, Kalaimamahu did not take back any part of the land he had given her, which was Makapala, in Kohala, Hawaii. He had always thought a great deal of her and of their eldest child, Kekauluohi o Mano, a daughter for whom his love remained strong until his death. After Kaheiheimalie died the property which was inherited by their daughter and their grandson, Lunalilo, remained as it was until the reign of Kamehameha III. He divided the lands in the Great Mahele of 1848, believing that the division would be permanent. It was said that he was the greatest of the kings, a royal parent who loved his Hawaiian people more than any other chief before him.

When, in 1809, Kanihonui, a nephew of Kamehameha, was put to death for committing adultery with Kaahumanu, Kaahumanu's wrath was aroused. She sought to recover from her anger but was unable to do so; and she considered taking the kingdom from the king by force and giving it to the young chief, Liholiho. Before she laid her plans for the war, a holiday for the purpose of surfing at Kapua in Waikiki was proclaimed, because the surf was rolling fine then. It was where one could look up directly to the heiau on Leahi, where the remains of Kanihonui were, all prepared in the customary manner of that time. It was said that only Kaleiheana, who was a Luluka, watched over the corpse from the time of death until it was decomposed. The chiefess had heard something about her lover's remains being there, and perhaps that was why the proclamation was made.

On the appointed day, chiefs, chiefesses, prominent people, and the young chief Liholiho went to Kapua. When all had assembled there, the king gathered his men together in readiness for trouble. He sent a messenger, Kinopu, after Kaahumanu's followers to find out what they were planning. It is said that three things were done at Kapua: surfing, lamenting, and more surfing; and it is said that they had intoxicants with them. Thus they whiled away the time until evening.

Before the company returned to Honolulu, Kaahumanu, surrounded by the chiefs, kept crying and looking up at Leahi. Keeaumoku, the father of the chiefess, had died during the 'oku'u epidemic, but Kalanimoku was there, watching over his grieving cousin. While the young chief and a group of chiefs were in their presence, Kalanimoku asked, "What do you think? Shall we wrest the kingdom from your father, make you king, and put him to death?"

Liholiho bowed his head in meditation before he looked at the gathering, and answered, "I do not want my father to die." This reply brought forth the admiration of all of the chiefs.

Kinopu, Kamehameha's messenger, returned before the company reached Honolulu and told Kamehameha all he had seen and heard, including the reply the young chief had made. When the king heard what the young chief had said he was touched and stated, "He is indeed a chief. He did not side with his guardian although he knew everything that had gone on. He chose patience rather than the kingdom. That is the nature of a true chief." Then the king asked of Kinopu, "What did the guardians and chiefs think of his reply?"

"They all admired him for it," replied Kinopu.

"Where are the chiefs?" inquired the king.

"When I left, they were getting ready to return," replied Kinopu, whose words caused the king to dismiss the men, except the usual guards. Then the chiefs arrived, talking about the young chief.

Liholiho was the most kapu of chiefs because he had inherited kapus from both sides. He inherited the *kapu moe* from his mother, Keopuolani, and the *kapu wohi* from Kamehameha, his father.

Those who had the *kapu moe* did not appear often in the daytime, lest the people be troubled, but usually went about at night. When two relatives were

51

at war and the fighting grew bitter, they could resort to the *kapu moe* to put an end to the fighting. For example, in the battle of Kakanilua between Kahekili and Kalaniopuu, Kiwalao put an end to the fighting by this means. When he appeared, those on both sides prostrated themselves. He also had the *kapu wohi*, the second of his kapus.

This *kapu wohi* was not like the other. It was considered a good kapu, for it permitted one to associate with men, women, and children. If one with the *kapu moe* came before one with the *kapu wohi*, it was needless for the latter to prostrate himself, for he could walk in the presence of the other. The back of a chief who had the *kapu wohi* was kept at a distance of about two fathoms. Only the person who fetched his personal belongings could pass to-and-fro there, and he kept slightly to one side of the back of the godly person. The kapu area was called *kuapala* because the *wohi* chief carried the *pala* fern and *'ie'ie* vines for the gods when the time for doing so arrived. The term *kuapala* included both the area and the persons permitted to walk behind the chief.

The *kapu wohi* was inherited by Kamehameha I; and both kapus were given to all the other Kamehamehas who reigned as kings, down to the present Kamehameha. Should their observance be continued today you would see how troublesome and unrealistic they were.

It is well, here, to explain that these kapus originated from the much-talked-of Haloa, who was perhaps like Judah among the Israelites. It is said that the two kapus were joined by Keakealaniwahine, a sacred chiefess of Hawaii who inherited the *kapu moe*, and Kaneikauaiwilani of Oahu, her royal mate to whom the *kapu wohi* belonged. Their daughter, Kalanikauleleiaiwi, inherited the two kapus.

If we understand the ancestral line of the chiefs, we know those who are connected with the family of Haloa, for we know the genealogies of the chiefs from Keakealaniwahine and Kaneikauaiwilani, son of Iwikauikaua. Iwikauikaua mated with Keakamahana and had Keakealaniwahine. Iwikauikaua mated also with Kauakahiakuaanaauakane and had Kaneikauaiwilani, and Keakealaniwahine and Kaneikauaiwilani had Kalanikauleleiaiwi. From them descended many of the chiefs of today.

The division of the kapus came about in this way. Kalanikauleleiaiwi dwelt with Keawe i Kekahialiiokamoku and Kekuiapoiwanui, Keeaumokunui, and Kekelaokalani were born. Keawe asked Kalanikauleleiaiwi for a kapu to be given to his first-born son Kaeamamao [Kalaninuiiamamao, by Lonomaaikanaka], and Kalanikauleleiaiwi gave him the *kapu moe*, reserving the *kapu wohi* for all of her own children. Kaeamamao dwelt with Kamakaimoku and had Kalaniopuu. Kalaniopuu dwelt with Kalola, and Kiwalao was born. Kiwalao dwelt with Liliha Kekuiapoiwa and Keopuolani, to whom the *kapu moe* descended, was born.

The descent of the *kapu wohi* came about thus. Kekuiapoiwanui dwelt with Kekaulike of Maui; and Kamehamehanui, Kalola, and Kahekili were born. Kekelaokalani dwelt with Haae and Kekuiapoiwa II was born.

Keeaumokunui dwelt with Kamakaimoku and had Keoua Kupuapaikalani. Keoua dwelt with Kalola and had Liliha; Keoua dwelt with Kekuiapoiwa II and had Kamehameha. Kamehameha dwelt with Kaheiheimalie and had Kamamalu and Kinauwahine.

Kalanikauleleiaiwi had other descendants, thus: She dwelt with Kauaua a Mahi and had Alapainui, and she dwelt with Lonoikahaupu and had Keawepoepoe. Keawepoepoe dwelt with Kumaaiku and had Keeaumoku Papaiahiahi, Alapai Maloiki, and Kaulunae. This Keeaumoku dwelt with Namahana and had Kaahumanu, Kaheiheimalie, Keeaumokuopio, Kuakini, and Piia (Namahana, Kekuaipiia).

Here is something else: Kaneikaheilani, a chiefess from Kauai related to the royal families of Lihue and of Kukaniloko, Oahu, went traveling to Oahu, Maui, and on to Hawaii; and she acquired a husband during these travels. It was said that her first husband, Kahalio, belonged to Kekaha, Kauai. Later, she dwelt with Kaaloaapii and had Kalelemauli. Kalelemauli lived with Haae and had Kamakaeheikuli and Haalou, both girls.

Keoua dwelt with Kamakaeheikuli, and Kalaimamahu was born. Kalaimamahu dwelt with Kaheiheimalie, and Kekauluohi was born. Haalou dwelt with Kekaulike, and Namahana and Kekumanoha were born. Kekumanoha dwelt with Kamakahukilani; and Kalanimoku, Kahakuhaakoi (Wahinepio, Kamoonohu) and Boki Kamauleule were born.

In this royal genealogy, we can see that Kaahumanu, as the senior of her generation, and descendant of Kalanikauleleiaiwi and Kekaulike and Haalou was right in lording it over her brothers and sisters and their younger cousins.

When Ii and his mother dwelt in the presence of the chiefs at Honolulu they lived in the home of the boy's namesake, Papa, at Kaoaopa. Among the other children there were two boys, Manuia, son of Kamauawahine by Alapai, and Kaniukahi, son of Nahili by Nakaiwahine. These two boys and Ii were the three who were to be placed in the court of the young chief Liholiho. The favorite pastime of the three was drawing ships in the sand, probably because there were many ships in the harbor of Kou [Honolulu Harbor], at that time. Most of the visiting ships were American, the British ships numbering half as many. Ships of other lands were not so often seen as they are today.

Liholiho did much mischief to the boys whenever he found them playing some interesting game. For instance, when they played *pahiʻuhiʻu*, which consisted of throwing a sharpened dart at a marker in the sand, the young chief would run from a distance and bang their heads together. All they could do was cry. They became very watchful for his approach, and when he came near them they all ran home, to the chief's great annoyance.

Sometimes Ii's mother sent him to the place where all the soldiers of the king were being trained to march with guns. The boy used a gun which had belonged to Kamakahiki, a *kaikunane* relative of his mother who had died, leaving his gun in the care of Ii's mother. For several days the boy went to the scene of marching, where the field was filled with adults and children.

Drilling in those days was not quite like that of today, for they had only half of the present knowledge. The soldiers stood in line from the front all the way to the back, and so it was with each line. At the proper command, those in the front row, which extended from one end of the field to the other, raised their guns in unison and fired. Then they placed the guns on their shoulders, turned left about face, marked time, and began to advance. So it went until the drilling period was over.

Before the drilling started, a proclamation was sent to the women of the court to fetch and spread grass on the field early in the morning. This proclamation required all the women who served in the court, chiefesses of lesser rank and notables, to fetch grass from Kawaiahao. When Ii's female relatives (*kaikuahine*) went to pull grass at the designated place, the boy accompanied them. Absorbed in pulling grass, they forgot about the boy, assuming he had gone home. When they left he was sitting among the *makaloa* sedges growing all around him, busily occupied in building a house of coconut midribs. He had no inkling that he was going to encounter trouble until he heard a voice say, "Here is the boy who runs away from you."

When Ii glanced up he saw Liholiho and the person who carried his possessions. Right then his peace of mind left him, because he realized that he was going to be beaten and might even die as a result. After he had been beaten for some time, the person who carried the possessions of the chief said, "Do not give such a cruel beating to the servant who will be your follower when he grows up."

When the boy was finally left alone, he did not realize it immediately. After a time, when the aches and weariness of the beating he had received lessened, he lifted himself up and peered about, then rose and returned home. He went into his namesake's workshed and lay down near Papa's feet without being noticed, and he remained there until the young chief's companion came to report the beating the boy had received from the chief. It was not until his *kaikuahine* glanced around and saw him lying there that they remembered about leaving him. The boy said nothing, nor did his mother. He understood the thing she had taught him, to be patient and forbearing.

After the drilling came practice with spears, a fearful sight. Those who were accustomed to spear throwing showed remarkable skill. The opposing sides met every evening with spears of hau wood, their points unwrapped. Perhaps the points were left unshielded to show how skilled the contestants were. To those who were experts, the spears were as bathing water; and the sport was greatly enjoyed.

When the boy and his mother boarded a canoe and left the harbor of Kou, he asked for and was given a paddle to wield. Earlier he had learned a little about paddling a canoe made of *wiliwili* wood that his parents had provided for him. It was his mother who taught him how to paddle, and he became adept at it. They landed in Ewa, where his parents performed all their duties and tasks in a few days. They returned to Honolulu in the canoe.

About two or three weeks after the trip to Ewa, on the day of Muku, the last day of the lunar month, all of the chiefs went to Waikiki to surf. When evening came they went to Leahi, where the royal parent, Kamehameha, had a house separate from that of Liholiho. Ii and Papa shared the house of the young chief. When the sun grew warm the next day, which was Hilo, Papa called to Ii to come and sit beside him, where he lay face down at their end of the house. The young chief, who occupied the other half of the house, was watching. Papa asked his nephew which he would choose between Kamokupanee (Expanding Island) and Lualewa (Without Foundation). The boy was unable to answer, for he did not understand the question. Then he was told that Kamokupanee meant the father chief, Kamehameha, and Lualewa meant the young chief, Liholiho. He was embarrassed about being asked such a question in the presence of one of the chiefs; but he replied, "The father chief is the wealthy one. The young chief has no wealth." Then he added, "Perhaps I shall remain with Lualewa."

When Papa replied, "This chief of ours is without wealth," the boy said, "The chief without wealth should be obeyed, and when he becomes wealthy, the servant becomes wealthy too." All of those present approved of this reasoning, the young chief included.

They remained there two days before the company returned to Honolulu, when Ii's mother heard of his reply to his uncle's question and rejoiced. It seemed that the purpose of Papa's question was to convey a lesson to his chief.

The daughters of Kamehameha's fishermen were increasingly skillful in the playing of the *'ukeke*, a musical instrument which was a thin piece of coconut stem and midrib held over their mouths. Crowds of listeners gathered down in Kakaako to enjoy their *'ukeke* strumming, and the boy was there every evening. One evening while he was thus occupied his mother sent someone for him, as Kaleiheana had arrived with a message from the young chief that Ii was to come to him. When the boy received his mother's message to come home, he was very reluctant to leave the gathering, and lingered for a time. He was sent for again and again, and he was torn between wanting to stay and wanting to heed the instructions of his parent. However, after his mother had sent for him three or four times, he put aside his desire to stay and watch the fun, concluding it was better to mind. His body accompanied the messenger, but his mind was with the fun. When he reached home, the chief's messenger had left.

His mother said, "So you have come home? Your uncle Kaleiheana has been here and gone. He came to take you back to the chief, to the place we have trained you for, to observe, to be obedient, and to take care. You do not belong to us, though we begot you. You must become the servant of the chief, Liholiho, and all of the chiefs whom your uncles serve. Do as you did before them and your chief. Since you have agreed to do as I wish and as your father has taught you, you have been summoned. We know that you will be mindful of all we have taught you."

As the boy talked with his mother, he forgot the pleasures in which he had been so interested. Before he left her he asked, "What must I do when I long for you and for my father, now that we are separating? Perhaps we shall never live together again."

His mother said, "Do not think of us. The chief alone must be your father and your mother. From him shall come your vegetable food, your meat, your tapa coverings, and malos."

The boy asked, "May I not come and see you sometimes when you are as near as you are now?"

"It will be all right to do so at the proper time," she replied, "but it would be much better for you to remain with the chief with no thought of us, whether we are as near as we are now or far away."

While they talked, the sun passed to the opposite side of Mount Kaala, and his mother said, "Night has come for you."

"Homai ka ihu (embrace me; literally, give the nose)," replied the boy. Thus ended their living together, and the boy stood up and went to the residence of the chief.

Before he reached the place whence the command to him issued, the thoughts of all the rules taught to him by his parents rose up in the boy's mind. He recalled this place he came to, a short distance from where the Hale Hookolokolo, or court house, later stood. There was a beach there, and heiau houses, each one enclosed with a fence. Wooden female images stood outside of each enclosure, with *iholena* and *popoʻulu* bananas in front of them. There were *maoli* bananas before the male images at the *lele* altar inside of the enclosure of lama wood. Back of the male images of wood was an *ʻanuʻu* tower, about 8 yards (*iwilei*) high and 6 yards wide. It stood on the right side of the house, and was covered with strips of white *ʻoloa* tapa attached to the sticks resembling thatching sticks. The *opu* tower was just as tall and broad as the *ʻanuʻu*, and was wrapped in an *ʻaeokahaloa* tapa that resembled a *moelola* tapa. The small lama branches at its top were like unruly hair, going every which way. The *opu* stood on the left side of the house, facing the images and the *ʻanuʻu*. Between the two towers and extending from one to the other was a fine pavement of stones. In line with the middle of the pavement were the gate and the house which was called the Hale o Lono, where Liholiho was staying. It was thatched with dried ti leaves,

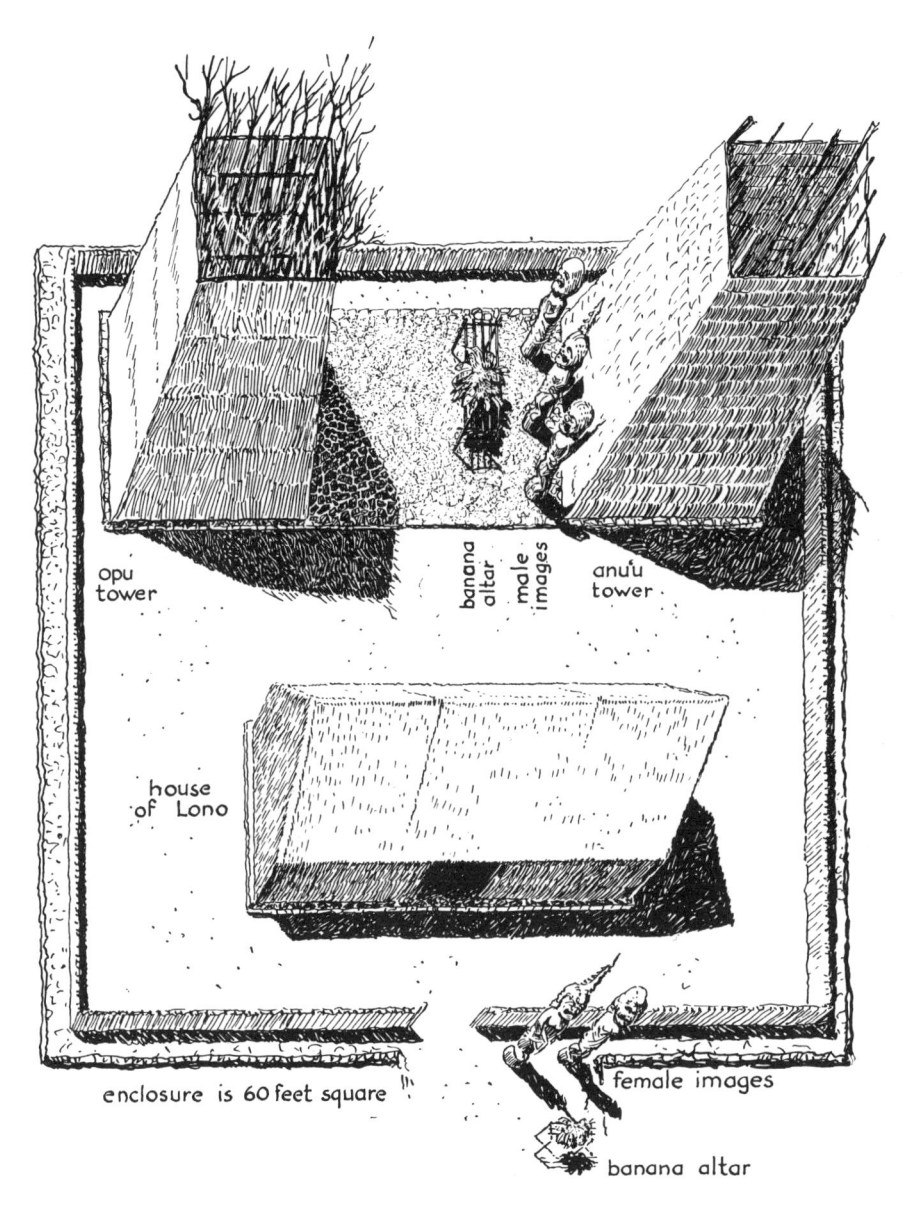

A Hale o Lono as depicted in the text. Drawing by Paul Rockwood.

just as Hale o Keawe in Honaunau, Hawaii, was thatched. Houses of this kind were all thatched with ti leaves, and all the posts and beams were of lama wood. The Hale o Lono was like a heiau. There were two others like it in the vicinity, one called the Hale Hui and the other, Hale o Kaili. The Hale Hui was the dwelling for miscellaneous gods and Hale o Kaili was for the god Kaili, or Kukailimoku.

As the boy drew near the Hale o Lono, he saw two crossed lama sticks outside the entrance gate. He knew that the tapa covering he wore must be removed before entering, and this he did although he was not yet near the houses. Then he walked to the steward's house just outside the enclosure and found Liholiho there waiting for him. When he was recognized by the occupants of the house and was told to enter, he went in and sat by the edge of the fireplace. He bundled his tapa and just sat as a stranger. The chief and people of the house treated him kindly.

Night had fallen, and the chief and the burning kukui-nut candles furnished the light there. After they had finished eating in the men's house, which was the one he had entered, the chief and the others stood up and went to the Hale o Lono. The boy departed with them, imitating their way of walking, just as his parents had told him to do. Thus began his knowledge of life in the royal court.

A few days after Ii went to him, Liholiho returned to his houses near Kaoaopa, where most of his attendants lived. On the plain, at the north side of the place, stood the house of the chief and that of his steward, Papa. They were not fenced in, but four stationary kapu sticks (*pahu puloʻuloʻu*) had been placed one at each corner, and these served as the enclosure for the houses. The boy had gone there frequently when he was little and had been taught how to walk and sit in the house and how to leave it. When the chief went there, all of his articles were given to the boy to carry, and thus he became the chief's companion. Before he picked the articles up, the boy tightened his malo so that he need not touch it again while his hands were occupied with the chief's things. As they walked along he kept to one side, for it was not proper to walk directly behind the chief, whose back was kapu (*kuapala*). The companion also avoided the chief's shadow lest his own shadow fall on Liholiho when the sun was in the east or in the west. So it was, at all times, with the shadow of the chief's house.

There were other kapus to be observed when going to any of the chief's residences. When one reached either the *puloʻuloʻu* markers or the gate of the enclosure he must immediately remove his tapa cloak or cape, bundle it, and cover it with grass—a sign of humility—before he entered. Sometimes the person entering must crawl to where the chief's mat was spread, passing between the chief and the kukui light, lest his shadow fall upon the chief. The gate and door of the house were very kapu, and no one was allowed to linger there except the chief. He could do as he pleased. When a *lelea* prayer was offered while the chief and his eating companions ate, everyone else knelt with his knees tightly together. They could not relax even slightly and could not move until the meal and prayer were finished.

Six members of the royal family had the kapu that required everyone to squat down (*noho*) as their possessions were carried past. These were Keopuolani and her son Liholiho and Kamehameha I, his son Kekuaiwa Kamehameha, and his daughters Kamamalu and Kinau. Five of them had stationary kapu sticks to enclose their houses, but Kamehameha I did not.

The other kapu chiefs were all revered, and kapus were observed in their homes. However, no one need squat down when the possessions of such chiefs passed by; they were covered with ti leaves or something else. These other chiefs were Keliimaikai and his son Kekuaokalani; Kaoleioku; and Piipii and her foster children Kapulikoliko, Kaiko, and Kahekili.

It was said of Keliimaikai that whatever he dedicated became very kapu. If it was a bathing pool, it became so kapu that men were not allowed to bathe there with malos on. Because of this rule, a bathing pool in the upland of Kawaihae was called Keliialaalahoolaawai (The chief who roused to dedicate the water). Also in Kawaihae was a kapu bathing pool called Alawai.

The house of Liholiho was named Hookuku; Kamehameha's house was named Papa; Keopuolani's, Kualalua; and Kaahumanu's, Kapapoko. While the boy was at Hookuku with the chief, he passed the heiaus where he and his attendant had been, and was reminded of his attendant and of their separation. After he had finished looking at the heiaus and had reentered the house, the chief asked him where he had been, to which he replied, "To the back of the heiaus, and then I returned."

The chief spoke again, "Those are the heiaus for healing which belong to you and to your uncle Papa."

When evening came they left Hookuku and returned to the Hale o Lono. As they traveled along the beach of Kuloloia from Kaoaopa, they saw many chiefs. Ii, who was carrying the young chief's spittoon in front of him, had a brush with death when somehow the cover slipped off, struck his knee, and bounced up again. He was able to catch it and so was saved from death, for had it dropped to his feet, his fate would have been that of Maoloha. As it was, he was criticized for forgetting the rule that the spittoon should be held at the back of his neck or shoulder, in which case the cover would not be stepped over if dropped. The boy became very nervous with chiefs watching him and talking about his narrow escape. When they reached home, the chiefs told some of the people there how he had passed the hill of death. Then they told him some of the other rules, and these were identical with those he had heard from his mother.

Ii's second escape from death was during a kapu of the heiau called Halelau. This was a long house, built with lama-wood rafters and posts. This house

A heiau house at Napoopoo, showing two Lono images. Photograph of an original drawing by Surgeon William Ellis.

for the god Lonomakua was thatched with dried ti leaves and surrounded by a fence of lama wood.

The kapu was imposed in the Halelau on the evening of Kane for the purpose of asking the blessing of the gods on their medical work. On the following day, Lono, the services and ceremonies were observed if the ceremony of the preceding night was successful. Pigs raised for the occasion were roasted (*kalua*), as was the custom. On the night of Lono, the kahunas prayed continuously in unison from evening until the next morning, Mauli, when the great kapu was to be lifted by the *koʻokoʻo* prayer. Before this prayer was given, Ii was told to go elsewhere in order to be out of the way, but the activities were so interesting he did not want to leave. The Halelau was some distance from the house where they all lived and another house stood between it and the Halelau. The boy went to the middle house instead of going home. The kapu was imposed with the words: "Kapu la, make la, a 'apu'e (It is kapu, it is death, a very strict kapu)." All talking and noises of every kind were silenced, under penalty of death.

No sooner was the kapu imposed than the boy felt a tickling sensation in his throat that made him want to cough. He held his throat with his hands until his eyes and throat were red, but finally he could no longer bear it. He coughed two or three times, but, fortunately, was not heard by those who had imposed the kapu. Those who were in the house with him were distressed, and one person dug a hole for him to cough into while another supplied a basin of water. When the kapu-freeing prayer was uttered, and the need for discomfort was over, he was greatly relieved. Had he been heard coughing, he would have been snatched from this world. Such were the many troubles that followed one about in the royal court.

The boy had seen all parts of the royal town and various places belonging to Liholiho before he went to live with him, and by this time had lost his fear of haoles, for there were many who constantly passed through the town from visiting ships. As he learned to associate with them, he found them pleasant.

One haole, a man called Namakaeha (Sore Eyes), was blind in one eye and his cheek was sunken on one side. He was a sailmaker and he was frequently seen at Kekumanoha's place, where he sat under the hau tree that shaded the front of the houses, sewing on sails. Later Akahi lived there, and there was a bakery on the south side of Richards Street. The children were in the habit of making sport of Namakaeha, mocking him until he was on the point of losing his patience, just as Elisha did.

One day, the children who habitually taunted Namakaeha, together with Ii, went to his place. When they called him a one-eyed haole with a lop-sided mouth and other epithets, he chased them angrily. The other children fled, but Ii stood still and let himself be caught. When asked, "Were you one of the boys who reviled me while I was busy with my work?" Ii answered, "I was standing with them but I did not say these things of you. I have done no wrong to make me run away with them. I only joined them to see what they did to you. I have no idea of hiding myself from you." His answer satisfied Namakaeha, who released him. Later the boy and the sailmaker became fast friends.

Thus the boy began to lose his country ways and to associate with haole residents and visitors. It was customary for the children to follow the haole men, who made friends with them and took them by the hand, in the daytime. But they avoided these men at night.

CHAPTER V

ACTIVITIES IN COURT CIRCLES

In his childhood, Ii and his companions knew many games to play, some of them the same sports which he was to see at the royal court. Some of the games he knew in the land of his birth were running, *maika* rolling, *puhenehene*, pulling or dragging a person, fencing, and quoits.

There was diving at Waikahalulu or at Puehuehu, places usually crowded with both chiefs and commoners. This was especially true of the junction of the stream below Makaho, where they went bathing. They also went sea bathing or canoe and board surfing at Ulakua, just makai of Koholaloa, when the waves rolled and broke perfectly. Only those who were skilled could perform these sports.

So it was with *koʻieʻie*, a water sport; with the sailing of coconut sheaths; with skimming stones on the surface of the water; with tug-of-war; and with the game of staying under water as long as possible. Surfing at Waikiki was greatly enjoyed by many, and so were *maika* rolling, sliding, pushing, running, throwing a stick and making it stand upright, *konane, puhenehene, uma,* wrestling, pulling with the fingers, hula dancing, and chanting. All of these amusements were commonly practiced by the children of that time but the boy saw some of them for the first time when he went to the royal court.

A place where men and women of every kind gathered in the evenings to enjoy themselves was called *loku*, and such places were known from the distant past. There were two *loku* much frequented at the time Ii was at court, one at the corner of King and Nuuanu Streets and the other at Kauanonoula, located at Merchant and Alakea Streets. The ghosts of earlier participants are now said to congregate in these places every evening from seven o'clock until midnight. Some of the amusements indulged in there were hula dances, chants, the recitation of narratives in chant form, and the telling of legends. Ii found the *loku* strange, for he had known none at home in Ewa. It was customary to announce in advance the nights when entertainments were to be held, and to explain what kind would be performed on a given night in a given place.

One of the games was *puhene,* a kind of guessing game wherein two teams played. The house was divided into two parts, with each team at one end. Five young and comely women, chosen for their chanting ability as well as for their beauty, were seated on each side. A rule was imposed that no one could cross over to the other side lest it be seen what was done with the object to be hidden, called a *noʻa.* The *noʻa* used in this game was a scrap of tapa twisted into a circle. It was hidden by a person who inserted a hand and placed the object in one of the gourd containers that lay in a cluster between the two teams. While this was being done, two persons stood and held the corners of a tapa curtain, screening the women who were hiding the *noʻa.* When it was hidden, the hands of all of the women grasped the curtain and rolled it up in front of them.

All of the women were like the lehua blossons of Makamakaole, over which the birds hover. They wore leis of *palapalai* fern encircling their heads and maile leis about their necks, and some wore the fern leis over one shoulder and tied together at the waistline under the opposite arm. The women placed their hands before them and kept their eyes cast down. They "sat at Muliwaa" (silent and unmoving). If those who were to guess where the *noʻa* was hidden found it, they won a point and one of the women stood up to chant. This form of amusement lasted all night.

Another treat for Ii was to go to the waterfront at Nihoa, the area now bounded at either end by Kaahumanu and Nuuanu Streets, to see the ships built by Hawaiians under the direction of haoles. It was indeed a sight to see all the ships lined up on shore like canoes. They had cabins astern, the size of the cabins depending upon the size of the ship. The boy climbed over each one, but always with an eye out for the watchman. He spent some time at Nihoa whenever opportunity afforded and then returned to tell all he had seen.

To his makai side as he faced east from Kaahumanu Street, the boy could see as far as the Hale Mahoe [as the Swan and Clifford building of the time of this writing was called]. In front of him was a house with double doors facing Ewa, with three small grass houses in front of it for the chiefesses. These were fenced in like Papa's house. Makai of them was the *mua,* or men's house, called Halehui, which faced Koholaloa and served Kamehameha I. A little makai of that was a small pond, and to the right of the houses and pond was a wharf of

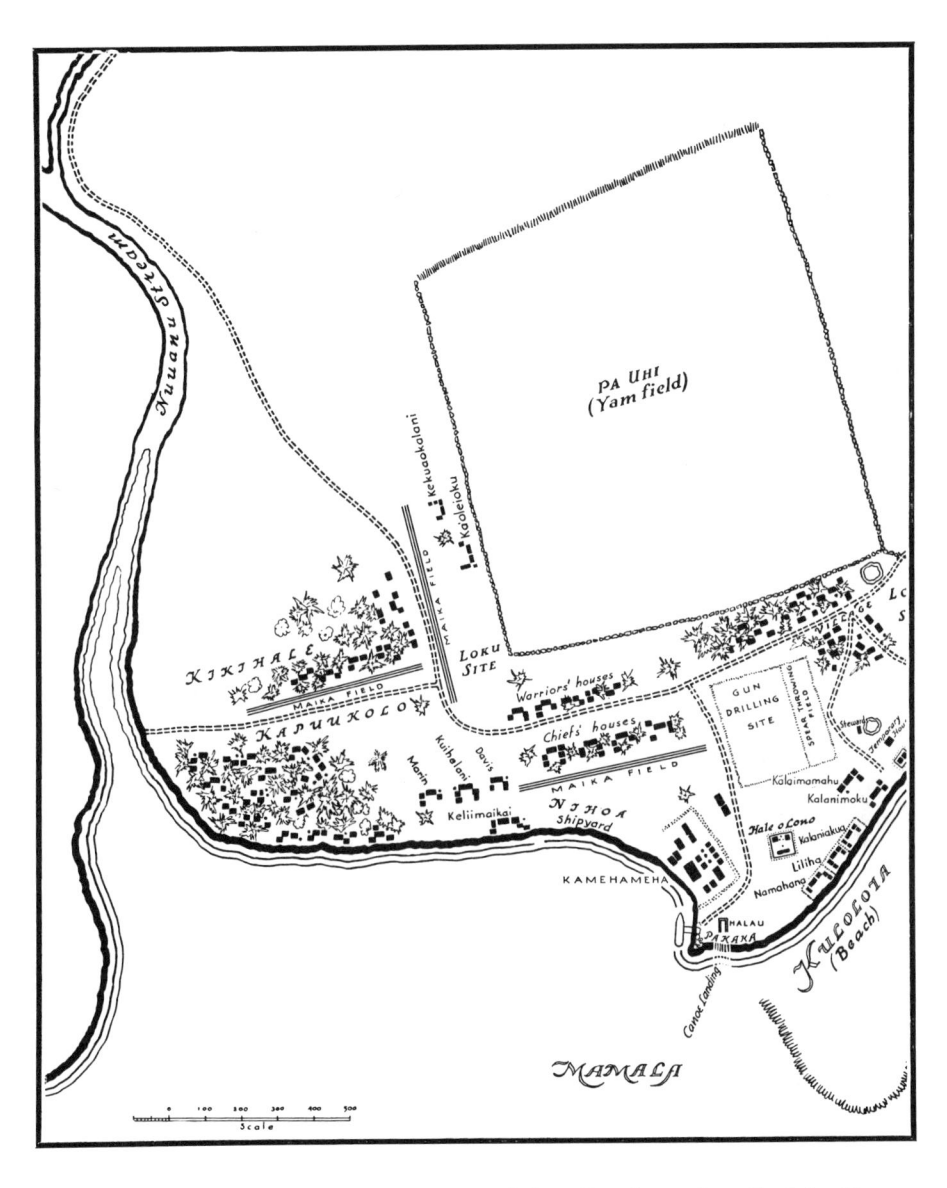

*The area from Nuuanu Stream to Kuloloia Beach as described by Ii.
Map by Paul Rockwood.*

rocks where a three-masted foreign-built vessel could be seen. This was the *Lelia Bird,* or the *Lelepali,* which had been bought by Kamehameha I, who named it the *Keoua.* The ship was tied to the shore by ropes, and a gangplank of boards reached from shore to ship. Here gathered the ship's crew and those who came to dive. One who was skilled in diving was admired for the trim way he dove into the water without a splash. Such a diver made only a soft sound as he came swiftly down, and only the gurgling sound of the sea was heard as he entered the water. Just makai of that place was a canoe landing, and eastward from there stood the canoe building shed of Kamehameha.

Just mauka was a large eating house called Kapapoko which belonged to Kaahumanu. And back of this were two storehouses, filled from top to bottom with gunpowder and guns. East of these were some houses in which were stored the belongings of Kamehameha, of the heir to the kingdom, and of the gods of the heiaus. About 2 chains away from the heiau houses was a vacant space approximately 4 chains square which was the *kahua* site used for gun drilling. Beyond this *kahua* site and east of the fence-enclosed houses of the king was the site for the practice of throwing hau wood spears. Here those who were skilled in this branch of Hawaiian warfare could be observed.

One who avoided being hurt by a hau wood spear and was clever in dodging and parrying was admired. The rules were not the same in all the schools that taught spear dodging, for the king had many more rules in his school than in those of the others. If an opponent was trained according to the king's rules, he would not be touched, no matter how many spears there were, because the man was trained in dodging from his head to his feet.

Kaoleioku was famous for his spear throwing. Because he knew just where to strike a dodging person, his spear did not miss. It is said that Kanepaiki was the best dodger. He was trained by one of Kekuhaupio's companions in arms, Keauhulihuli, who was famous for his courage and spear dodging. Kanepaiki's skill was his ability to see all the spears coming toward him and to parry them. Spear dodging practice kept the men trained for warfare. Such performances led the children to go about with spears of bulrush stalks.

Maika playing was done on a 12-foot wide site which extended from the place where Dr. "Not-a-Minute-Lost" Stangenwald had his office on Fort Street to the iron works at Ulakoheo. Crowds of chiefs and commoners gathered on all sides, and Kamehameha I joined them.

A *maika* stone resembles a wheel whetstone in shape, but it is small enough to be held in the palm of the hand. *Maika* stones were not thrown with an overhand motion but with an underhand one.

Kanekoa of Waikiki and Maloi of Honolulu were the strongest of the *maika* players. Maloi was skilled in throwing the stone upward, and he made it fly through the air for about 10 fathoms from the point from which it was thrown before it dropped to the ground. Kanekoa played in the ordinary manner. His strength was equal to Maloi's, however, and they were so evenly matched that one did not win over the other. Those who placed their bets on them did not profit.

A player held the stone to his forehead and ran from one end or the other of the field to a good spot from which to toss it. A man who acted as a pointer indicated where the stone first hit the ground, and waved his right hand to show where it came to a stop before he gave the signal for the next player to begin.

Another way of playing *maika* was for two or more persons to play on the same field at the same time. Still another was to have stakes placed at each end of the field. Then one player rolled his *maika* stone from the stakes which acted as markers at one end toward those at the other end of the field, while the other player rolled his to the spot where the first player's stakes were. If he had finished throwing and his stone touched the ground and began to roll before the other player's stone hit the ground, he won a point. If it did not roll before the other's stone touched the ground, then that player won a point. The first to reach the goal won two points. If his opponent was not strong in rolling his *maika* stone, he would never win a point. He was no better than a strong man who sent his *maika* stone off the course. Those who placed their wagers on such stopped at once.

There were two kinds of foot racing, one on a short course 30 or 40 fathoms long, and the other on a long course, perhaps 3 miles or more in length. Those who placed their bets knew by the flags which one of the racers was faster.

Once Naihe, son of Lonohiwa, an attendant of Kamehameha, and Kaaipaai raced to a draw. They were both fast on a short track and were asked to race, for they were famed for their speed. They stood at the starting point, with a flag at the goal. The one who got there first to grasp the flag, which fluttered among the people who were betting back and forth, won. The two stood at the starting point as though they hesitated to run together, and finally they ran singly, first one then the other. This stalling of theirs caused the race to be called off. Some of the gamblers believed that they were afraid of each other.

Gambling was common in foot racing, canoe racing, surfing, boxing, hand wrestling (*uma*), pulling with the fingers, wrestling, dragging a person, sliding, playing *puhene, puhenehene,* and *konane.*

Betting became a pitfall for those who did not know the scheme secretly followed by the experienced bettors. If there was to be a *maika* contest or a foot race, it was customary for the contestants to be kept at home until the day of the contest, watched over by their assistants, lest a contestant be harmed by the backers of the other side. Many bettors who had not yet laid their bets and paid them to the assistants visited the homes of the contestants to examine their physiques and the way they sat or stood. Bets were placed on the contestant who appeared to be the stronger in rolling the *maika* stone or the swifter in running.

A gambler who won would then bet his winnings with someone else, until he had accumulated a great heap of things. Such a person was called a *lau'au'a*, meaning that he was a sharp bettor. If he did not win, he started an argument. If he was a *lau'au'a*, it was better to return his property, or a fight would result. Those who lost to him blew their noses instead [their tears flowed and their noses ran].

Soon after Naihe and Kaaipaai had their race the king started off the work of braiding sennit ropes for ship tying, there on the *maika* playing site. There were two boards for rope twisting at either end of the amusement ground, and each of the two boards had three persons to turn it. One heap of fibers was laid over three furrows, and there the fibers were divided into strands. One of the boards moved along as the three big strands were twisted into one, through the center of the board that moved forward. The moving, twisting board stayed in front of the other, converting the strands into one big rope strong enough to tie to a ship. The actual work of rope-making was done by a Lascar called Kalani, who resided with Kamehameha. It seems that rope-making was his business.

Kamehameha, with the members of his court, also gave much attention to farming, especially in Nuuanu, from Niolopa to Hapuu. He also farmed at Ualakaa in Manoa, in Waikiki, and in Kapalama.

When Kamehameha went to Nuuanu, mounted on his horse, Kawaiolaloa, many of the children, including Ii, followed him with great interest. They found innumerable people all over the farming area, from down below the present road at Niuhelewai to the bend in the road where the houses of the Portuguese now stand. The bulrushes were as nothing, for they were cleared away in a single day. Some men cut the rushes, some dug them out, some built mounds, and others covered the mounds with the rushes. Much food was provided for the noonday meal of the workers, who then resumed their work until evening. The actual planting was reserved for the caretaker of the land.

So it was on the following day, at Kahoikekanaka, close to Kamanuwai at Peleula. It, too, was teeming with men, though there had been more people at Nuuanu. The men, scattered systematically from a spot on the upland side to a place on the seaward side, dug and beat on the banks with dried coconut-leaf stems. The next day they trampled in the wet patches and planted taro. When the workers and Kamehameha ate, Ii shared in the food, for among the men in the crowd were his mother's own brothers. All he did was watch the horse, but actually he just wanted to be there.

After these projects, three schools for *lua* fighting (*pa ku'i-a-lua*) were established by Kamehameha, and perhaps there were some smaller ones. Hahakea was the instructor at one of them, Namakaimi was the instructor at another, and Napuauki and his assistant were teachers at the third. At the school taught by Napuauki and his assistant were twenty-four boys from Kamehameha's court who were trained for more than two months. Among them was the king's own son

Kekuaiwa, who was older than the chiefess Kinau. Ii also attended this school, as did Kekuanaoa, father of Kamehameha IV and V. Twenty-three of these boys are dead at this writing.

Earlier, some of Kamehameha's warriors had been organized into a company called the Kulailua (Knocked Over). It was so named for the force by which the discharging of a rifle on the shoulder made one fall backward. One had to bring the hand around to ignite it. Like the pushing back, so was the igniting. Strange were the doings of those days. It was natural to feel strange, for they were not accustomed to the methods of the foreigners. But, as has been pointed out, in the ancient method of spear fighting they were unequalled.

We have already seen some things accomplished under Kamehameha, but some not mentioned previously were fishing, canoe-making, paddle-making, and the like. His craftsmen were as well cared for as were his farmers, and there were many of them. His wish was to obtain prosperity for the people.

Here let us return briefly to farming. The places Kamehameha farmed and the houses he lived in at those farms were show places. His farmhouses in Nuuanu stood several hundred fathoms away from the right side of Kapaehala, a knoll on the western side of Nuuanu Street and Hanaiakamalama House. Perhaps the location was chosen to enable him to look both inland and seaward to his food patches. Some elevated houses seem to have been for that purpose. So it was with Puupueo, directly below Ualakaa. He dwelt part of the time at Helumoa in Puaaliilii, Waikiki (in the house mistakenly called Kekuaokalani; Kuihelani is the correct name) to till the famous large gardens there. He also lived in Honolulu, where his farms at Kapalama, Keoneula, and other places became famous. These tasks Kamehameha attended to personally, and he participated in all the projects.

Kamehameha was often seen fishing with his fishermen in the deep ocean, where the sea was shallow, and where fish-poison plants were used. He took care of the canoe paddlers who went out for *aku* fish, bringing in supplies from the other islands for them, and sent ships to-and-fro fetching nets, lines, *olona* fibers, and other things. Part of his goodly supply of such necessities he divided among his chiefs and among those he had conquered. Because of his generosity, all of the chiefs worked too and gave him a portion of the products of their lands.

According to Kamanawa's counsel, Kamehameha had divided the large *ahupua'a* tracts and the smaller *'ili'aina* tracts of land all over Oahu among his chiefs. Kamanawa was the twin brother of Kameeiamoku and perhaps they were the origin of the name Namahoe, The Twins. Parcels of land at Waikiki, where the chiefs liked to live because of the surfing, were given to chiefs and prominent persons. Other *ahupua'a* all over the island of Oahu, which Kamehameha had won after the battle of Nuuanu, were also divided.

For the benefit of the young people of today and those of the future, the land divisions were as follows: The *'ili'aina* land of Kaneloa in Waikiki and also the *ahupuaʻa* of Punaluu in Koolauloa to Keliimaikai; Hamohamo and the *ahupuaʻa* of Kaaawa to Keawe a Heulu; Kaluaokau and Pau and the *ahupuaʻa* that includes the two Laie's to Kalaimamahu; Kalaepohaku and a part of Halawa for an *ahupuaʻa* to Isaac Davis; Pahoa and the other part of Halawa for his *ahupuaʻa* to John Young; Kanewai and a *kalana* land division of Moanalua to Keeaumoku; Kapunahou and Moanalua for his *ahupuaʻa* to Kameeiamoku; Waialae together with all the large *ʻili kupono* within the lands of the king to Kaahumanu.

The lands of Maui, too, were portioned out after the battle of Iao. Those of Hawaii were divided after the death of Kalaniopuu at Waioahukini in Kau. Kamehameha's own land divisions on Hawaii were Hamakua, Kohala, and North Kona. After the battle of Mokuohai, all of the lands from Kauai to Hawaii were united by Kamehameha I. The benefits and blessings that came from his patient acquisition of land are ours in the lands we live on today.

Kamehameha had three sons and two daughters born to him during his residence on Oahu. Kinau, by Kaheiheimalie, was the older of the daughters and Nanaulu was the younger. The oldest of the boys was Kekuaina, Aliipalapala came next, and Kamoakupa was the youngest, perhaps. Three or four of his children died in Honolulu, where they were born, before his return to Hawaii. Nanaulu was still an infant when she died; one lived only a few days; another, only a week.

Kinau and an older child than she were born at Waikiki. Kinau's eyes rolled about, but she was one of the king's brightest children. To a person who did not recognize her, she would say, "O man, get away at once, for I am a chiefess." When the person heard this, he left her presence immediately. Because she warned them, some people were saved. She was obedient to her elders and observed all the wishes of the heir of the kingdom. Her elders praised her for doing all that was right.

Kamamalu, by Kaheiheimalie, was older than the children born on Oahu. She was born at Kawaihae, Hawaii, about 1802, at the time when the *hula kalaʻau*, or stick hula, was popular. This was before the *peleleu* fleet built for Kamehameha's proposed invasion of Kauai came to Kahuhuki on Oahu. During the king's residence on Oahu, Kamamalu lived in Liholiho's household as his betrothed, for they were mere children then. Ii saw her from her infancy until she dwelt with the heir of the kingdom as his wife, when she was about twelve years old and Liholiho was about seventeen or eighteen.

While Ii was at court, there were two other occasions when sports and games were held in the royal town of Honolulu. These occurred when the *makahiki* gods went forth from the *luakini* heiau at Leahi.

There were two gods, the *akua loa* (long god) and the *akua paʻani* (god of play). They were both 18 feet long and each had a carved semblance of a human head on the top. At the necks were attached cross sticks, about 54 inches

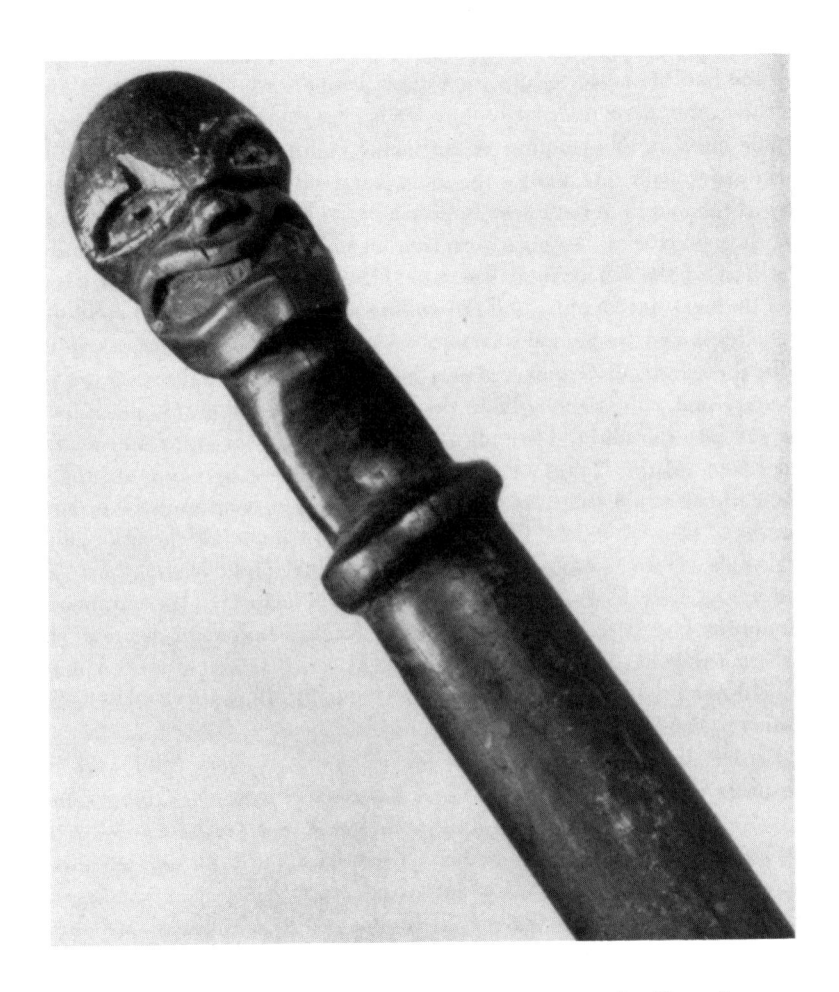

The head of the original makahiki image given by Kamakau of Kaawalao to the missionaries. In Bishop Museum.

long, to which were fastened fine white *'oloa* tapa the length of the poles with spiral feather leis hanging from end to end and *'iwa'iwa* fern fastened over them from one end to the other. The fronts of these long poles faced backward when carried, so that the "wife" could be seen. [This was the wife of Lono, according to the tradition of Lonoikamakahiki. It was he who made a circuit of the island of Hawaii after the loss of his wife, competing in various games and sports.] Because she had been lost to him, such processions were held each year and circuits of the island made in order to look for her.

The *makahiki* ceremonies began in the month of August, called Hilinehu in the Hawaiian calendar, before the gods came out of the *luakini*. On Hilo, the first day of the month, a kapu was imposed in the evening that lasted throughout the next day, or Hoaka. No pigs were roasted on that day; but on the following day, the first of the Ku days, called Kukahi, pigs were roasted. The kapu was lifted on the next day, Kulua, and the ending of the kapu was called Kauluwela. Then the chiefs and people gave themselves up to pleasure-seeking.

In the month of October, Ikuwa by Hawaiian count, the king declared a single kapu night, called Kuapola, in the *luakini*. The kapu period extended from evening far into the night. They all gathered at the *kuahu* altar and waited for the appearance of the Huhui (Pleiades) over the forest or mountain top. Then the priest whose ritual this was called out as follows, mentioning the names of the months: "E———e la'a ko hanai, hanai po, hanai ao, ia hiki Uliuli, ia hiki Melemele (O———sacred will be your feeding, night feeding, day feeding till [the star] Uliuli arises, till [the star] Melemele arises)." He continued until all the months had been named, as follows: Kaelo (January), Kaulua (February), Nana (March), Welo (April), Ikiiki (May), Kaaona (June), Hinaieleele (July), Hilinehu (August), Hilinama (September), Ikuwa (October), Welehu (November), Makalii (December).

Before the months were called off, coconuts of every kind were broken open, a procedure called "Wahi ka niu o Kuapola (breaking of the coconuts of Kuapola)." Afterwards the *kuahu* altar was closed, and pleasure-seeking ceased. Fishing and farming stopped, as well, for the homes had been well supplied with necessities in anticipation of the *makahiki*.

If the watchers were fast asleep when the Pleiades arose, and they rose so high that it required the lifting of the eyes to see them, then the appropriate time for the utterance of the *hanai* ritual mentioned above was missed and the time for the utterance had to be changed. The work for that night ended after this ritual. If a man returned under the eight or nine hours he could reasonably be expected to be away for the kapu Kuapola, he might return home to find a wrongdoer with his wife. This might lead a husband to kill one or both of the offenders. Women of that time suffered cruelly because of such wrongdoing.

At dawn the *makahiki* gods were taken to the beach, which was crowded with bathing chiefs and commoners. Some had composed chants based on personal details they had heard about others, and these compositions were shouted from early dawn. One person shouted until he came to the last line, then everyone joined in, like this:

Ke lewa wale nei no mawaho	Hanging suspended outside
Ka ukana Kumaʻaiku.	Was the bundle of Kumaaiku.
I hewa nui hoʻi ka hunone	He was at fault to tease
ʻAʻohe i haoa iloko hale.	Instead of putting it in the house.

CHORUS

Na ipu ʻekaeka puapuaʻa,	Soiled containers, like "pig" clouds,
Na ipu ʻekaeka puapuaʻa,	Soiled containers, like "pig" clouds,
Na ipu ʻekaeka puapuaʻa,	Soiled containers, like "pig" clouds,
Na ipu ʻekaeka puapuaʻa.	Soiled containers, like "pig" clouds.

The fun increased and first one group and then another shouted throughout the morning until the time the *akua paʻani* was set up on its site.

From about three to six in the late afternoon, the field was crowded with people. Anyone who was prepared to compete in boxing was chosen. When two were ready, they stepped in out of the crowd amid the shouts of the people and exchanged blows until one fell down. From the time of the first blow between them the crowd cried, "Ah!" with each blow; and when one fell, the "ahs" were prolonged. The late-comers knew by the rising of the voices into a prolonged "ah-h-h!" when a boxer had fallen. The voices crying "Ah! Ah! Ah!" were like an invitation to hearers to come. None who could cry "Ah!" would remain at home or at the task that occupied him when two boxers stood before the spectators.

The boxers sized each other up before striking. If they were both skilled and neither could knock the other down, the spectators' cries indicated as much to the late-comers. The methods of one boxer differed from those of another; and it was said that they were like fishing shelters, one standing here and one there without being joined together, but both common sights. One might fall when the other was skilled in punching even without knowing any rules, and such people became famous for their punching ability.

While the games were going on, the *akua loa* (long god) was brought to the gate of the enclosure surrounding the house of a chief of *niʻaupiʻo* rank. (Such chiefs could make one wilt by having one's back scorched by the sun.) The person bearing the image said, "Greetings." Those from within the enclosure replied, "Greetings, greetings to you, O Lono." Then the bearer of the image came in and stood by the doorway of the house, where he was handed an ointment made of masticated coconut wrapped in a bundle for the annointing of the stick, accompanied by the words, "Here is your annointing, O Lono"; but the actual annointing was done by someone from within the house.

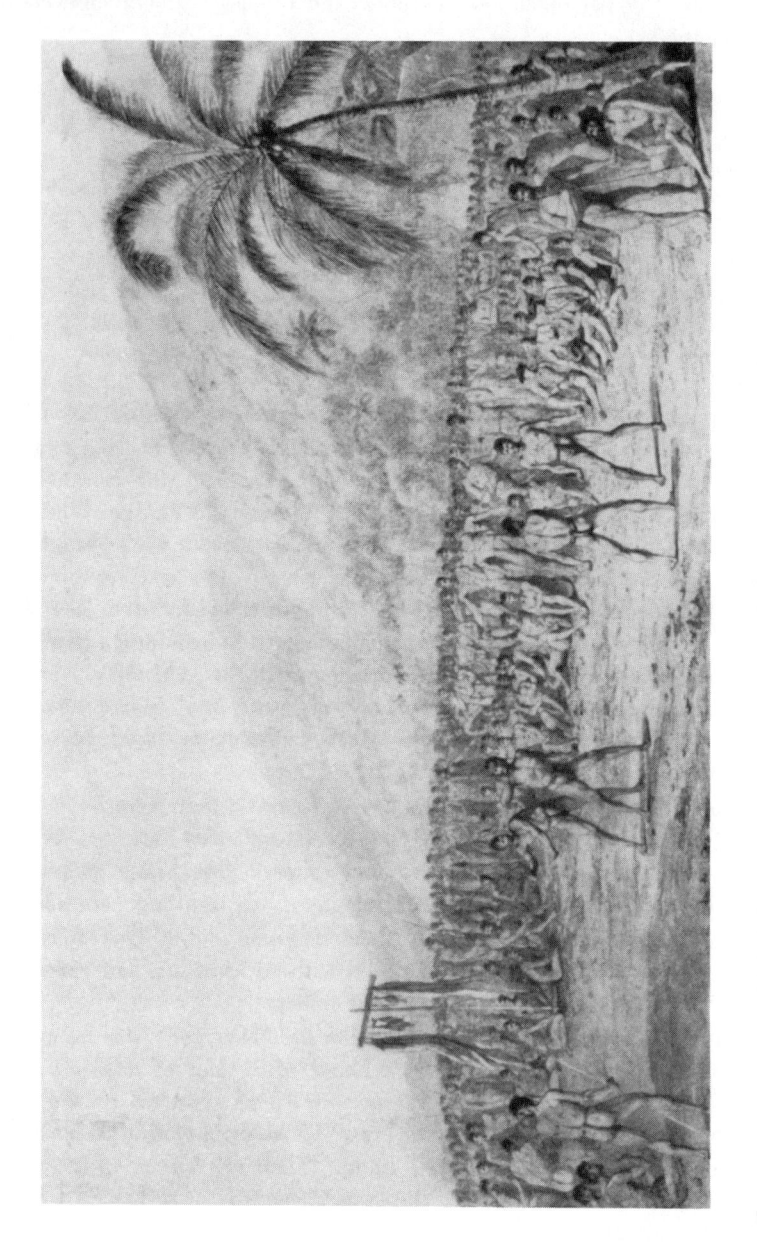

Makahiki boxing scene by John Webber. Original in Bishop Museum.

In the meantime, foods were prepared for the wooden god, to be eaten by the man who carried it. They consisted of a cup of *'awa* and banana or sugar cane to remove its bitterness, and some *'a'aho*, a pudding made of coconut and pia starch thickened by heating with hot stones. This food was laid on ti leaves to be eaten after the other foods. Then a side of well-cooked pork was given him with some poi. The chief fed the carrier of the god with his own hands, so that the hands of the carrier did not touch any of it. After this feeding of the god, the bearer was ready to depart and said, "Farewell, O friends." Those of the household answered, "Farewell, O Lono." Then the whole company left the *hale mua* and went to the field to wait for the chiefess of *ni'aupi'o* rank to present her gift to the god. Such a gift might consist of a pig and a malo of fine *ninikea* tapa or perhaps sometimes only the malo. The gift was accompanied by the words, "This is for your annointing, O Lono. Hearken to our plea." If the chiefess was married and had no children, the plea was for a child.

If there were many *ni'aupi'o* chiefs at the place, there would be many to feed the attendant of the god. The attendant was never overcome by the effects of the *'awa*, and this was believed to be because the god prevented it. Perhaps it was to keep the people deceived with the foolishness of men, for it was only the work of men. It has also been said that the attendant who was fed had fasted two days prior to this feeding.

In the evening of the day on which the wooden gods departed to go on their circuit of the island, the chiefs who had fed the attendant remained secluded with their possessions from daylight to dark. The attendants of the gods carried them facing backward when they traveled. Therefore it was said that the eyes of Lono remained upon the activities of the people when the gods left the presence of the chiefs for the circuit of the island. The procession went from Honolulu toward Ewa, and when the procession reached the boundary between Honolulu and Kapalama, the *akua loa* stopped with its two *alai* markers, two sticks that were used to mark the area that was made kapu for the god. This area was forbidden to the people, but not to the attendants. As the *akua loa* stood on its designated place, the persons in charge of the land of Kapalama brought all the taxes of the land. If the taxes were sufficient, the tapa of the *aku loa* was gathered in (*papio'ia*) and the god proceeded to the next *ahupua'a*. The *akua pa'ani* was placed where the *akua loa* had stood to inspire the men to box.

From the time of the closing of the *kuahu* altar until the gods returned no canoe was allowed to sail and no one was permitted to go to the mountains. The time was spent in waiting for the return of the gods and their attendants. While waiting, those who knew how to reckon time figured out how long it would take to get ready and what day the gods would arrive. When the gods returned to the *luakini*, the two persons bearing the *akua loa* and the *akua pa'ani* approached from the right, while the person bearing the *akua poko* (short god) came from the left. When the *akua poko* finished its journey from the lands designated for its visit, such as Kailua and Kaneohe, it returned to the *luakini*. On its way back, it received no more gifts from lands whose taxes had already been collected. The return of this god was called *papio'ia* (the-gathered-in).

Many people followed the procession on its tour over the land, among them the boxers, and all partook of the foods that were contributed by the people of each place. Ii followed the procession of the gods as far as Waipio in Ewa, and thus learned the customs of the *makahiki* period.

In imitation of what he saw on his journey from Honolulu with the god of play, the boy made two images that looked very much like the *makahiki* gods. Beside them he placed ferns and a clump of bananas bearing fruit.

For four days there was boxing with the boys from Waikele. The matches were held in front of the images, starting about four o'clock in the afternoon. Then, because the visiting boys plotted to take the images, they were put away in a safe place.

At noon of the fifth day the battlers met at a designated place and fought back and forth with stones. One of the Waipio boys was struck by a Waikele boy, and so the battle was postponed until evening. Then those of both sides gathered. Kaapuiki, wearing his dark red shoulder covering, was on the side of the opponents, and when Ii threw his stone, it struck Kaapuiki on the eyebrow and made him cry. This ended their devilish behavior; but Ii, having been told that the other was the son of a sorcerer, was frightened. Later he learned that the report was not true.

After this "battle" of the children a sham battle between adults took place on the southwestern side of Kupapaulau at Waikele. Two chiefs who had gone from Honolulu to Puuloa with some chiefs of that locality landed at Aioloolo in Waikele, and the battle was staged between them and residents of Waikele that very afternoon. The two sides gathered at a place above Aioloolo on the slope of the hill leading down to Kupapaulau.

The spectators noticed that both sides were equally skilled in stone-throwing and in dodging the stones that flew back and forth. No one was hurt or harmed, and the skill of the participants and the chiefs who arranged the sham battle was praised. It seems that the chiefs watched to see how skilled their people were in battle.

At about the time of the sham battle, a proclamation came from Kawelo, the overseer of the land of Waikele, for the men of the land to fetch the double canoe beached at Kupahu, on the northeastern side of Halaulani in Waipio. Because this proclamation came from Kawelo, who said the order was from Kalanimoku, the men of Waipio made ready to detain the canoe. They felt that the command should have come from their own leader, Papa.

When Kawelo and the men of Waikele had taken their places from prow to stern of the canoe and the command, "Go ahead," was given, the canoe did not budge. It was being held back by the men of Waipio. Kawelo's men tried again to make it go forward, but to no avail, so Kawelo asked the Waipio men why they held on. Kaimihau answered, "You cannot do this, for we were not told of it by our leaders. If Kalanimoku had made this request through our own leaders, we should have heard of it and therefore done nothing to prevent the removal of the canoe. If you persist in the idea of taking the canoe, day may change to night and night to day without its budging from its resting place. All things left here at Waipio are protected, from the sea to the upland, and we shall not let them go unless we hear from our own leaders." O companions, see how well the people served their leader. The peace of the land of Waipio was well known while the high chiefs were in charge and up to the time of Papa's death.

Here is a wonderful thing about the land of Waipio. After a famine had raged in that land, the removal of new crops from the taro patches and gardens was prohibited until all of the people had gathered and the farmers had joined in thanks to the gods. This prohibition was called *kapu 'ohi'a* because, while the famine was upon the land, the people had lived on mountain apples (*'ohi'a 'ai*), tis, yams, and other upland foods. On the morning of Kane an offering of taro greens and other things was made to remove the *'ohi'a* prohibition, after which each farmer took of his own crops for the needs of his family. These occurrences were wonderfully similar to the things spoken of by David in Psalms 96:1-8. It was right to offer thanksgiving; but the ideas of that time were erroneous.

CHAPTER VI

FOREIGN INFLUENCES

It is said that there had developed a great argument between Kamehameha and Isaac Davis, one of the well-known haole men who were with the king during his battle at Koapapaa in Hamakua, Hawaii. When the first Russian ship to visit Honolulu arrived in about 1808, visitors noticed the friction between the two men. It was not generally known why they had disagreed, thereby ending their pleasant association to hoist the banners of animosity. However, they did not openly quarrel, because Kamehameha would not countenance that. Finally, they put an end to their disagreement, and had become friendly by the time the ship departed from Honolulu.

That same year, or perhaps later, Kamaholelani arrived from Kauai with gifts from the islands of Kauai and Niihau sent by Kaumualii. This event was like the coming of Huia to Kawaihae, Hawaii, with such bundles while Kamehameha was living there. Its purpose was to preserve friendliness and was inspired by Vancouver's suggestion that it was better to be friendly and to look to each other's welfare than to fight. Their early peace with each other was wonderful, before the peace of this archipelago with many foreign powers. Wonderful are the deeds of the Unseen One, O companions.

Kamaholelani, the chief from Kauai, was graciously welcomed by Kamehameha, and upon his return he took gifts for Kaumualii. Apparently the way was being cleared before Kameholelani's return for a face-to-face meeting between

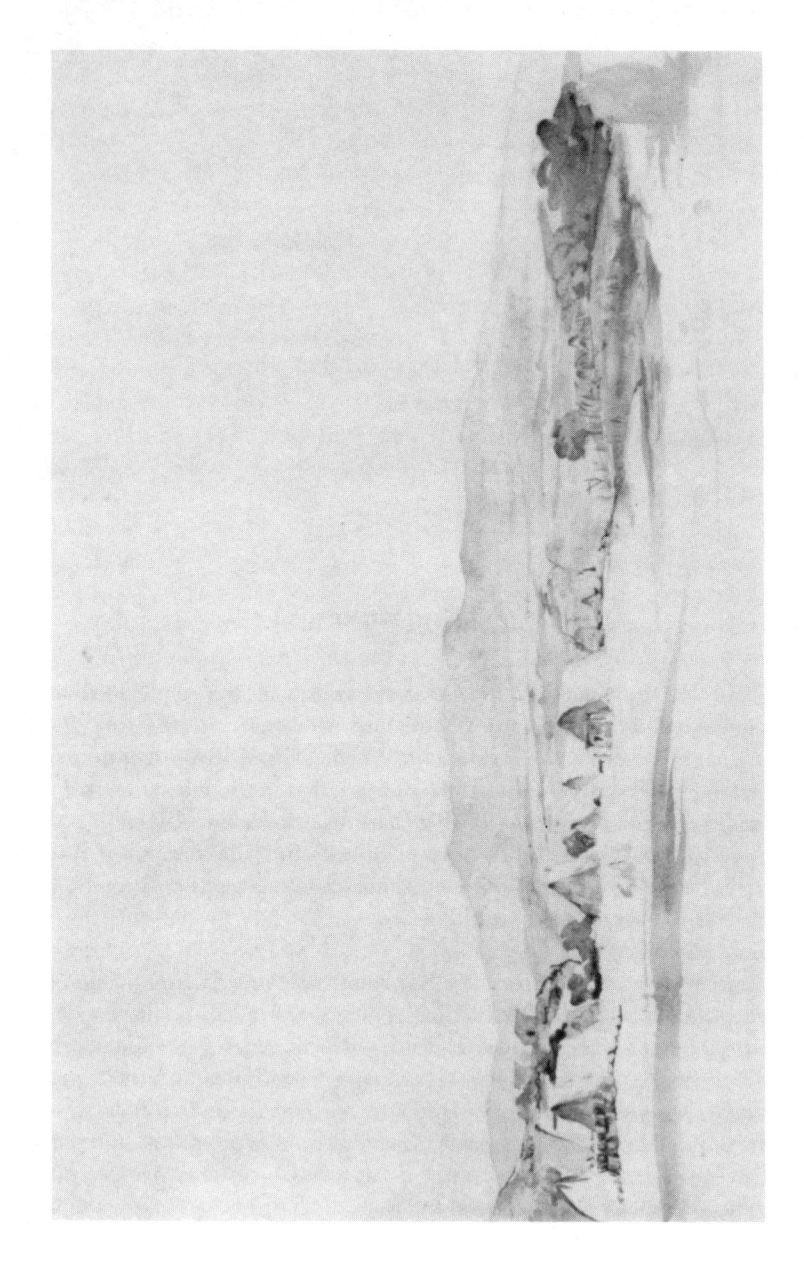

Copy of sketch by John Webber of a village on Kauai. In Bishop Museum.

Kamehameha and Kaumualii. In an effort to keep the peace, three messengers were sent—Kihei, Kekela, and Keaweopu—to meet with Kaumualii.

It was in the year 1810, after the death of Keliimaikai, Kamehameha's younger brother, that a discussion was held between the chiefs and Kamehameha pertaining to the advisability of Kaumualii's coming to meet him. Meanwhile the chiefs plotted to have Kaumualii put to death when he arrived, not in the presence of the king, but after he had seen the diving pool of Waikahalulu. However, Kamehameha did not approve of the plot, for he had often heard of the hospitality accorded to the chiefs of the eastern islands when they went to Kauai.

The meeting was postponed until they could meet with the counselor, Kalaikuahulu, who had gone all over these islands from the east to the west and who had earned a reputation for skill in reciting genealogies when the chiefs were in Lahaina in 1805. His fellow contestant there, a native of Borabora, lost the match with Kalaikuahulu. When Kalaikuahulu arrived, a meeting of chiefs was called again to discuss the matter. These chiefs were Kalanimoku, Ulumaheihei, Naihe, Kuakini, Kaoleioku, Kaikioewa, and Kalaikuahulu. After the king had spoken on the question of killing Kaumualii, Kalaikuahulu stood up and approved of the king's reluctance. He said, "It would be a serious thing to have Kamehameha called the bloody-handed king because of the death of one who has been kind. I say the best thing for the king to do is to meet his kinsman when he comes to this island and lay in his hand a fishhook and line, a symbol of the fish of the dark sea which the king has brought hence. I say that Kaumualii shall not die in his own native haunt, but where he seizes the hook and line, there eventually shall his corpse be found."

This was approved by the entire company. The meeting ended with a proclamation, and word was sent to the Kauai chiefs to come to Honolulu. Nathan Winship, the captain of a foreign vessel, who knew the chiefs asked Kamehameha's permission to fetch Kaumualii. His request was granted, and Winship set sail for Kauai. It took about a month to make the necessary preparations for those who were coming to Oahu.

Most of Kaumualii's chiefs hesitated to come to Honolulu lest they be killed, as rumors indicated. But Kamaholelani was not fearful, nor were Luia, Kaiahua, and others who knew Kamehameha's nature and good deeds. Kaumualii agreed to come, but made no decision about the date of departure. Then a person who was known for his sound thinking was summoned from Kaukaha in Napali, Kauai, to attend the discussion meeting. When the reasons for this hesitation were presented to him, he set forth his thoughts, saying, "O chief, if you listen to these people who would restrain you, we shall be without a homeland. But if you go to see your "older brother" we shall keep the land. You shall not die when you see him face to face. As you go to the ocean to fetch fish, so shall you return to build fine houses. When the heir of the kingdom comes, you will meet him on this shore. Therefore, put aside all doubtful thoughts."

This prophecy made them all agree to make the trip. After sailing two days, anchor was dropped outside of Mamala at noon; and the captain met with Kamehameha on shore. The report of Kaumualii's coming spread everywhere, and the town made all preparations to welcome the guests. Fishing canoes arrived from the lands of the chiefs at Ewa and from the king's lands.

That afternoon, the wharf at Pakaka and other places were crowded with people who were to make ready the canoes and boats of the king and chiefs who were to go out to the ship. There were two double canoes, three rowboats, and one single canoe. The king selected four men to man the single canoe in which he and Kekuaokalani rode. They boarded on shore before the canoe was lifted up by men standing in rows from prow to stern. With one hand each, they set the canoe afloat in the sea. The paddles of all the craft dipped together, led by the single canoe with Kamehameha sitting at the stern, a suckling pig in front of him. Those on board the ship watched the approaching canoes, for they had received a report that Kamehameha was coming on board.

When the canoes reached a spot in the harbor just outside of Ulakua, the single canoe went alone into Mamala channel. Passing the surf of Awalua, it proceeded to Kukuluaeo, close to the surf. It was not noticed by those on board the ship, for they were busy watching the double canoes and boats for sight of the king. Kamehameha's canoe, which was on the seaward side and about half a mile away when the other canoes drew close to the ship, caught the crest of a wave and rode in, reaching the ship ahead of the other craft.

Kamehameha hastened aboard and stood inside of the railing with the pig in his arms. He freed the pig as Kaumualii stood up, and it ran immediately to Kaumualii. Then the king said to Kaumualii, "Homai ko lima (Give me your hand)." Thus they greeted each other kindly and with true affection. The king stayed on board ship only long enough to greet all of the chiefs of Kauai, then announced his return to shore saying, "I shall go ahead and send canoes for you and your ruler." With that statement, he pointed out the place where they were to land.

While Kamehameha returned to shore, those on board talked much of his skill and graciousness. Meanwhile canoes from the harbor were speeding along toward the ship to take those on board ashore. Kamehameha saw the first boat coming from the ship, followed by another one. After the first of these boats came ashore the cannons were fired. The voice of a child was heard to wail on the second boat. It was Kahekili, the son of Kaumualii by Namahana, who was afraid that they were going to be killed and who behaved as any child would. Not long after the visitors landed, the sun set and all the fishes—which had been loaded on canoes afloat at a place now called Ainahou—were borne into a roofless wooden house close to the shore. As dusk descended, the canoes returned to their berths.

Kaumualii and his company, including Kamaholelani *ma*, were received in the houses close to Pakaka. Kalua and Puaaiki were in Papa's house at Kaoaopa. The following days were spent in visiting among the chiefs and members of the chiefly families from the island of Kauai.

It is said that several days after the landing of Kaumualii he went up to the house of Isaac Davis to while away the time and converse in English. It was probably on that occasion that Davis warned Kaumualii, saying, "Do not go up to Waikahalulu, lest Naihe destroy you." This startled Kaumualii and caused him to shorten his stay in Honolulu. When he asked Kamehameha's permission to go home, they discussed the reason for his request, the matter of each maintaining his individual position until death and the question as to what heirs would succeed them. Kalanimoku was there to discuss these matters with them and said to Kaumualii, "Take care of the chief Liholiho, who belongs to you and to your cousin Kaahumanu. Liholiho shall be the heir." Thus we can be thankful for the soundness of the prophecies uttered before Kaumualii came hither.

When their personal possessions had been made ready, the Kauai company returned to their island. They took with them brotherly affection as chiefs of a united land, parents of the people, and associates of those from foreign countries. Perhaps this was to establish in this archipelago the true religion, whereby we are now seeing the rapid growth and increase of righteousness.

When the travelers departed in peace, Papa detained Kaulapohu, a friend of Kahee's, asking him to remain a while and return with Papa's canoes which were to carry goods for the attendants of the chief Kaumualii. The canoes were filled with brown *pa'ikukui* tapas from Halawa, Molokai, and with nets and fish lines. From Waipio in Ewa and from some lands of Hawaii came tapa made of *mamaki* bark, *'ouholowai* tapas from Olaa, and so forth. After all was ready, Opunui, Kuaena (the father of Ii), Kaulapohu, and their canoe men left. When these people reached Wailua on Kauai where Kaumualii was then living, enjoying the large streams of that watered land, all the things brought by this second company were displayed.

Opunui, the head man of the double canoe called *Halemanu*, died there; and it is said that riotous living, pleasure-seeking, and extravagance were the causes of his death. So it is that the bones of the traveler are at Waihoikaea, which lies above Nounou, on the east side of the hill. Soon after the death of Opunui, Ii's father took charge, and everyone returned to Honolulu alive and safe. Those who returned from Kauai told about Opunui and about the beauty and abundance of that island, where, it was said, Opunui's father had some relatives. Opunui was admired by the people of Wailua for his good-heartedness during the days he lived among them.

Soon after Kaumualii returned to Kauai, Isaac Davis died, and it was said that he died as a result of his warning to Kaumualii. This sort of reasoning was customary when the people were pagans, but so much for the worthless. Many chiefs and notables mourned Davis, including Kamehameha and the company of warriors who watched over him. The funeral procession went from Davis'

Copy of sketch by John Webber of a beach scene on Kauai. In Bishop Museum.

dwelling at Aienui to Kewalo, where his body was deposited on the land of Alexander, a haole who had died earlier. At the time of his death, Davis was an old man with white hair and other signs of age.

Alexander was the first to brew intoxicants in these islands. At Makaho he brewed such a great quantity that it filled the three-masted ship *Keoua Lelepali* when, for the last time, the king returned to the island of Hawaii, his homeland. There was a great quantity of intoxicants on Oahu, and many were the stills found in Awa, Waiawa, Ewa, and some other places. Among those who visited these places was Ii. He had a relative who assisted in the work, and he learned something about it from him. It was interesting to see how ti root was converted into a strong liquor. When the root was boiled on a stove, the liquid came forth like the flowing of sweat from a bud. The hand was wetted with the first drippings and then waved over the flames, when the drippings burned brightly. The first brew was called *lolo*, the second *kawai*, and the last *kawai hemo*.

According to the feeling of that time, the Creator had made all things for the benefit of man, to do with as he pleased. This belief would suit the ignorant, who do not seek the Holy Scriptures. Perhaps intoxicants should be used by the few who are skilled physicians to help in the ailments of men when other medicines fail. This would be the will of One who created plants and trees of all kinds, that man may glorify Him.

Before he went to live in the court, it was Ii's custom, in the dusk of eventide, to go to Kumelewai to show his parents what he had received that day. When he brought some intoxicants, he was asked where he got them, and he answered, "From Hookalo." After he drank two glassfuls, his senses became blank. At midnight he and his male attendant went from his parents' house to that of the attendant, which was about two chains away. When day came, his attendant told him they had been haunted by a ghost that night and that he thought he had seen it. The boy answered, "I did not see it. If I had, perhaps I should have been afraid." The often-heard stories of ghosts frightened him, and if he had heard the voice crying at midnight, he would have been unable to sleep unless the doors of their house were closed. O companions, in things like this I would have you parents, foster parents, and guardians of children remember that talk of ghosts and legends of haunts make the children afraid of such devils. Thus the children may disappoint us by being fearful of non-existent things. They should fear the Heavenly King. Thus shall blessings remain, with fear of doing wrong against the Holy Laws.

When Ii told his parents of the episode they said, "You must not become addicted to drink and forget all that has been taught you, now that you are going to dwell in the court. You know what Maoloha did. Do not imitate him, but listen to everything that your namesake teaches you. It is well to pay attention."

Ii remembers these things and recalls the intoxication of chiefs and chiefesses. Unfortunately he did not learn their chants, which were never written down.

At one time, in the sea below Kaholoakeahole, there was a gathering of men from the court and other chiefs, about forty or fifty in all. Kalanimoku was at the head of this rum-drinking group, which remained there from noon to afternoon before landing on the shore in front of Kalilikauoha's house. It seems that the group decided to form a drinking line and that the one who poured for them was Eeka. Each person ran and sat down, with his thighs on either side of the one in front of him until all were seated. Then thirty-one gallons of intoxicants were lifted over those excessively stupid people.

We can remember how animal-like men can be during such stupid behavior. Perhaps their ignorance is more understandable than that of people of today, for they did not know what God is like, despite the fact that they were a religious people. They worshiped in ignorance, as Paul said of the people of Athens. We now have rules of conduct acquired through the wisdom of the Holy Scriptures. Those who think wisely, though they are ignorant and know not the Scriptures, are like them.

In the year 1810 a young haole youth named John Rives debarked from a foreign ship, perhaps American, and went to Kaoaopa in Honolulu. Papa received him in his home. He was liked because of his youth and boyish ways, and was considered a good associate for the young chief Liholiho, who took a liking to the newcomer. He gave him the name Luwahine (Old Lady), after Kaahumanu, who was known by that epithet. The foreign boy grew to be well known to the chiefs. He learned very quickly to speak Hawaiian, perhaps because he was young and there were few haoles around him. The captain and the crew of the ship he came on did not bother themselves over him.

When Luwahine started a school to teach English, three classmates were chosen for the chief. These boys whose heads Liholiho used to bump together were Ii, Manuia, and Kaniukahi. A fourth was the person who had been nursed at the breast with him. So together they learned their ABC's and other things which Luwahine wrote and gave to each of them. These were very hard to learn and to pronounce, for the letters and sounds were strange.

Luwahine taught six days and then said, "We shall have no school tomorrow because it is a day for us to rest from our labors." He did not say that it was the Sabbath Day, a day for God, who worked six days and rested on the seventh. Luwahine was a Papist. He told them to wear clean clothing on the day of rest, and their parents provided these. It was not necessary for him to say anything to Liholiho, for he had good clothing, dressing like a foreigner from top to bottom. He had a fine appearance. After three or four weeks the school was abandoned because Luwahine had been unjustifiably rude in his speech to the young chief, and they were no longer able to get along. In anger, the haole youth told Liholiho that he was going to find one of the poisons in Hawaii, all of which he knew, with which to kill the chief. This threat brought out the fire in the young chief. When the two ceased to live together, the haole youth, who sought another place to live, was cared for by Kaahumanu and her younger sister Kaheiheimalie. He later dwelt with a wife and had two daughters, one named Kahoa after Kaahumanu and the other, Oana, after Kaheiheimalie. Perhaps he named them so because of the generosity of the chiefesses in caring for him. As Liholiho had befriended him and had named him for one of them, they treated him with kindness.

Another haole companion of the king, who was generally known as Naoa, was not as proficient in the Hawaiian language as was Luwahine. For one thing, he stuttered. After Naoa had lived at Kawa for some time, he became physician to the chiefs. Perhaps he did know something about treating the sick, but he was not too well versed. When a flag was raised to summon him, he sailed on a double canoe to the place of the chiefs.

About the year 1811 a certain English ship said to belong to a company in Oregon, berthed in the harbor of Honolulu. On this ship were some Scotch people, the first ever seen in these islands. The owners of the company, who had heard that all of the islands had been united by their good friend Kamehameha, had sent people to meet Kamehameha personally and discuss with him their need for men to work in the great river region in Oregon. Kamehameha consented, and 100 men were sent back on the ship. This was the first time that Hawaiians went to Oregon to kill animals for their fur.

The ship to carry the laborers came twice, and on each trip a man belonging to the retinue of the heir of the kingdom accompanied the ship on its return voyage. The first to go was Nanamake, and the second was Uluhua. Other chiefs did likewise because they desired clothing and other goods. No purse was held fast where foreign clothing was concerned.

There were few English ships in the harbor then, but American ships came frequently. Many Hawaiian women boarded the ships coming to port here. They did not think that such associations were wrong, for there was no education in those days. The husbands and parents, not knowing that it would bring trouble, permitted such association with foreign men because of a desire for clothing, mirrors, scissors, knives, iron hoops from which to fashion fishhooks, and nails. Some women, most of them wives of foreign residents, were seen wearing men's shirts and beaver hats on their heads. They thought such costumes were becoming to them.

Several years earlier, a search for fragrant woods had been made in the mountain forests. It was first thought that the fragrant *naio* wood was the one desired by the traders; but when some of it was taken to China, it was found to be the wrong wood. When it was learned that *'iliahi* (sandalwood) was the wood in demand, the mountain forests of these islands were diligently searched for it. In fact, the time of most of the men was taken up with the cutting of sandalwood for trade in China. This activity brought many ships to Hawaiian ports, mostly American. While Kamehameha lived on Hawaii after his last return there many sandalwood trading ships were seen, and it is said that the ship owners grew wealthy.

Three three-masted vessels sailed to China with sandalwood in 1812: the *Albatross,* the *O'Cain,* and the *Isabella* under the commands of Nathan Winship, Jonathan Winship, and William Heath Davis. Each ship took ten men from here to help unload. When the ships returned and anchored outside of Mamala, boats from Ulakua went out to take the homecoming men ashore at Pakaka. These men were dressed in the red garments of soldiers and wore shiny hats, hence looked like haoles off of men-of-war instead of like Hawaiians. The men, women, and children who had come to look at them were scattered along the beaches from Kakaako to Pakaka and in other places, for never before was such a sight seen in Honolulu. "Kupanaha no! (How strange!)" the people exclaimed. However, these adornments and whatever else the returning men had were taken by Kamehameha.

About three or four days after the ships returned, the captains were permitted to set up a place for a celebration and feast. They built canvas booths at Kapauhi, the king's yam garden, where nothing was growing just then. On the night after everything was made ready, rockets soared to the sky from the ships, sending down a shower of sparks when they burst. There were loud shouts in the town that night, and none could go to sleep until late. It was the Fourth of July for the Americans, and wonderfully well do they observe that day of victory. But "children do not know how to count the nights (kamali'i 'ike 'ole i ka helu po)," and what did the people of that time know of the Fourth of July!

At noon of the following day, the canvas booths were filled with haoles and guests invited by the captains to come to the feast. But Kamehameha did not go there. We know how he had guarded his kingdom before this, when Kaahumanu was filled with bitterness toward him because of Kanihonui. During the haoles' celebration, he was surrounded by guards, Ii among them, as he had been at that other time. But the king was not startled by the shouts of the men, women, and children who ran after the yellow, green, and red streamers scattered before them.

CHAPTER VII

PLACES AND PERSONS ON OAHU

Perhaps it would be well to follow the Honolulu trails of about 1810, that they may be known, and to determine whether the houses were many or few. Let us begin looking.

The trail from Kalia led to Kukuluaeo, then along the graves of those who died in the smallpox epidemic of 1853, and into the center of the coconut grove of Honuakaha. On the upper side of the trail was the place of Kinau, the father of Kekauonohi. His houses were made kapu after his death, and no one was permitted to pass in front of them. Piopio and others were in charge.

The trail came out of the coconut grove and went on to Kaoaopa. Mauka of the spot where it came out of the coconut grove was a bare place, like a plain, and below this spot were Keopuolani's houses. Back of her houses was a long stone wall, beginning outside of the grove and going north to the edge of the pond of Umukanaka, as far as a cluster of houses there.

The trail went by Papa's heiaus of healing, and in front of them was Hookuku, the residence of the heir to the kingdom. His houses were separated from all the others there because of the strict kapu surrounding them. Four kapu sticks were set up, one at each corner, about 2 chains away from the houses; and the trail was about 5 fathoms beyond the sticks. When those approaching drew near to the kapu sticks, they observed the rules we have mentioned previously.

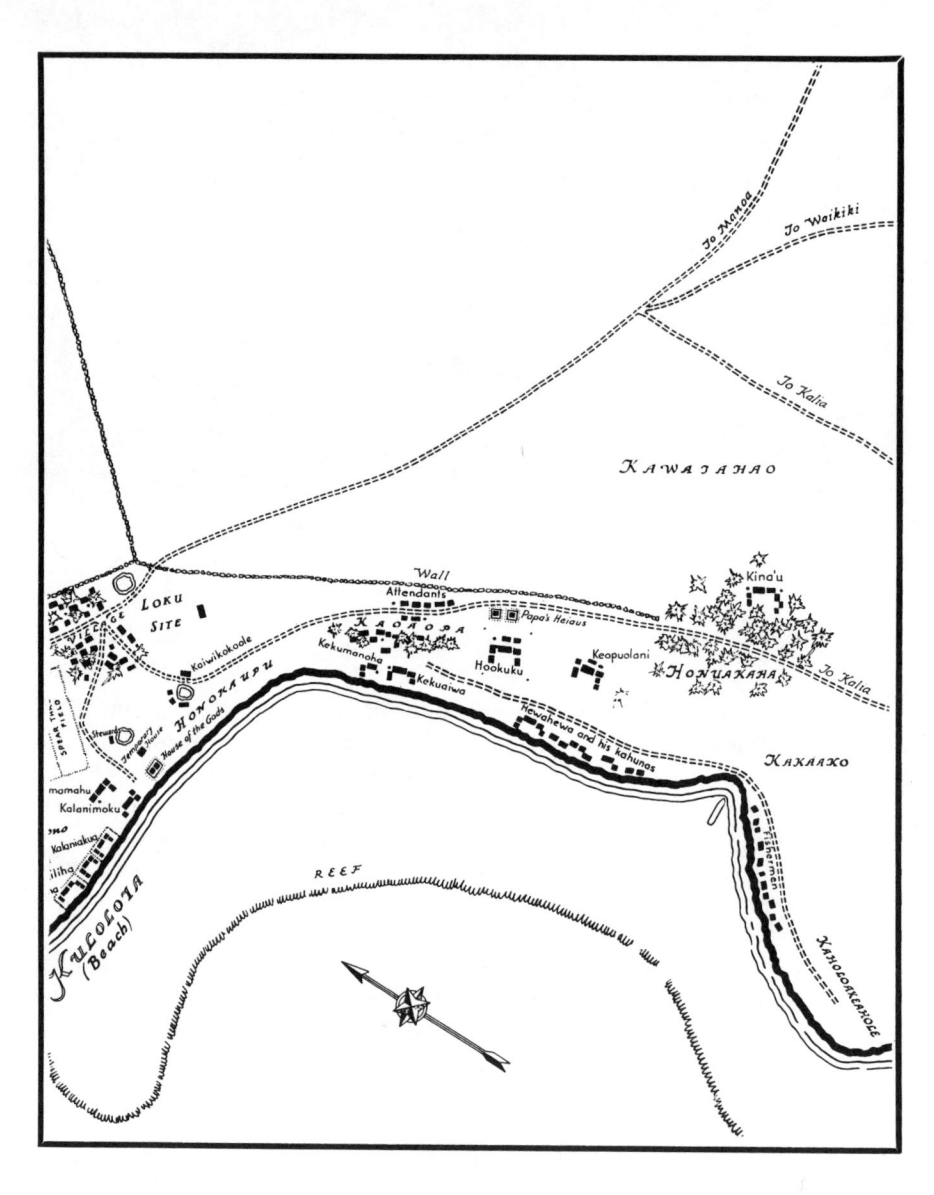

The area from Kuloloia Beach to Kakaako as described by Ii.
Map by Paul Rockwood.

We have spoken of Kaoaopa before as the location for the homes of attendants to the heir to the kingdom. Their houses stood on both the makai and mauka sides of the trail, set apart from the others like those of the heir. From the makai side of Kaoaopa was a trail to the sea at Kakaako, where stood the homes of the fishermen. Below the trail lived Hewahewa and his fellow kahunas. The trail led to the spot where the ship *Namahana* was berthed, then went on to Kaholoakeahole. The *Namahana* was in the charge of Leleahana, father of Abel Wahinealii, and was berthed on the north side of Naahu's place, where Halakika later resided. North of where this trail branched off from Kaoaopa, and close to the home of Ii's mother, was a coconut tree on which the boy made a swing. Here he and his companions whiled away hours each evening. The person who could chant the most pleasingly swung the most often.

Also on the north were Leleahana's houses, then those of the attendants of Kekuaiwa, son of Kamehamcha. Kekuaiwa's home was set apart with four kapu sticks. Next came Kekumanoha's place, then a vacant place that reached as far as the bathing pool of Honokaupu, above Queen Street, north of a pier at the corner where Queen and Alakea Streets now meet. There were two houses above this bathing pool which belonged to Kaiwikokoole; and north of the pool was one house, on the mauka side of the trail. Many bathers gathered often at this pool.

The trail went on above the spring of Honokaupu to the *loku* site at Merchant and Alakea Streets. Just above this spot it joined the trail from Waikiki which came over a wall and branched off to the two drilling sites mentioned earlier. Beyond them, to the west of the drilling sites, were the king's houses. A trail joined the one from Waikiki above the field where *maika* rolling and foot racing were held, on the mauka side of the king's houses, and came out at Pakaka.

West of the Honokaupu spring was the pond owned by Mataio Kekuanaoa, where the coconut trees later grew. The houses of the king's stewards were there, in the charge of Kamokupanee. Makai, and south of the drilling field, was a temporary house for those of the Kulailua company. On the makai side of the temporary house were the houses of the gods Kalaipahoa, Kihawahine, and others. Just beyond the houses of the gods were Kalanimoku's houses, close to the edge of the sea. The trail there was always used to reach the drilling field, for by going between the houses of the gods and the heiaus one escaped death. Mauka of Kalanimoku's houses were Kalaimamahu's houses, and there he had died. Next to Kalanimoku's houses were those of Kalaniakua, Liliha, Kekauonohi, and Namahana.

Let us return to where the trail from Waikiki met the trail from Honuakaha, mauka of the Honokaupu spring. The trail ran on from there until it reached above Aienui, going by the big stone house of Kimo Pakaka, or James Robinson. It went to the *maika* field of Kikihale, and then on to the stream above

Lepekaholo (Liberty Hall). Adjoining Kikihale and stretching from Kaumakapili to the south side of John Meek's yard was the *maika* field of Kalanikahua. On the south side of Kalanikahua were Kaoleioku's houses and those of Kekuaokalani, son of Keliimaikai. Each side of this *maika* field was bordered with houses, as was the *maika* field of Kikihale. A *loku* site at King and Nuuanu Streets, mentioned before, was where the two *maika* fields joined, and that place was without a house.

On the mauka side of the place where the trails met at Honokaupu, houses occupied both sides of the trail. The stone wall mentioned before ran on mauka of the church at Polelewa to the upper corner of King and Nuuanu Streets. Then the stone wall turned and went on up to Beretania Street. The fence on the mauka side was made of hau wood, and it led to the corner of Emma Street. There it turned and came down to meet the edge of the trail from Waikiki. That was the enclosure of the yam farm called Kapauhi mentioned earlier.

The trail to Nuuanu began at Kalanikahua and led north of Kaumakapili Church to below the little stream which flowed out of Kamanuwai pond. There the trail turned slightly to the right, went along the edge of the pond, and down into the water. Then, coming up on the bank onto Waiakemi, it led on to Waaakekupua, along the bank of the taro patches, to the Pauoa stream, up to Pualoalo, and on to the gap at Nuuanu Pali.

Our description of the trails of the royal town is finished, but we have not yet told of the trails going to lower Waikiki, Kamoiliili, and Manoa. A trail led out of the town at the south side of the coconut grove of Honuakaha and went on to Kalia. From Kalia it ran eastward along the borders of the fish ponds and met the trail from lower Waikiki. At Kawaiahao a trail passed in front of the stone house of Kaina, late father of Kikaha. The trail went above Kalanipuu's place, along the stream running down from Poopoo to the sea, close by Kaaihee in Makiki, to Puu o Manoa, then below Puupueo, where a trail branched off to go to upper Kaaipu and Kahoiwai, and another to go below Kaahulue, to Kapulena and Kolowalu.

The trail from Kawaiahao which led to lower Waikiki went along Kaananiau, into the coconut grove at Pawaa, the coconut grove of Kuakuaka, then down to Piinaio; along the upper side of Kahanaumaikai's coconut grove, along the border of Kaihikapu pond, into Kawehewehe; then through the center of Helumoa of Puaaliilii, down to the mouth of the Apuakehau stream; along the sandy beach of Ulukou to Kapuni, where the surfs roll in; thence to the stream of Kuekaunahi; to Waiaula and to Paliiki, Kamanawa's house site. The latter was named for the Paliiki in Punahoa, Hilo. Perhaps that was where Kamanawa lived when the king resided in Hilo during the battle called Puana, prior to the building of the great *peleleu* fleet.

From Paliiki the trail ran up to Kalahu, above Leahi, and on to the place where the Waialae stream reached the sand. The trail that ran through Kaluahole

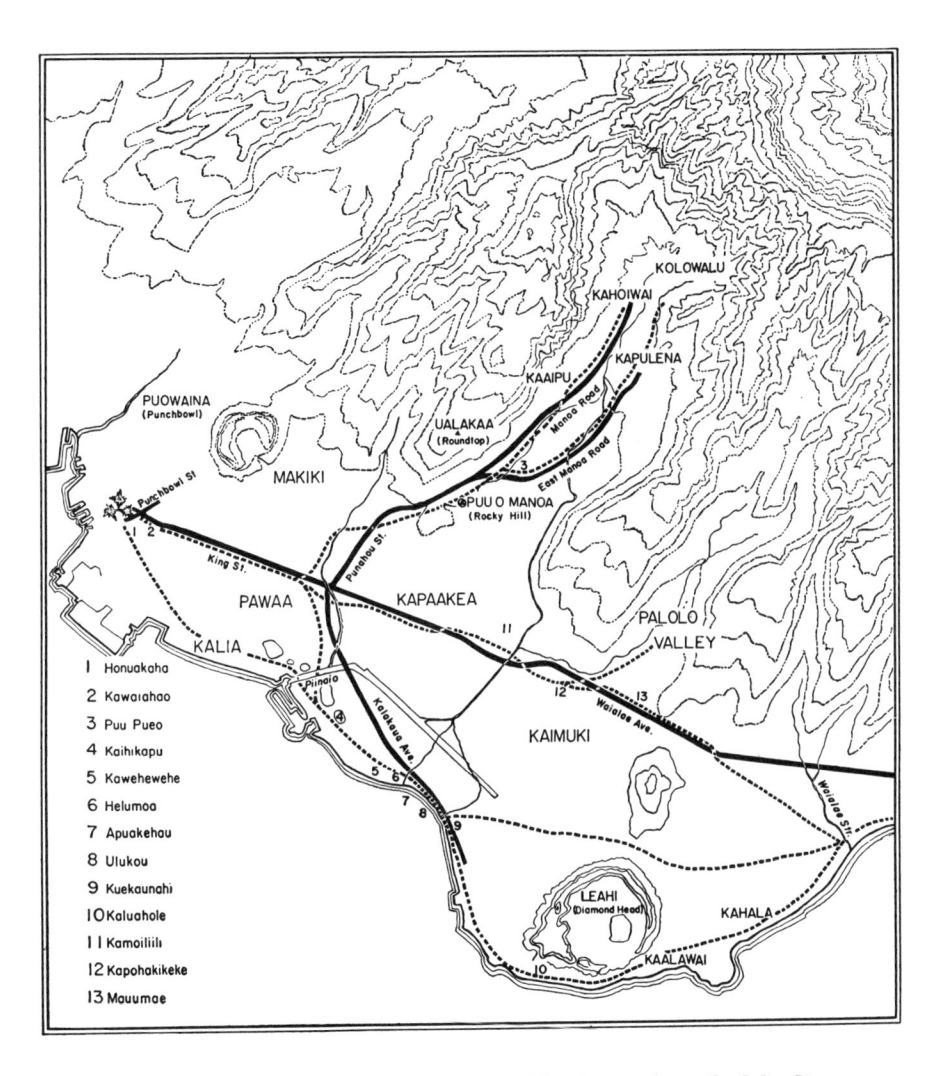

*The trails from Punchbowl Street to Waialae as described by Ii.
Map by Gerald Ober.*

went to Kaalawai, up, over, and down into Kahala, to meet the other trail at the place where the stream reached the sand. There they met the mauka trail that came from Ululani's place in Pawaa to Kapaakea, then up to Kamoiliili, and to Kapohakikeke, where it left the trail that went up to Palolo, and continued on to Mauumae, above Kaimuki where a pole later stood to serve as a mark for ships. From there it went down to, and along the upper side of, the taro patches and the pools of Waialae to join the other trails at the sand and go along Keahia and on to Maunalua, to the sea of Koko, to Makapuu, and so on.

Let us now examine the remainder of the places in the royal town, for we have not yet seen them all. There were many people living in those other places. Perhaps we should glance first at the spot below Kikihale's *maika* field. Many people who lived here at Kapuukolo were fishermen who fished with draw nets and with the many other kinds of nets needed in their profession.

Kuihelani was an important person there, for he was of high station. He had many people to serve him, his wives were many, and his household was large. Ii went often with his mother to see Kuihelani, who was related to them, perhaps through Kaaloakaulani or perhaps through their *makuahine*. This large family was related to the family of Luluka. Perhaps that was why the mother and the boy went to these places often and were known by many of the people in the household of each wife, who lived there as a retainer. Because of his skill in handling the property of the king, Kuihelani attracted prosperity to himself. The keeping of a multitude was as nothing to a man so wealthy. The king's faith in him never changed, for the king's lands in his charge were cared for by his kinsmen, and they were obedient to Kuihelani's commands. Therefore the kinsmen also held good positions and were well known.

Among these people was the Spaniard Paula Marin, a friend of the king, who lived wherever the king's relatives lived. On his place—which was surrounded on the sides, back, and part of the front by Kuihelani's property—he had two or three horses, one a mare, and a young cow. Marin was very fond of fishing, perhaps because he saw Kamehameha doing it. And he was also an expert in the stick hula.

Makai of Kuihelani's own home was Keliimaikai's home, which was on the coral point where the first custom house stood. On the south side of this place was berthed the *Kaaloa*, a ship belonging to Kuihelani, which lay at the extreme north of all the ships previously discussed.

Near the *Kaaloa* and in the vicinity of the custom house at the beach was a house for the very first Chinese ever seen here. There were two or three of them and they prepared food for the captains of the ships which took sandalwood to China. Because the faces of these people were unusual and their speech—which is now commonly heard—was strange, a great number of persons went to look at them.

On the south of Kuihelani's residence was that of George Isaac Davis and his company of people. The chiefs' places extended from there, above the *maika* field to the Honokaupu trail junction. Near there, too, were the houses for the king's stewards, and above that group of houses were the houses of the warriors. These stood on the upper side of the trail. Among the chiefs' houses were those of Kuakini, of Kaiko, and of Kaukuna Kahekili, Kaiko's younger brother.

Let us turn to look at the trail going to Ewa from Kikihale, up to Leleo, to Koiuiu and on to Keoneula. There were no houses there, only a plain. It was there that the boy Ii and his attendants, coming from Ewa, met with the god Kaili and its attendants who were going to Hoaeae. When the *kapu moe* was proclaimed, they all prostrated themselves on the plain until the god and his attendants passed by.

When the trail reached a certain bridge, it began going along the banks of taro patches, up to the other side of Kapalama, to the plain of Kaiwiula; on to the taro patches of Kalihi; down to the stream and up to the other side; down into Kahauiki and up to the other side; turned right to the houses of the Portuguese people; along the plain to Kauwalua, Kalaikoa's house of bones; down to a coconut grove and along the taro patches of Kahohonu; over to the other side, and from there to a forded stream and up to Kapapakolea, an established resting place for travelers.

From there the trail went to Kaleinakauhane, then to Kapukaki, from where one could see the irregular sea of Ewa; then down the ridge to Napeha, a resting place for the multitude that went diving there at a deep pool. This pool was named Napeha (Lean Over), so it is said, because Kualii, a chief of ancient Oahu, went there and leaned over the pool to drink water.

The trail began again on the opposite side of the pool and went to the lowland of Halawa, on to Kauwamoa, a diving place and a much-liked gathering place. It was said to be the diving place of Peapea, son of Kamehamehanui of Maui who was swift in running and leaping. The place from which he dove into the water was 5 to 10 fathoms above the pool.

There the trail led to the taro patches in Aiea and up the plain of Kukiiahu. Just below the trail was the spot where Kaeo, chief of Kauai, was killed by Kalanikupule. From there the trail went along the taro patches to the upper part of Kohokoho and on to Kahuewai, a small waterfall. On the high ground above, a little way on, was a spring, also a favorite gathering place for travelers. From there it continued over a small plain, down the small hill of Waimalu, and along the taro patches that lay in the center of the land. Above this trail was the home of one of the two haole men previously mentioned, the men to whom the boy's attendants spoke.

Paula Marin had a place there also. It could be seen near the edge of a low cliff going down to the upper side of a grove of cactus plants, said to have been first brought to Hawaii by Marin.

Trails of leeward Oahu as described by Ii. Map by Paul Rockwood.

The trail went down to the stream and up again, then went above the taro patches of Waiau, up to a *maika* field, to Waimano, to Manana, and to Waiawa; then to the stream of Kukehi and up to two other *maika* fields, Pueohulunui and Haupuu. At Pueohulunui was the place where a trail branched off to go to Waialua and down to Honouliuli and on to Waianae. As mentioned before, there were three trails to Waianae, one by way of Puu o Kapolei, another by way of Pohakea, and the third by way of Kolekole.

From Kunia the trail went to the plain of Keahumoa, on to Maunauna, and along Paupauwela, which met with the trails from Wahiawa and Waialua. The trail continued to the west of Mahu, to Malamanui, and up to Kolekole, from where one can look down to Pokai and Waianaeuka. There was a long cliff trail called Elou from Kalena and Haleauau on the east side of Kaala coming down to Waianae. There was also a trail called Kumaipo which went up and then down Makahauka.

Below Kumaipo trail in the olden days was a stronghold named Kawiwi. At the time of a battle, a boy was posted there as a guard every night. He was often hungry, for the lord of the stronghold did not supply him with food. This caused him to change his allegiance and give the place over to the rebels. This he did by calling out "Hake. Come up the ladder. Let two come, let the second stay back, let one come along. Hake, hake. Come up the ladder. Let three come up, leave the third, and let two continue up." The boy kept up the cry until the stronghold was filled with men, and its lords were taken captive by the rebels. O friends, if it is true that the boy did this, it proves what the Holy Scriptures have pointed out (Luke 10:7) that "the laborer is worthy of his hire (E pono ke uku 'ia mai ka pa'ahana)."

The stronghold of Kawiwi was part of a mountain ridge lying between Waianae and Makaha and overlooking Kamaile. The trail, Kumaipo, went down to the farms of Makaha and the homes of that land. A branch trail which led up Mount Kaala and looked down on Waialua and Mokuleia could be used to go down to those level lands. It was customary to have dwelling places along the mountain trails that led downward from here into Kamaile, as well as along the beach trail of Makaha.

There were many houses at Makaha, where a fine circle of sand provided a landing place for fleets of fishing canoes. The trail which passed by this sandy bar was the one from Puu o Kapolei, which had joined the beach trail from Puuloa and from Waimanalo. It then went along the shore all around this island.

A place where robbers operated was located between Nahikilalo and Makaha. The robbers remained in a cave while their watchman kept a lookout from the top of the cliff. When he saw one or two travelers, he called, "Malolo kai e (Low tide!)." When there was a large company, he called, "Nui kai e! (High tide!)" Those who traveled alone or in pairs were robbed, but those who came in a large company went unmolested.

The trail led to Kaena and all the way to Waialua. From Waimanalo to Kaena traveling by noonday was very unpleasant because of the heat of the sun and the lack of wind over some stretches of sand on the trail. A chant was composed about the intense heat of the sun:

Ua wela i ka la e	Scorched by the sun
Makua la.	Is Makua.
Kuano no o Kea'au e,	Parched is Keaau,
Ua nopu i ke ahe la,	Cooled only by the breeze,
Ke Kaiaulu kamalamape.	The light Kaiaulu breeze.
O Poka-'i aumoe hine,	Darkness is met at Pokai,
I ke hau e Ka'ala la.	There the dew of Kaala.
Hale'au'au o Kauna la,	There is Haleauau, Kauna,
O Pule'e i Malamanui,	Pulee at Malamanui,
Kauka'opua, kai o'Ewa,	Kaukaopua, the sea of Ewa,
'Ewa e la!	There is Ewa!

Makua which also has a fine sand beach and a landing for fishing canoes, was a usual resting place for travelers and a place to spend the night. The morning was cool for the journey on to Kaena. Kahaiki and Keawaula, the land that has the fishing grounds for *aku* and for *'ahi* fish, were close to Makua.

At Makua there was a trail up the mountain and down to Kawaihapai, where it met the trail from Kaena. It was said that this was the trail on which the "red-eyed one" became lost, but it might have been another one. A red-eyed person who went from Mokuleia intending to go to Makaha, mistakenly went by way of Kawaihapai, thereby arriving at Makua instead. Hence the saying, "Makole iho hewa i Makua (Red-eyed one goes by mistake to Makua)."

When travelers arrived in Kaena in the morning, they escaped the heat, for they were cooled by the Moae breeze. They rested at Waiakaaiea until afternoon, then continued traveling along the level places of Kawaihapai and Mokuleia, thence across the mouth of the Kaiaka River and over the sand to the plains of Paalaa and Kawailoa to Kamani, a village with a pond, the boundary walls of which separated it from the Anahulu River.

On the opposite bank lies Maeaea, a sandy beach with a canoe landing and a good harbor for ships. A village stood at Leepoko Point, and nearby were the ponds of Ukoa and Lokoea, with many homes about them. Between the sandy stretch of Maeaea and the houses at Ukoa, on the seaward side, was the trail from Kamani to the place in front of the sluice gate of Lokoea, and on to Koolauloa.

From the stream of Anahulu and from Kamani, above the houses and taro patches, a trail stretched along in front of Kuokoa's house lot and the church. This trail went on to meet the creeks of Opaeula and Halemano, the sources of the stream of Paalaa, on down to the stream of Poo a Moho, and on to the junction where the Mokuleia trail branched off to Kamananui and Keawawahie, to Kukaniloko, the birthplace of chiefs. Just below the main trail was the descent to the stream of Kuaikua, where there was a diving place and a place for travelers to rest. Beyond was Paka stream and the *maika* field of Kapalauauai, which lay beyond the pond belonging to the village. There the trail met with the one from Kolekole and continued on to the stream of Waikakalaua, Piliamoo, the plain of Punaluu, to a rise, then down to Kipapa and to Kehualele. A trail ran from this main trail to Kalakoa, Oahunui, and other places much visited, such as Kukaniloko. From there it extended to the digging place of Kahalo, then went below to Paupalai, thence to Lelepua, and to Kahalepoai, where the legendary characters Kalelealuaka and Keinohoomanawanui lived. Then it reached Kekuolelo, the stone in which the *niho palaoa* was hidden, then went on to Puunahawele and Pueohulunui, where it met with the Waialua trail.

All of these places mentioned had large populations. The land was rich, and there were many trees in olden times. Who has "closed" these places today? We do not know enough to say, "It was so-and-so." But there would be commercial wealth in the trees of these mountains if they were fenced off from animals. So it is with the planting places of every poor person. The person who manages these mountains and valleys could become prosperous.

Here we shall discuss what befell certain personages of Honolulu.

First, let us speak of the death of the chiefess Kalaniakua. She died by suicide because of shame at the frequent jibes from Liliha about "homeless chiefs, who dwell under my protection and that of my *kaikunane*, Kamehameha, whose kingdom this is. They destroyed our child, these captives whom we brought here from Iao." Liliha spoke thus, perhaps, because Kalaniakua was pregnant by Kamehameha and the child died in her womb.

One day Liliha secretly sent her grandson, Liholiho, to go and cling to Kalaniakua's back while she sat in the open talking with a company of women. While they were absorbed in conversation, the young chief clung to Kalaniakua's back until she reached around for him and placed him on her lap. When Kalaniakua repeated this, Liliha, who was watching was filled with wrath. [Being of highest kapu, Liholiho had the right to climb upon Kalaniakua's back.]

O companions, let us seek the reason for the two women's opposing each other. Liliha was born to Kalola, the daughter of Kekuiapoiwanui, and Kamehameha was born to Kekuiapoiwa II, the daughter of Kekelaokalani. Kekelaokalani was the younger sister of Keeaumoku and of Kekuiapoiwanui, who were born to Keawe and Kalanikauleleiaiwi. But Kekuiapoiwanui set aside the junior relationship in the family for Kekelaokalani's children, it is believed. Well, then, if Kalaniakua was the offspring of Kekelaokalani (*ina na ua Kekelaokalani la o Kalaniakua*) why was she singled out to be despised? It would have been different if she were related through the Maui chiefs Lonoapii, Kiha a Piilani, Piikea, or Piilaniwahine.

The descendants of the ancient chiefs of Maui, from Kamalalawalu down, became as nothing when they were taken captive at the battles of Iao and Keoneula. So it was with those of Oahu who were taken captive by Kahekili, who gave the island of Oahu to Kamehameha (*ua haʻawi aʻe ʻoia ia Oahu no Kamehameha*). When Kalanikupule, son of Kahekili, resisted and Oahu was invaded, Kalanikupule was rendered helpless at Nahuina and entered headlong into death at Wahiawa. Set aside were the benefits enjoyed by Kahekili's sister Kalola, and the only thing to do was to dwell under the protection of Kamehameha. Thus perhaps it was with Kalaniakua.

We know that grief weighed heavily upon Kalaniakua for the things Liliha had done. Therefore, she asked Kekumanoha to prepare some poison for her so that Liliha should have no more to say of her. The idea dwelt in Kekumanoha, who talked it over with his sister Namahana. They were both sad over the matter; but the poison was prepared for Kalaniakua's suicide, as this was her wish. Her death was heard of, but the motive was unknown at the time. She died at Kuloloia, in the enclosure of Kekauonohi, later acquired by Haalelea, on the south side of Mokuaikaua. The place was filled with chiefs, besides Kalaniakua, Liliha, and Kekauonohi, who was then but a small child. It is said that Kalaniakua's body was secretly hidden by Kekumanoha.

Let us study the act of this chiefess who was unhappy over her wrong deeds. They were wrong because of, first, her great regard for her own rank; second, her lack of respect for the kapu of Liholiho; and, third, her destruction of the unborn child of Kamehameha. Applicable here is Solomon's saying, "The wicked is driven away in his wickedness: but the righteous hath hope in his death. (Hoʻokukeʻia ka mea hewa iloko o kona hewa; Lana hoʻi ka manaʻo o ka mea pono i kona make ana.)"—Proverbs 14:32.

The good royal mother Namahana, mother of Kaahumanu *ma*, also died at Kuloloia, where she had a home. During her life she was known for her self control, and she was considered the best behaved and the noblest of persons. As she was beautiful in appearance, so were her deeds. Perhaps that was why she was espoused by Kamehamehanui. As we have seen, they were both the children of Kekaulike, and so they were brother and sister through the one parent. When Kamehamehanui died, Namahana was taken at once by Keeaumoku, who was a relative and who is said to have been a handsome man.

Namahana was a fine old lady when she died. A younger cousin of Namahana's children, who was present at her death, was named Kuloloia for the place in which Namahana died. This was a custom of those who loved their chiefs in the olden days. While the cries of lamentation arose and Namahana's body was on view, someone came from Waialua or thereabouts to die with her and share the same grave, which was another ancient custom with some who loved their chiefs and sought peace of mind. The heir to the kingdom was kept at Waikiki during the period of mourning, for Honolulu was defiled by the royal corpse.

Certain afflictions befell several chiefs of this period. One of these chiefs was John Adams Kuakini. Kuakini knew how to speak some English and many white people went to his home all the time. He is said to have become lame as a result of associating in sin with Kaoo, wife of Kuihelani, a relationship which continued until it was noticed by Kuihelani's servants. When he was discovered, Kuakini ran away and in so doing jumped over a wall and broke some bones in his foot. This was the origin of the blemish which this chief carried with him until his death and which changed a fine, handsome person into an old man. Thereafter, when he fought with his wife and she ran away from him, he could not pursue her because of his lameness.

The right side of chief Kaiko's neck was pierced by a spear just above the collar bone, and he was left with a sunken scar. He was self conscious about the scar and kept that side of his neck covered with a tapa garment. But when intoxicated with rum,

Ahuwale mai la ke kualono e,	The mountain top is exposed to view,
Ka nahele mauna Lolokuʻi a.	The forest on the mountain of Lolokui.

Kanepaiki, who was admired for his skill in dodging spears, had a scar on his forehead. It was said that he was once struck by a stone tossed by Hinau in a children's fight. It did not injure any of the nerves when it entered his skull, and he recovered fully. However, because of the scar he kept his forehead covered with hair which he allowed to grow long on top and brought down over his forehead. Even when he was drunk and fought, his scar ("*noʻa*") remained hidden.

It was said that because he killed lizards, Kahiko's affliction came to him. Such was the talk of that time, for there were many gods and many lords in that period.

A fearful thing happened, when the eyes of a young man called Nawaakoali were taken. He was the son of a member of the court, one of the Kulailua company. Papalima was the keeper of the god Kaili in the coconut grove of Honuakaha at the time Nawaakoali's eyes were snatched out and blood and slime poured out. Hearts were filled with pity and sorrow over his trouble. It was said that the reason for his misfortune was adultery; but in truth, it was due to that unenlightened period.

CHAPTER VIII

KAMEHAMEHA'S RETURN TO HAWAII

It is now time to speak of Kamehameha's return to Hawaii. In about 1812, while all of his chiefs and people were assembled from one end of Honolulu to the other, an announcement was made of the king's desire to return to his homeland. He ended the schools for *lua* fighting; and all of the ships were made ready, including the *Keoua Lelepali*. Several months passed in preparation for his return.

The Hawaiians had already begun to build ships like those of the foreigners, for they were superior to canoes. The idea was a good one, and their ships were well built; but they lacked the skill to sail them in the ocean. This lack of skill is evident even today, when there is much knowledge and wisdom about other things. They were skilled, however, in craftsmanship. Some made iron blocks for ballast, and some of these blocks were used in making anchors. These were wooden cross pieces nailed together and had four pieces of wood extending from the cross pieces alongside the iron block that was set up between them. The lengths of the ropes that lay along the wooden pieces corresponded to the height of the block. Ropes were wound around them, securing them to this block with a hole in it. A rope was inserted in the hole and added to the other ropes that stretched along the block from the cross pieces and came out through the binding ropes. This was the hauling rope for the anchor. When this thing was let down into a suitable spot in the sea, the ship remained stationary. When the rope was a little slack, the anchor held fast without moving when the wind blew and the billows beat against the ship. There was wisdom in those "childhood" days.

Ii did not know that the king was ready to sail, but he observed the fine appearance of the first company preparing to go. When the king permitted Liholiho to go on the canoe of the god Kukailimoku before the rest of the royal company left Oahu, Manuia and Ii went with him, for they tended to the young chief's personal belongings. There were three of them on the *pola,* or platform, of the canoe, and the man who proclaimed the kapu stood in front with the *kapuo* stick. Many canoes accompanied the young chief and the god who headed the procession, but no canoe preceded that of the young chief, so why did they need a man to proclaim the kapu as they sailed the sea? Was it to place a kapu on the wind, or on the ocean billows?

After leaving Honolulu, they landed at Hanauma Bay, which was a good place to wait until the wind was better for sailing to Molokai. The wind observers climbed up to Kuamookane and to Ihiihilauakea, which is located in front of Kuamookane, on the west side of the bay. Hanauma faces the southeast and is well sheltered and rather shallow on the upper, sandy side. As it is surrounded by cliffs except for the entrance, it is an inland bay.

After two or three days of waiting for the wind to lessen, Ii was seized with a longing for his mother. He was standing with Manuia at the edge of the cliff and looking toward Leahi and Kaimuki, which lay in full view, when this longing came to him and prompted him to say to his companion, "I have a yearning for my mother." The remark was repeated to others, but with their minds filled with love for parents and friends, they did not wait to tell the young chief about it. They left the company and went to Kaoaopa, where they saw the person they greatly longed to see. When greeted with the customary "O 'olua mai nei? (Is that the two of you?)" they replied, "Yes." When they were asked whether they had permission to leave, they replied that they hadn't but explained, "Because we were so filled with love for those left behind, we came. We saw that that company would not be able to go soon from this island and that Kamehameha's departure is uncertain. Perhaps he is waiting to see when we are going to sail." When they were told it was wrong to leave the chief they replied, "We are going back tomorrow." They were then told that the king had left the day before and to return immediately but they were determined to stay, and so spent the day there.

Before dawn the next morning the canoe watchers saw that canoes carrying lighted touches surrounded the *Keoua,* which lay directly outside of Waikiki. That morning the king's ship entered the harbor of Kou and at high sun, the young chief's canoes returned from Hanauma. The two boys who had departed from him the day before were relieved when they saw Liholiho's canoes. Then they learned the reason for the king's return. The *Keoua* had sprung a leak and taken in considerable water.

When the break that caused the leak had been repaired, the vessel was made ready to sail again. This time the young chief boarded the ship and the two boys were on board with him, as were Kuihelani and Kahanaumaikai, both of whom the king had placed over Oahu. The god went by canoe, at the head of the canoe fleet. The other canoes sailed and landed where they chose.

By the time all the chiefs and other passengers whom the king had selected were on board, the shore was filled with onlookers. When the sails had been dropped from the yardarm, guns were fired to bid farewell to the land and the people of the island. There was a great cheer from the shore and from the ship, and loud wailing. After that the sails were set in place and the prow of the ship turned about toward Mamala, the channel that leads out of the harbor. Thus did they leave Honolulu again and go out of Mamala. The *Keoua* was navigated by Captain J. M. Harbottle, and there were many other haole men who helped to handle the ship for the king. These men were all related to the king in some way and had received lands from him. They were like the people who were born in the islands, and each had a wife and children.

The ship left the harbor about twelve noon. At four o'clock in the afternoon it developed another leak, so about 20 miles from shore it turned back. The water that leaked in turned black, for it had reached the place where the powder was stored. (This event gave the younger brother of H. K. Kapakuhaili his name, Kapaulapulu, or Wet Powder.) The haole men were trying to stop the water from the inside but were unable to check it. When the king heard of this new trouble from Kaleiheana, Waipa was ordered to examine the leak, for Waipa's knowledge and skill were known to all. He took a piece of canvas and rubbed it with beef fat. Then with nail and hammer in hand and a rope tied securely about him, he was let down into the sea and reached the spot where the water entered. When the ship was turned about so that the prow would be away from the billows, he nailed the treated canvas over the break, putting an end to the trouble.

Here was a Hawaiian whose skill exceeded that of any haole man on the ship. A story has already been told [by Kamakau, in the *Kuokoa* for July 20, 1867] of Waipa's successful building of a ship on which he sailed with the *peleleu* fleet. He was a descendant of Lonoakai, a man of chiefly blood.

Kaleiheana saw that the leak was checked and went to report to the king, and as they ended their conversation, Waipa appeared to report that the break would hold until they reached Maui, where they could examine the trouble again. The king did not agree with Waipa, however, and ordered the ship to turn back.

When the ship moved shoreward, not far from Kupikipikio and Kaalawai, it was almost night. Again, the *Keoua* was surrounded by canoes with lighted torches and anchored outside of Waikiki to enter the harbor of Kou the next day.

While the *Keoua* went shoreward, the other ships moved as in a procession beyond the reef two or three miles off-shore. Then they, too, returned to land. They appeared to sail in the formation of canoes in procession.

The king was undecided whether to sail on the *Keoua* again after two mishaps, and he finally decided to wait for the sandalwood trading ships to return from China. The company had not long to wait, and no sooner had the trading ships arrived than the news went abroad that the king was going home to Hawaii on the foreign ships. Because of this, Papa did not take Ii to sail with him on the young chief's ship. The boy was ordered, instead, to sail on Papa's own ship, and the ship's master was asked to care for the boy. Some chiefs and people sailed on the ship called *Makanimoku* (*Albatross*); others, with Liholiho and his people, sailed on the *Ogena* (*O'Cain*); and all of the king's wives went with him on the ship *Enepalai* (*Isabella*), the captain of which was William Heath Davis.

Apparently there was mutual understanding and cooperation between the Hawaiians and the foreigners, which is an indication of the good deeds of our first ruler. He inspired two governments to befriend each other and associate kindly in a manner pleasing to all who would dwell in unity. The saying, "Ua mau ke ea o ka 'aina i ka pono" (The life of the land is preserved in righteousness)" was most fitting, and its application continues to the present day, though the people of that time knew nothing of the ideals of today. Whence came his wisdom and this desire to do good deeds? Perhaps from his skill in warfare and his religious nature. His unenlightened worship led to the coming of the light of truth. Perhaps he was like Cornelius when he saw the true light, and thus learned religion from Vancouver. So it was that the true light came from foreign lands, the United States and Europe. And here it is, burning brightly with us.

When the king's ships arrived at Lahaina, the people of the island of Maui met with the king. They expressed their affection for him with innumerable gifts. It is said that so many things were heaped before him that the gifts and the food stood in huge mounds. The breadfruit grove of Lele, from one end to the other of Lahaina, was filled with men, women and children, come to see their good king. At this time, Kamehameha and his queen, Kaahumanu, placed his son Kekuaiwa Kamehameha and Kahanui (Keeaumoku) in charge of the whole island.

After he had seen the people, the king sailed to Molokai to see again the *maika* field Kaakeke. As had the people of Maui, Lanai, and Kahoolawe, those of Molokai who came to see their king brought gifts from their island, which was famed for its net-making. A net was started and finished on the back of a person walking to the place where the gifts were to be offered. By the time they reached the spot it was ready to lay down as a gift. In this way the tax of the land was paid.

The *Keoua Lelepali* which had been forced to return repeatedly to the harbor of Kou was among the ships at Lahaina, perhaps because of the alertness of its captain. It is said to have been faster than any of the foreign ships except the *Isabella*. On board the *Keoua* were Captain William P. Kalaimoku, two or three haole men, and the sailors. It was during this trip that the mate of the *Keoua*, a haole who could not swim, fell overboard and drowned. The fishermen who searched found him lying clothed in the depths, and he was brought on board. His funeral was held in Lahaina, where he was buried. His death was regretted, for he was well liked and admired for his goodness and graciousness.

It is well to speak briefly here of the many people, both Hawaiian and haole, who have perished because they did not know how to swim. Therefore, our children of today should learn the art of swimming. Though death is victorious over all mortal beings, "no one who takes care of things ever loses them to the rats."

After the king had rested and enjoyed himself, the company moved on to Hawaii. Before going on, the king heard that the young chief's ship, the *O'Cain*, was crowded with people; so he drove most of the men and women into the sea by waving his club and sword, for he desired to protect his young chief from being crushed. He excepted Heulu's wife because of her good deportment.

All the ships left Lahaina at the same time. When, at Kamaalaea, they met the gusts of the Mumuku wind, coming from Ukumehame, the sails of the foreign ships were taken in, but not those of the *Keoua*. She left the others far behind, except the *Isabella* which kept close to her until night fell. Thus they sailed until they arrived in Kailua, Kona, Hawaii.

After the king's company had gone, Papa's ship, on which Ii was to sail, was made ready to leave Honolulu. Before the boy departed, he conversed lovingly with his mother. His father had gone ahead with the fleet of canoes because he was determined to be with his son.

The mother prepared the needed supplies for her son, filling two large gourd containers, which were taken aboard the ship and put in the charge of Nahoounauna, the mate, and his wife Kaupe, and Captain Kaunakakai. The boy's mother asked them all to take care of her son until he reached his namesake. She also spoke to her *kaikunane*, Hoomakaukau Keawekolohe, the father of Kaopua, because he was the overseer of the two other remaining ships that were sailing to Hawaii from Honolulu.

On the afternoon of the day before he boarded the ship, to be separated from his mother and his personal attendants, Ii received two glasses of *lemu hao* ['*okolehao*] from a friend of his. This was only the second time he had come in contact with this intoxicant, though in later times he grew to be familiar with it. On this occasion, he was tipsy in the presence of his mother and he chanted this chant:

Hiki melemele ka ʻopua i ke kai,	The clouds appear yellow over the sea,
He kai kuehu lani na ka malie,	A sea that is the hue of the clear sky,
Ua kakaʻulae holo a ka laʻi,	The *ulae* fishers sail out in the calm,
ʻIkea keʻele, ʻikea.	The keel can be seen, can be seen.
He aka mauli lani no luna,	A sky is reflected from above,
He hauli no na kuahiwi,	Shadows are cast by the forest,
He pane lae no na mauna,	Covering the brow of the mountain,
Ke hele nei i kuʻu maka,	They move before my eyes,
Ua aʻa me he ʻoloa la.	The light appears in patches like *ʻoloa* tapa.
Kulu iho nei au i ka po,	Night descends and I am drowsy,
Lulumi ana ka hiamoe.	I am overcome by sleep.
Hoʻala mai ana iaʻu ke koʻekoʻe maka huʻihuʻi,	A damp coldness rouses me,
Make i ke anu, make i ke anu o Kawanui,	I am chilled with the cold of Kawanui,
I na hau lumaʻi waʻa o na Maihi	With the dew that fills the canoe [hulls] of Maihi
O ka uka wale i Hainoa la.	In the distant upland of Hainoa.

He chanted with his mother until one chant was finished, then began another and another until they had chanted five or six, for the boy had become quite an expert in this art under his mother's tutelage. Chanting was an important custom with the chiefs, and sometimes continued through the night, and different chants were appropriate at midnight, at dawn, and when day had come. Ii's mother went with him or with her *kaikamahine* from one place to another, to Kaahumanu, and to other chiefesses. The boy's attendants composed chants in his honor until dusk, preliminary to a fond farewell. Unfortunately the boy was unfamiliar with their chants, hence they are now unknown. The company gathered in the same house to spend the night, and it was the light of day that woke them.

The ships were ready by nine or ten o'clock in the morning, and the canoe was waiting to take the boy on board. He bade farewell to his mother, sisters, attendants, childhood playmates, relatives who had come to Honolulu from Ewa and Waianae, and his oldest sister, who had gone to live at Waialee in Koolauloa. He boarded the canoe in their presence while they chanted his name chants. It was a good way to express sadness at parting. As soon as he was on board his ship, Hoomakaukau's ship, the *Apuakehau,* took the lead. In broad daylight the next day Papa's ship reached Kawaihoa at Maunalua.

As these ships had no boats or canoes, the passengers had to swim to shore and back when the ship was at anchor. Anchors such as those described earlier were used during this voyage.

The next day the ship *Kaailipoa,* owned by Kalanimoku and captained by W. Sumner, reached Kawaihoa. This ship had arrived from Waianae in the evening of the day the other two ships left Honolulu. The captain and his Hawaiian wife, Kauila, met the owner of the ship and remained ashore in Honolulu until the next morning, when they came on board again. That night the ship sailed to join the others. This two-masted ship was handsome indeed. There were two foremast sails at the prow, two at the top, and one between. The sails at the stern were on the main mast. The ship was rather high, with port holes near the stern.

The *Apuakehau*, with all of the king's stewards aboard, had come in from Waianae early on the same day as the *Kaailipoa* did. The captain of this ship was a Lascar, who in his ignorance had first taken it past Waianae. This was a very handsome ship, with three masts, rather low and longer than the others. There were three sails at the foremast, three in the center and three at the stern. The *Apuakehau* anchored for two days at Kawaihoa, waiting for Mr. Solomon, a haole man who lived at Niu and who had been asked to take the ship to Hawaii. He was a carpenter who also knew navigation. At noon of the next day, when Solomon's canoe reached the ship, he said, "This is a fast ship if the sails are unfurled. It is sailing that makes the ship go forward." Early that evening, all of the sails were unfurled, and the ship sailed from its berth with the sea rippling behind because of its great speed. It vanished from sight beyond the point of Ihiihilauakea. Hoomakaukau *ma* passed from sight and could no longer be seen from Oahu.

After Papa's one-masted ship had remained at anchor for about five days, it too departed. A whole night was spent in mid-ocean, and by the next night the vessel had reached Punakou, Molokai. Day found it at Kahalapalaoa, where it caught the Maaa breeze and went right along to Lahaina, where "na hono o Piilani" (lands of Piilani) were seen. They went ashore there at Lahaina on a canoe that came out to the ship. The boy saw black *kala* seaweed from Mokuhinia, and this recalled the familiar seaweeds of his birthplace.

It was wonderful to see the breadfruit and coconut groves of Lele, thriving from one end to the other. Boys were surfing on the north side of Pelekane, with banana trunks for surf boards, and Ii watched with delight. Adults were surfing outside of Uo.

On the evening of the second day there they sailed away, to be met by the strong gusts of wind of those lands, extending from Olowalu to the points of Papawai and Kamaalaea. The wind was so strong that it tossed up a cloud of dust. The ship heeled over, but the master knew how to cope with this wind. The descent of night hid that side of the islands between Puuolai, Maui, and Molokini Islet. The next day the ship arrived outside of Kaelehuluhulu, where the fleet for *aku* fishing had been since the early morning hours. The sustenance of those lands was fish.

When the sun was rather high, the boy exclaimed, "How beautiful that flowing water is!" Those who recognized it, however, said, "That is not water, but pahoehoe. When the sun strikes it, it glistens, and you mistake it for water. This is not like your land, which has water from one end to the other."

Soon the fishing canoes from Kawaihae, the Kaha lands, and Ooma, drew close to the ship to trade for the *pa'i'ai* (hard poi) carried on board, and shortly a great quantity of *aku* lay silvery-hued on the deck. The fishes were cut into pieces and mashed; and all those aboard fell to and ate, the women by themselves.

The gentle Eka sea breeze of the land was blowing when the ship sailed past the lands of the Mahaiulas, Awalua, Haleohiu, Kalaoas, Hoona, on to Oomas, Kohanaiki, Kaloko, Honokohaus, and Kealakehe, then around the cape of Hiiakanoholae, which was two long points of land. At first it seemed that these two were the only jutting points of land, but then more were seen, extending as far as Kapalilua. After Hiiakanoholae Point, Kaliliki Point was passed, and then the many houses that covered the land from Honuaula to Auhaukeae were visible. Anchor was dropped outside the reef at Honuaula, and the eyes of those aboard ship traveled over the land from Kaliliki to Honuaula, a land of rough aa and smooth pahoehoe, adorned with growth.

Kamakahonu was a fine cove, with sand along the edge of the sea and islets of pahoehoe, making it look like a pond, with a grove of *kou* trees a little inland and a heap of pahoehoe in the center of the stretch of sand. A stone wall ran inland from the right side of Kamakahonu, and on the other side of that wall there was sand as far as a rock promontory. This sandy stretch, called Kaiakekua was a canoe landing, with some houses mauka of it. The rock promontory above Kaiakekua is the Pa o Umi. Beyond it are the sands of Niumalu, and next, the spot where Hulihee Palace now stands. On this land, Kalakee, was the first site of the king's residence, and his house was called Papa. Outside of the enclosure, by the edge of the sea, was a spring called Kiope. Its fresh water came up from the pahoehoe and mixed with the water of the sea. It was a gathering place for those who went swimming and a place where the surf rolled in and dashed on land when it was rough. It was deep enough there for boats to land when the tide was high, and when it was ebb tide the boats came up close to its rocky pahoehoe side. From there the sea was shallow as far as the spring of Honuaula, where there was a house site on a raised pavement. There the young chief lived. Just makai was a patch of sand facing north, where canoes landed, in front of the heiau of Keikipuipui. A Hale o Lono faced directly toward the upland, and toward the north there was a bed of pahoehoe which reached to the sea, where there was a surfing place for children. To the south was where the waves dashed onto the land. West of the Keikipuipui heiau was a surfing place called Huiha, north of Kapohonau. Later, a heiau was built there by the king.

Perhaps because the ship was anchored so far to the south, the north side of Keikipuipui heiau seemed to be adjacent to Kiope spring. Some women standing there in *paʻu* dyed with turmeric were noticed by Ii, who spoke aloud, "How is it that those women are standing so close to the heiau wall?" He was told that this only seemed to be so because of the position of the ship. The women were Kailipono and Kamakaeheikuli, *kaikuahine* relatives of Papa. Those on shore had recognized Papa's ship and, perhaps, had gone to the spot near the edge of the sea to get a good view of the ship and the boy. When next he noticed the women, they were approaching in a canoe. Then wailing was exchanged between them and Kaupe, Nahoounauna, and the boy. The sun was sinking toward the islet of Lehua by this time, and the women urged that the boy go ashore with them, telling him of Papa's illness.

Ii went with them, and the canoe landed where the water was shallow. Then the women led the way to the main trail. They went past the Kaaipuhi spring, between the houses on both sides of the trail, and on until they arrived at the mauka side of the Honuaula cave. On the upper side of this trail, about 5 or 6 chains from where their canoe had landed, was a small group of houses standing apart. Where the houses began on the south side of the trail that ran through the village another trail branched off, ascending the mountain and leading to the food patches. A stone wall to protect the food plots stretched back of the village from one end to the other and beyond.

The boy and the two women stood at the enclosure entrance of the house in which Papa lay ill. As this was a men's house, *mua*, and only men were permitted there, they waited a little while, until Kuike, a kinsman of the boy, came out and learned who the boy was. The boy was led through the entrance and in through the door of the house where his namesake lay, beyond the *ukuwai*, or center of the house.

Each gable end of the *mua* was set apart by logs that reached from the spot opposite the door to each side of the door. Ii guessed that these logs were used as pillows, for the few occupants of the house were lying down from one end of the house to the other. The middle of the house was used as a passageway. Papa was lying on his back against the wall on the mauka side of the entrance, and the boy went to sit by his uncle's left shoulder. After the preliminary greetings, Papa asked, "Where is Malamaekeeke, your father?"

"I thought he came ashore with all of the others, including the god, before you arrived," answered the boy. But the uncle said that this was not so.

Papa then talked with the boy as follows: "You have come, just as your mother and I wished. You must serve both of our chiefs, Kamehameha and Liholiho, but you are to fulfill your choice by remaining with this chief of ours, Liholiho, for you already know how to behave and what to do. As we have lived with the king when he was poor and when he was rich, so must you. Mind all of the chiefs, because they are all ours. Stay with me tonight, and tomorrow go with your uncle Kaleiheana." Kaleiheana was next to Papa in the service of the young chief, followed by Keawekolohe Hoomakaukau and Manuia, their *kaikaina* relatives by Kamano. Nahili was the one under Papa in serving the king.

Papa's food and that of the others in the house was kapu because they were of the medical profession. The next day when the sun was warm, the boy realized that he had not seen his uncle eat any food and that he, too, had gone without eating. Perhaps it was his illness that made Papa go without eating, or perhaps there was nothing he could share with the boy.

A View in Owhyhee, with one of the Priest's Houses.
Published Jan. 1. 1782, by G. Robinson.

The boy embraced his uncle and went out in tears. He sought out Kaleiheana's residence, and there he met Kalamanamana, Kaleiheana's wife. Kaleiheana was still in the men's house at the other side of the steward's house. Kaupe had been with Kalamanamana since leaving the ship, and Ii found that her husband, Nahoounauna, had taken all of the boy's clothing into the men's house. After resting a while, the boy went on to seek his uncle Kaleiheana; and together they went to see Liholiho. When the young chief saw the boy enter with Kaleiheana he was very happy and so was Ii. In a little while, the young chief, who had not yet eaten, ordered the stewards to serve food. When the food and the eating companions were ready and they had begun to eat, the young chief said, "Give the boy some food." Kaleiheana refused, saying, "He shall eat in the steward's house." The boy held the kahili, as he had done before, for it had been his duty on Oahu to hold the kahili and tend to the spittoon. After the chief had eaten, the boy went to eat at the steward's house, a custom that was to be continued.

In a few days Ii's father landed with his canoe, in company with other canoes which belonged to the young chief. The boy was glad to know that his father was alive and to see him again face to face. He was fonder of his father than of his mother. Their faith in each other was mutual; and so was learned this fixed law of this era of education.

The Hawaiian- and foreign-built ships that had waited with them at Kawaihoa on Oahu were all hauled ashore, as was the custom with canoes. Perhaps it was necessary because of the lack of brass in their building. Two of the ships had been blown by the wind all the way to Kauai, perhaps because their captains lacked skill. It was decided by the king and the captains who conveyed the chiefs to Hawaii that the *Keoua* should be filled with sandalwood and sold with its cargo, for it was showing signs of age. The articles obtained through the sale were to belong to the king. A fine haole man from one of the foreign ships took it to China.

Before the king and chiefs went to Kahaluu for a year, there were seen some strange coconut trees in the midst of a coconut grove. The leaves of some of them had been bent over the dried nuts and plaited from the base of the leaf to the trunk, thereby holding up the nuts. This was truly an uncommon procedure and one not seen by Ii anywhere else. We were told that no one was allowed to take the dried coconuts. All the chiefs who owned groves were on Oahu, and perhaps that was why the caretakers of the land protected each chief's grove. Not long afterwards, when the people who were to consume the nuts returned, such bound-up trees were seen no more.

Soon after the decision was made to sell the *Keoua*, the masts of the king's canoes were erected, and it was told abroad that he was sailing to Kahaluu. So those who were going, either by canoe or by foot, made themselves ready.

The boy accompanied his young chief in the canoe fleet his father had brought from Honolulu, and landed at Kahaluu. However, when the sun was about to set and the father was ready to return by canoe to Kailua, the boy insisted on going with him. The father was opposed to the idea of Ii's leaving the young chief, but the boy said, "That may be so, but you and Kaleiheana are being allowed to stay at Kailua as you wish. Though we have come to this island for the same reason, to serve Liholiho, the chief is not yet settled. Therefore, it would be well for us to go back together until we know what he is going to do." At these words Kaleiheana agreed that the boy go with them. They landed at Kailua, at their place in Papaula.

The following days were ones of intense famine in Kailua, and the followers of the young chief suffered. The boy and his father went to stay for several days with a resident from nearby Keopu. It was here that Kaiwikokoole, a *makuakane* of the boy, met the lad and his father when he came with the king's farmers from Kuahewa. They brought food from the store houses of the king, kept for just such times as this.

Kaiwikokoole was said to be one of the boy's fathers, but the boy's features were not like his. Kaiwikokoole, who had taken care of the boy while they were on Oahu, owned some of the houses that stood close to the bathing pool of Honokaupu in Honolulu. This *makuakane* of the boy conversed with his father about their living in the house of a friend, and he asked permission to take the boy and keep him for some days because of the great famine. So it was decided that the boy should go with him, leaving his father in the house of their friend. In the upland of Kuahewa he lived on a farm where the tree ferns grew, located above the long trail mentioned before. This was a war trail when Umi the chief was victorious in battle. On the huge farm was a large number of *'ai alo* (men who ate in the king's presence) appointed by Kamehameha to take charge of the work. The boy was comfortable there with his *makuakane* Kaiwikokoole, because he had known him before. His teachings were like those of the boy's parents. Whenever Kaiwikokoole went to work at farming, about a quarter of a mile distant, the boy went with him; and when he laid down his implement to rest, the boy took it up to cut off fern leaves and the like. When Kaiwikokoole took back the implement, the boy returned to the house to look for something else to do.

Whenever it was announced that taro stalks were to be cut, a company traveled to Puaauka for this purpose, and the boy was allowed to go along. On the first of these trips he was shown some taro called *uia*, growing by a house site, with corms which reached the middle part of the upper arm in length and were about a foot and a half in circumference. Men who went to cut taro stalks at that time also examined them.

When the taro-cutting company paused to smoke tobacco, the boy watched them puff smoke out of their noses and mouths and tried to do likewise. He almost choked to death, and it took him two hours to recover. So does trouble befall one who is unaccustomed to such things. His *makua* did not hear of his trouble when he returned to their house.

The boy lived in the upland with Kaiwikokoole for some time before Kaleiheana sent a messenger to fetch him. The messenger was named Kalaikane and he was a *kaikunane* relative of the boy's mother, whose name was the same.

Papa's health had become much worse after the king and chiefs had left for Kahaluu. His friends and the boy's father had gathered at Pahoehoe in Kaumalumalu, near Kailua, to be with him. The boy and his companion arrived there at dusk, to find that Papa could no longer speak clearly.

Papa, who wanted to go to Hookena, his land in South Kona, was carried aboard a canoe in the harbor, but the time for the *makahiki* celebration was drawing near and canoes were prohibited from sailing. They were waiting for the gods to be set up before the Hikiau heiau after their circuit of the island. Everyone was filled with fear of the kapu, but the boy's father felt a great pity for Papa, who fretted aboard the canoe, so he made ready to sail. However, he was strongly urged to wait until the chiefs had heard of Papa's wish.

When the king and the chiefs heard how Papa was they gave permission for him to leave, knowing that this was his last illness. However, when he received permission from his chiefs to sail, Papa no longer wished to do so because the wooden *makahiki* gods were about to arrive. Or perhaps his desire ceased when permission was granted.

After the kapu days had passed, the gods arrived at Hikiau, the most important heiau in the district of Kona. This was, I believe, the king's first year on Hawaii after his return from Oahu. It has been said that the king spent the thirteenth year of the century at Lahaina; but if that is an error, this event took place in 1813.

Papa's journey for the benefit of his health led to Hookena, his own land. There a ti-leaf thatched house was erected for healing purposes—a house of green ti leaves, according to the prescribed medical treatment. While Papa was lying there in this small hut, a strange rising of the sea brought water into the house and wet the patient. Only once did this happen.

It was doubted that Papa would recover, for he remained the same. When the boy climbed one of the coconut trees in the grove to get himself some nuts, he heard a cry from the woman Kamakaeheikuli, asking, "Who is climbing the coconut tree? Naipuawa [Papa's son by Kamaua], the boy whose tree that is, is dead. Who is this?" When she was told that the climber was Papa's namesake, she said, "It is all right then, for he [Papa] is still alive."

The chiefs who resided at Kaawaloa from the time they came from Kahaluu to await the gods at Hikiau, listened for news concerning the serious illness of Papa. When the time for the patient to depart this world was near at hand, he was borne on a litter to the dwelling house and laid down. A few days later, he turned away and left his wife and all his people. A messenger was sent to so inform the chiefs.

Fifteen days after his death, Papa's heirs and assigns met at the sea shore of Waipunauliki in Napoopoo to discuss what best be done. With the consent of the king, Nahili and Keawekolohe were appointed to divide the lands of the deceased from Hawaii to Oahu. None disagreed with the divisions, which had the king's approval. Only the widow's interests were opposed, and she sought some other means of gaining a livelihood.

When the king returned to Kailua from Kaawaloa, the boy went to live with the young chief. They were with Ii's uncle, Kaleiheana, who carried out his duties of caring for the canoes brought from Oahu. While he was away because of Papa's illness, Kaleiheana left a substitute in Kaia, who had accompanied Nahili from Oahu. It was at this time that Kamehameha acquired Kamakahonu.

CHAPTER IX

KAMEHAMEHA'S COURT AT KAMAKAHONU

Kamehameha's first residence at Kailua was at Kalakee, as we have mentioned. There stones had been heaped up like a wall at the edge of the sea to make a foundation level with that of the inland side. This was done in order to set apart the makai trail that came down from Pa o Umi, a trail used since remote times. The place where the heir of the kingdom lived, close to the heiau of Keikipuipui, which was on its western side, had also been built up.

Kamakahonu was formerly the place of Keawe a Mahi, the *kahu* of Keawe a Heulu. When Keawe a Heulu died, it went to his son Naihe, who, it is believed, caused the death of Keawe a Mahi. Kaawa, a favorite *kahu* of Naihe is said to have been responsible for the king's residing there. It was customary for Kaawa to ask whoever massaged him, "What is your desire?" and to grant whatever the person asked. It was thought that the king had perhaps mentioned to Kaawa his desire for Kamakahonu when he and Naihe were in Kaawaloa, where they then lived, though Keawe a Mahi was still living and dwelling on the place.

At last his great longing was satisfied, and he moved into Keawe a Mahi's house. He built another house, a *hale nana mahina 'ai*, on the seaward side of Keawe a Mahi's residence from which to observe the farm lands. Facing directly upland toward Kuahewa, this house was like an observation post, for the site had first been built up high with stones. It was located on the west side of Ahuena, a heiau that stood beside Kamakahonu, on a spot where canoes could be seen

117

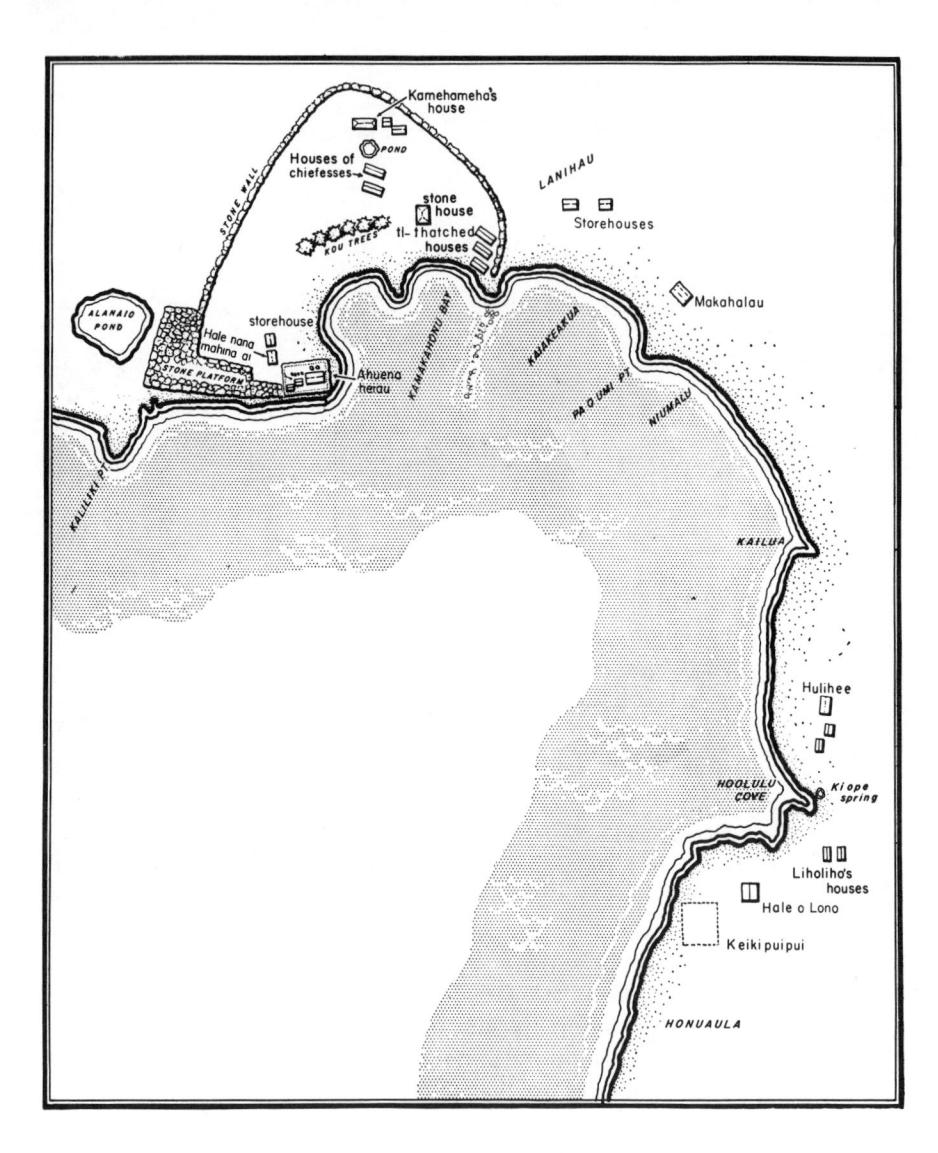

Kamakahonu and environs as described by Ii. Map by Paul Rockwood.

coming up from South Kona and from the vicinity of Kailua in North Kona. Perhaps the king's great desire for Kamakahonu was because it was a place celebrated for the constant appearance of fishes. Sometimes *kule*, fish that burrow in the sand, appeared from there to Honuaula, for there is sand from Kaiakekua to outside of Honuaula, where small ships anchor.

Honuaula has a cove that opens to the south. When the Kona wind blows, it is not a safe port because of the huge waves from the south, depending upon the force of the wind. Perhaps that was how the ship *Kekauluohi* was driven ashore at Kaiakekua at one time. When the Kona wind blows, it is a time for those who are proficient to go surfing.

At Kamakahonu, the king erected three houses thatched with dried ti leaves. Just north of the sleeping house (*hale moe*), and extending a little beyond the front of it, was an eating house (*hale 'aina*) which belonged to Kaahumanu. This house had two openings in the gable end toward the west, and close to the second opening was the door of the sleeping house. A third opening was in the end toward the upland.

There were three openings in the sleeping house. The one in the middle of the west end, one which served as a window on the upland side of the southwest corner, and one mauka of the window. This window lay beyond the men's house (*mua*) on the south. The door mauka of the window was the one entered when coming from the men's house.

The door of the men's house closest to the sleeping house was the one used to go back and forth between these two houses. There was also a door in the end wall on the west side of this house, and two small openings in the south seaward corner, one on the upper side and one on the lower side of the corner. These faced the many capes of Kona and took in the two extremities of this tranquil land and the ships at anchor. However, should the ships be more to the ocean side, only the masts were visible. A fifth opening was a little on the seaward side of the northeast corner, where the upland side of the men's house extended a little beyond the sleeping house, and it was only through this entrance that the men went in and out. It was near the door that was used to enter from the sleeping house. Near the door facing westward in the *mua*, was the king's eating place. On the upper side were large and small wooden containers that served as bowls and platters, together with a large poi container always filled with poi from the king's lands.

The trail that led in and out of Kamakahonu was south of the *mua* at the beach, as previously described, with pahoehoe at both ends and sand in between. The men's eating house, the sleeping house, and the women's eating house were at the end of a 7- to 8-foot stone wall that ran irregularly from there to the shore at the back of the *hale nana mahina 'ai*. Outside of the wall was the trail for those who lived oceanward of Kamakahonu. Immediately back of the wall was the pond of Alanaio, where stood some houses. There, too, was the start of the road that goes to Puu o Kaloa and on as far as Kiholo, where it joins the road from the upland that is called Kealaehu. The upland road runs from South Kona through the middle of the *ama'uma'u* fern belt, and this is thought to have been the road by which Kauhiakama traveled all the way around the island in a few days.

Two eating houses were built for Kaheiheimalie and her daughter, Kekauluohi, opposite the three houses thatched with ti leaves. They stood back of the *kou* trees growing there at Kamakahonu, both facing northwest. Kaheiheimalie's eating house had two doors, but Kekauluohi's had but one door. In front of her house was a bathing pool, at the upper bank of which were some small houses and that of the king.

Because Kekauluohi was kept in seclusion the door of her house faced the stone wall. Her guard was Hika, just as Luheluhe and Kauiki had been the guards of Mokualoha (Kaahumanu). Thus this woman was kept under strict kapu by the king and did not go abroad in the daytime. There were no restrictions at night, for the sacred chiefs were then free from this kapu.

A stone house was built between the three houses thatched with ti and those of these chiefesses. Its builder was either a Frenchman or a Portuguese named Aikona. He was skilled in such work, and this was the second stone house he had built.

Aikona's first stone house, which was built in Honolulu before the company left Oahu, stood near W. N. Ladd's stone house. On its north was the first custom house. For this house, the chiefesses and men and women of the royal household brought earth for mortaring from Kanelaau. They formed a large procession, and by time for the morning meal, the earth was in such a great heap that they had enough. This well-built house was the only large stone building of that time. Marin's house was built like it, for Aikona was his son-in-law, through marriage with Miela, Marin's oldest daughter.

When Aikona began building the end and side walls of the house at Kamakahonu he built a third wall between them and arranged stones in the center of this middle wall to form a door. The walls rose together until the house, from one end to the other, was finished. When Aikona later removed the stones set up in the doorway of the center wall, the doorway looked like the fine arched bridge of Pualoalo at Peleula in Honolulu. As he removed the stones, Aikona explained that had they been piled inexpertly the whole house might have collapsed. This house was well completed. In the stone house were stored the king's valuables and those of Aikona. These valuables were kegs of rum and gunpowder and guns, of which the guns and powder were placed on the inside near the inner wall. Rum distilled on Oahu accounted for most of the freight aboard the ship *Keoua* when it returned to Hawaii. It was first unloaded at Kaawaloa and left there at a house with stone walls and a roof thatched with pili grass, in charge of Hanaki, the watchman. This house was enclosed by a stone wall and surrounded by a grove of coconut trees and other plants near the canoe landing called Awili.

Soon after the building of the king's houses at Kamakahonu, two ti-thatched houses were built for the young chief at Papaula in Honuaula. One was a *mua* for the heir of the kingdom; the other, a *hale 'aina* for his young wife. The name of the woman's eating house was Kawaluna; that of the husband was Hookuku.

Two or three storehouses, some work sheds (*halau*), and work houses in which women could print their tapa were also built. There were two kinds of work sheds, all thatched with pili grass, behind the white sands of Kaiakekua and the brine-covered sands close to the pahoehoe. Behind these houses was the trail that went up to the plains, to the area overgrown with thickets, to the bottom of the mountain slope, to the region where the *'ama'u* ferns grew wild, and on to the mountain.

In the storehouses were piled bundles of surplus *pa'u,* malos, and tapa sheets. These had been given to the chiefs as *makahiki* taxes that were presented to the gods when they made a circuit of the island every twelfth month. Because the profit received from these taxes on the land was so large, combined with the king's personal shares from his other lands, goods were piled in great heaps. If one looked into the storehouses, one saw small, large, extra large, and medium-sized bundles and wooden bowls filled with hard poi. There were separate bundles for women and for men. Consequently, separate storehouses were provided for the food to be eaten by each sex. There was no separation of the fishes, however, because either men or women could take what they wanted.

Two more houses were built at Pa o Umi, one of which was a *maka halau* [a house built so it could command a view] thatched with pili grass. One of its doors was toward the three houses thatched with dried ti leaves, and it faced the long land points to the south. It was a common sight to see canoes coming and going, for it was the place of arrival and departure for canoe freight. If they sailed at night they went along with the dew-laden breeze; and when it was day the Eka breeze bore them along, as did the Maaa breeze of Lahaina. Though a canoe can carry much more than can a horse, perhaps it may be compared to a horse that hauls a wagon a long distance.

Later, another storehouse was built in Kamakahonu, on the north side of the *hale nana mahina 'ai*. It had stone walls and was constructed like a *maka halau*. The upper of its two stories was for storing tapa, *pa'u*, malos, fish nets, lines, and *olona* fiber; and all other goods went into the lower story. The thatching was of sugar-cane leaves, the customary thatching on the houses along that shore. Dried banana trunk sheaths were used for the inside walls and were cleverly joined from top to bottom. Banana trunk sheaths were also used in the *hale nana mahina 'ai*.

The houses along the beaches of that land of tranquility looked large and solid because the foundations were on raised platforms of stone, some higher than 4 feet. Furthermore, there was no gale such as blew in Lahaina and some other places to push the houses over. The only strong wind that blew along these beaches was the one that came from the upland occasionally, called the Kuhonua. Although coconut leaves were bent over sometimes and *'i'iwi* and *'apapane* birds blown by the wind were seen perching on coconut or *noni* trees and on stone walls, no house was ever damaged. The Kuhonua winds blew for only a few hours at a time, after which the customary calm of the land returned. A little more frequent was a cold wind from Kekaha, the Hoolua. Because of the calm of that land, people often slept outside of the tapa drying sites at night. It is said to be a land that grows cold with a dew-laden breeze, but perhaps not so cold as in Hilo when the Alahonua blows.

Ahuena heiau as it looked after Kamehameha restored it. Photograph of an original sketch by Louis Choris in Honolulu Academy of Arts.

After these houses were built, another heiau house, called Ahuena, was restored (*ho'ala hou*). This house stood on the east side of the *hale nana mahina 'ai*, separated from it by about a chain's distance. The foundation of Ahuena was a little more than a chain from the sand beach to the westward and from the rocky shore to the eastward. Right in front of it was a well-made pavement of stone which extended its entire length and as far out as the place where the waves broke. Behind Ahuena, the surf turned right and broke on the pahoehoe as far as Kaliliki.

The east side of Ahuena was in line with the row of pahoehoe mounds at the mauka side of Kamakahonu. A trail began there at the mound of pahoehoe at the east corner of the men's house and ran along close to the beach from that southeastern extremity of Kamakahonu for a chain or more, then turned right and went on to the southwest of the mound of pahoehoe in the center. On the eastern front of Ahuena, and close to it, was a canoe entrance, where canoes would come up to the shore right in front of the *hale nana mahina ʻai*. There was also a landing place by the mound of pahoehoe in the center and another by the line of pahoehoe mounds on the mauka side of Kamakahonu. This landing place was between the pahoehoe mound in the center of Kamakahonu and the front of the three houses thatched with dried ti leaves.

Ahuena house, which was a heiau, was enclosed with a fence of lama wood and within this fence, toward the front on the west and facing inland, there was an *anuʻu* tower. A row of images stood along its front, as befitted a Hale o Lono. Images stood at the northwest corner of the house, with a stone pavement in front of them that extended as far as the western gate and as far as the fence east of the house. On the west side of the outer entrance was a large image named Koleamoku, on whose helmet perched the figure of a plover.

In the center of the house was a fireplace for cooking bananas. Opposite the door at the back wall of the house, in line with the fireplace and the entrance, was a Kane image. This image was of the nature of an *ololupe* god, a god who led spirits; and that part of the house was his place. All the bananas cooked there were laid before his *kuahu* altar, where those who took part in the ceremonies prayed.

This is one of the prayers:

Ololupe ke alakaʻi uhane,	Ololupe, guide of spirits,
Pau ai kamahele,	Destroying traveler,
He kanaka he ʻkua e Kane.	[Destroy] the man [and] the spirit, O Kane.

There were many more prayers of that nature. Prayers of today are much better than those of yesterday. Indeed, the old religion even condoned killing.

A secret council met there to discuss matters pertaining to the government and to loyalty and rebellion. This was a continuation of the practice on Oahu. The council said that the *ololupe* god would perhaps be charged to bring hither the spirits of the rebellious to be destroyed.

The members of the council—Kamehameha I, Liholiho, Kalaikuahulu, Nahili, Haleino, Kaioea, Keaweopu, and Kuhia—met together every evening, except for Liholiho who, on the nights of Kane and Hilo, went to Hikiau heiau to observe these kapu periods. Ii accompanied the heir to the kingdom everywhere, and together the two entered the house where the others were gathered. The boy would lay before the king the things he had brought from their dwelling and go outside of this house, called a *halehui ʻilimaiʻa*. After the meeting was over he fetched his chief's things again.

Here it would be well to discuss the practices that destroyed people in the olden days and destroys some persons even now. The thing that seems improper to the writer is the great faith that some persons have in such benighted practices in this time of enlightenment, for each dies of the sin he himself commits.

In olden times sorcery was believed to have much mana and there were many kahunas who practiced both *ana'ana* and *kuni* sorcery. The practices of the *kahuna kuni*, however, were seen in the open, and such kahunas were regarded as good. Their ceremonies were performed where the dead body lay in the presence of those who mourned him. *Kahuna kuni* uttered their prayers over the ashes of the offerings they had burned to destroy the person who had carried off the *maunu*, personal "bait" such as a lock of hair or fingernail parings, used in the *'ana'ana* sorcery that caused the death. The filth-eating *kahuna 'ana'ana* were different and are said to have been destroyed along with the persons who had brought them the *maunu*. However, it was really fear that killed the victim.

This was true also of the *kalaipahoa* images, noted for the deaths they caused. They were aided by the bananas and taro placed on the *kuahu* altar before one or more of the images. If a rat or a lizard died when it ran over the altar while the dedicated offerings lay there, it was understood that the offerings had produced mana. Many people have seen these gods flying like shooting stars, and such stars were called *ke 'kua hana*. The term *akua hana* was used for the gods who were thus strengthened with food offerings. The body of the chosen *kalaipahoa* image was scraped and the scrapings were taken and secretly fed to the intended victim. This created the term *akua hanai* (fed the god). As this was a common practice, chiefs and commoners alike were constantly filled with dread of it.

The idea of death was always present. Everywhere men were filled with jealousy and anger, as with the heat of fire; and death was the only way to appease them. Thus killing and depriving gave some protection against evils, except those from the *akua hana* and the secret practice of *'ana'ana* sorcery. Many died from one end of the land to the other in those benighted times. Many were secretly destroyed, and the reason for their deaths realized only when news was heard that so-and-so had died suddenly. Fear was the cause of such deaths, not mana.

Such a death was suffered by Kaoleioku in 1818 in Honolulu. It was said that he was killed by the *akua hanai*, being secretly fed the poison god in his food during his evening meal. He slept until midnight, awoke to smoke tobacco, then fell into a final sleep. Kaoleioku's fate became generally known through gossip. So we see there was great fear of this thing, which is probably why the king guarded Kalaipahoa in his sleeping house when he was in Hilo prior to the voyage called the great *peleleu*. Ololupe, the god who guided spirits to death, was equally feared.

So it was when Naaimakolu, the son of Kahilipa of Molokai went to dwell with Kekuaokalani, son of Keliimaikai. He was skilled in waving a flexible hand kahili, arching it this way and that, and making it go around; but all of these led to death. A certain way of shaking out a tapa shoulder covering was another means of bringing about death. It was said that those who did not know about this method of causing death died, but that those who did know about it lived. At that time death was a matter of the greatest concern, but it is very different now. Death is as nothing to us because the time of righteousness and blessings in the worship of Jesus Christ, King of kings and Lord of lords, has come. Pitiful were those things done by the people in the time of unenlightenment and those persons who lived and died in that period without knowing enlightenment and peaceful association.

CHAPTER X

LIFE IN KONA

Before the king restored Ahuena house, a two-masted ship arrived in port. Mr. Maikuli, an elderly man, and Mr. Anana, a young man, were the agents for this ship, which belonged to the Hudson's Bay Company. The vessel had a spar with the stern mast and three topsails with the forward one. The fourth sail, a large one, was at the base. It was like a man-of-war, low and fine in appearance, with the muzzles of cannons showing around the sides. When they were needed, they all projected at once. Bayonets were kept at the sleeping places of the crew. Perhaps these weapons were used to repel the Nouwaiki [?] people, who were said to be fearless. This was indeed true, to judge by the appearance of those who had arrived earlier.

It is said that a hundred Hawaiian men were taken to labor in the Northwest at that time, but the payment received by the king for graciously giving these men away is not known. Hawaiians still live on those shores.

It was some people of the Hudson's Bay Company who helped King Kamehameha III in 1842. Perhaps some among us knew Haalilio and Richards, the messengers who sailed for freedom.

Before the two-masted ship left Kailua, the agents associated with the king and Liholiho. They taught the heir to the kingdom how to play whist, which was new to him and which was to become widespread. The only card game the people and chiefs had known before was "Nuuanu." The agents lived

127

in John Rives' houses, back of the king's storehouses, which were on the right side of the trail leading up to the farm lands of Lanihau. These men lived in the islands for about two years, then were seen no more.

It was the agents who suggested that Liholiho learn English. They fostered the idea until a haole man was found to teach him. This man had landed at Kahoolawe some years before after a ship on which he had been the mate was wrecked at sea. With some other men from the ship, he managed to make a raft out of pieces of the mast, and this carried them to land, where two Hawaiians dove for fishes and obtained food for them to eat.

It is believed that the man chosen to be Liholiho's teacher was an American, for his ship, the *Marshall*, was from the United States. This good man lived with the heir to the kingdom for some time, and taught him some English words and how to write them. He used this knowledge to obtain bottles of rum from ships' captains. Apparently he wrote only for rum, nothing else.

After the king had been in Kailua for two years, the person who had taken the *Keoua Lelepali* laden with sandalwood to China to be sold returned. It is said that he gave into the hands of the king $10,000.00. If that was true, it was the first profit the king had received from his kindness to the Americans and their ships. This was the first flow of money into the kingdom. However, greater amounts come in nowadays.

At about that time Alexander Adams arrived. [In 1816 Adams landed at the island of Hawaii from the brig *Forester* out of London. The *Forester* was purchased by Kamehameha, who renamed it the *Kaahumanu*, and Adams remained in the service of the king as the ship's captain.] Adams was often seen passing to-and-fro before the door of Kalanimoku's house, wearing a serge suit, a coat and trousers of dark cloth. He looked about twenty-five years old at the time.

The year 1817 had not yet passed when a Spanish [Argentinian] ship arrived. Some of the men, including the captain and the mate, looked like Englishmen and spoke both Spanish and English.

The captain of the ship went to see the king and, with some men who accompanied him, spent an enjoyable time there. The king opened a barrel of *mole hao* ['*okolehao*] for them, and this attracted the foreigners, who gave money to the king for it. Several thousand dollars were spent in Kona during the time that the ship remained there. Finally, the ship and all the freight on board were sold to the king for an unknown sum, and the crew left to scatter about the island.

There were two ships of this kind [Argentinian]. The second to arrive was a two-master, with a double prow. When it came, the larger ship had already been sold to the king. The second ship did not remain in Kailua long, but left to appear later at Kauai. Soon after its departure a man-of-war arrived, seeking the two ships, and the king learned that they had been stolen. The two ships had caused speculation when they came, for they were not like any of the other ships that had come to Hawaii.

Because the crews had deserted their ships and vanished into the mountains and other places, they were not found by the man-of-war, which confiscated the ship which had been sold to the king but nothing else. A month later, after the man-of-war and the reclaimed ship left Kailua, news came that the double-prowed vessel had been found at Waimea, Kauai. When its captain was found in the house of a Hawaiian, he was taken to a suitable place and shot to death.

This was the second time that prosperity came to this people during the rule of the first king. It is thought that several thousand dollars were cast on shore by those of that stolen ship before it was retaken. All the clothing on board also went ashore. While the ship and those who had stolen her were at Napoopoo, the king, realizing that hundreds of dollars were being poured into the area, built two houses thatched with green ti leaves for the money that the natives of the place were expected to give him. He received a heap of money in that gift-giving, which was a customary thing. He was clever in getting money by such planning and through his hospitality to strangers.

Whenever there was a meeting in the Ahuena house in the evening, the king instructed the heir carefully as to how to do things, describing the lives of former rulers such as Keakealaniwahine, Kalaniopuu, Koihala, Kamalalawalu, Kauhiakama, and Hakau. Thus Liholiho learned the results of abuse and disregard of the welfare of chiefs and commoners and about farming and fishing and things of like nature. In the discussions with the king the heir derived understanding which has passed down to his heirs of today. We can see the power of the law of the privy council and the executive councils in this time of education. This should remind us of the good work of that first king. The secret council was continued in Kailua after the king returned from Oahu, and it continued until his death.

As already mentioned, Liholiho made journeys to the heiau Hikiau to impose the kapu. He sailed by double canoe to Hikiau every evening on the nights of Hilo and Kane to observe these kapu periods. While others paddled, Liholiho and the person who carried his possessions just sat on the *pola* platform built on the booms that held the canoes together. One canoe was securely lashed to the other by cleverly braided sennit cords which formed a pattern worked out by those trained in this art. They sat by each *pepeiao* [comb cleats to which the booms were lashed] because it was higher at these places. The *pepeiao* were cleverly made to hold the thwarts (*wae*) inside of the canoe. The *'iako* booms were carefully selected. *'Ohi'a* was preferred for the curved booms with the hump in the middle, and the humped side was at the top. The ends of the booms, which were placed over the *pepeiao* of the canoes, were straight.

In double canoes, the one on the right was called *ekea* and the one on the left, *ama*. Some double canoes had three *'iako* booms made of *'ohi'a lehua* wood, but longer canoes had four or five *'iako* made from mature, tough wood. Other booms, called the *ke'a*, were used in front and in back. These lay very close to the stern and bow pieces of the canoe. Between the rear *ke'a* and the large *'iako* boom at the front of the canoe were the three other booms that helped hold the canoes together. At the end of the *pola* platform, which was at the rear *ke'a*, were two poles tied fast to the three booms and the rear *ke'a*, but there was no platform at the front boom and *ke'a*. The mast was set up directly on the large *'iako* boom in front, held by a slab. The two poles of the platform were joined to either side of the slab and lashed fast with ropes from front to back. This was to protect the bundles of tapa and other precious possessions. These poles were tied with ropes that were wound and looped to make it easy for one person to undo the platform and carry it ashore, or unship it in case of disaster.

A double canoe of the type used by Liholiho. A model in the American Museum of Natural History.

We shall not discuss the masts and sails of ancient Hawaii, for those have been written about in the books of the foreigners since the time of Lono (Captain Cook).

The paddlers of a double canoe sat from prow to stern on each canoe and paddled in unison. If they began on the left, they all paddled on that side, and when one person made a banging sound with his paddle, it was a signal for all to change to the opposite side. If, after two dips of the paddle, the person made another sound with the blade of his paddle, then everyone from prow to stern on both canoes changed again. This was an attractive sight.

To keep a single canoe from overturning, alternate persons paddled on opposite sides. This craft shot ahead just as a double canoe did; and it, too, was attractive to see. Paddling takes strength, and good arms for paddling are admired.

There were rules for refloating a canoe that had overturned at sea, thereby saving it and its occupants from destruction. This art was taught to members of the court of the king in Kailua, and thus Liholiho learned how to refloat a capsized canoe.

This is the nature of the art of binding so as to right a double canoe. When a suitable place for training exercises was reached, one of the two canoes was filled with sea water and allowed to sink. Then the men stood on the sunken canoe and hauled on ropes attached to the *muku* (outer ends of the booms) of the other canoe, overturning the two together. With both canoes upside down, like a canoe capsized naturally, all the men swam about in the sea as they would if a canoe were upset. They all clung to the bottoms of the canoes and tied ropes to the boom end of the one indicated by the instructor. Then they pulled together on that canoe while standing on the *muku* of the other. The canoe with the ropes attached turned over, emptying itself of sea water. Then the men climbed onto the empty canoe and tied the ends of the two or three rollers (*lona*) carried as equipment to the *muku* and to other places on the booms of the swamped canoe and tied these ropes to the *pola* platform between the canoes. Then the ropes were drawn around at the rear of these *lona* to the empty canoe. Ropes were attached from both ends of these *lona* and knotted to resemble a fishnet. On this were placed rescued baggage and equipment, as well as persons suffering from cold and cramps; and a fire was started to warm them.

When they were warmed and their stiffness was gone, the instructor made the men sit with their paddles from front to back in the hollow body of the drained canoe. Two men sat in the canoe containing water, one in front and one in back, hence it seems that the swamped canoe was also afloat. The instructor called out, "Go forward five dips of the paddle." Then he counted, "One, two, three, four, five." As he began to count, the canoe started forward. The man at the back of the swamped canoe stood dipping the water out with his paddle while the water spilled out from the stern, owing to the movement of the canoe. Then the instructor called again, "Paddle back five dips with the stroke that makes the canoe go backward." This caused the rest of the water to spill out at the prow, until there was none left. Thus did they seek salvation in time of trouble.

It is said that there were two things that made it impossible to right a capsized canoe: the breaking off of the booms and the smashing of the canoe. When either of these things happened, the occupants were doomed.

When a single canoe overturned, its supplies and equipment were gathered together and taken care of by one man while the others righted the canoe. To do this, one man stood where the float of the outrigger joined the forward boom and another, where it joined the rear boom. They held fast to the ropes attached to the free ends of the booms and forced the float downward. Then they climbed the booms and, watching the movement of the billows, turned the canoe, thereby spilling out half or a third of the water. When they let go of the booms and the canoe, it floated. Then the rest of the water was removed with the bailer.

Akalele, a man famed for his paddling strength, is said to have come from Kauai and to have lived with our first king. One night the king left Kawaihae and set forth with his double canoes. Daylight found his company outside of

Kekaha, and they rested a little while at Kailua. Akalele was alone on a single canoe about 6 fathoms long and filled with baskets of sweet potatoes, fowls, dogs, and such gifts as people brought who came to see the king on the beach in Kona. When they arrived at Kahaluu, or Keauhou perhaps, the single canoe began to race with the double ones, to see which could first reach their goal, Awili in Kaawaloa. So they raced, the king with his canoe paddlers, Akalele alone. Although the single canoe was loaded with goods, the king desired this race.

A paddle on one of the double canoes made a rattling sound at the prow, and the contestants began to paddle. The canoes kept together past Kahoopaheehee Point and beyond Honalo. As Kanaueue Point was passed, they were still together, and they kept together at Naawaawa. At times one of the double canoes would be slightly ahead of another, and Akalele kept up with the outrigger of the last canoe. Then Akalele caught up with the outrigger of the foremost canoe. Each canoe strove to win; but first one, then the other, fell behind as far as Keawakaheka, where they turned shoreward. After they passed Keopuka and reached Kalaemano at Kaawaloa, they again turned shoreward. Near the harbor of Awili, where there is a narrow channel only large enough for a single canoe, the king called out, "O Akalele, turn your canoe into the narrow entrance! Glide in on a wave!" Akalele did as he was told and was first to arrive at Awili. The others took the longer way around and found him there carrying the things ashore. The king helped Akalele because he was a stranger.

Kualii, a paddler from one of the double canoes, is said to have leaped into the sea and found himself barely able to walk because he was out of breath and leg weary. This man was accustomed to such work; but against Akalele, the strength of a multitude was as nothing.

Perhaps Akalele would have grown to be a great favorite of the king, had he remained with him longer; but he chose to return to Kauai. When he was ready to leave Hawaii, a wind storm was blowing; and he was warned not to sail. However, he sailed anyway, boasting to those on shore, "When did the wind ever carve a paddle?" as he patted his blade. The warnings proved prophetic, and his strength failed against the wind. He who elevates himself shall be humbled.

Kawaimomona was also a strong paddler, but his strength was not tested as was that of Akalele. It is said that with a single stroke Kawaimomona could make a canoe come gliding in on a wave.

Kepaalani, too, was known as a strong man, but his strength was not put to the test in the same way as Akalele's. When his canoe left the harbor of Kailua to go to Kawaihae, he paddled without pausing to rest until he reached shore. Because of this ability he became a favorite of the king, and it was thus that he received the whole of Puuwaawaa and the fish ponds Paaiea in Makaula and Kaulana in Kekaha. It is said that he was not very good at paddling according to rules, but this was not so important as the fact that he landed where he wanted.

Rules for canoe paddling were customarily observed in ancient times, and Kamehameha had been trained until he was skilled at it. In paddling either on the right or on the left he moved his paddle from the outside inward. He was also taught canoe surfing, in which both he and Kaahumanu were most skilled, board surfing, and so forth.

In Puaa, North Kona, is a famous surf called Kooka, where a coral head stands just outside a point of lava rocks. When the surf dashed over the coral head, the people swam out with their surfboards and floated with them. If a person owned a long narrow canoe, he performed what was called *lele wa'a,* or canoe leaping, in which the surfer leaped off the canoe with his board and rode the crest of a wave ashore. The canoe slid back of the wave because of the force of the shove given it with the feet. When the surfer drew close to the place where the surf rose, a wave would pull itself up high and roll in. Any timid person who got too close to it was overwhelmed and could not reach the landing place. The opening through which the surfer entered was like a sea pool, with a rocky hill above and rows of lava rocks on both sides, and deep in the center. This was a difficult feat and one not often seen, but for Kaahumanu and the king it was easy. When they reached the place where the surf rose high, they went along with the crest of a wave and slipped into the sea pool before the wave rolled over. Only the light spray of the surf touched them before they reached the pool. The spectators shouted and remarked to each other how clever the two were. This art was held in esteem at that time, and so the surfing places were constantly filled with men and women.

The surf of Huiha at Honuaula in Kailua proper, directly above the place where ships anchored and just seaward of Keikipuipui, was rough when it rose. A person who had just learned to surf was afraid of it, but those who were skilled regarded it as fun. The landing place for this surf was a circle of sand. The water swirled gently as it went out from the shallows, and it was there that the surfers came in to reach the sand circle.

Huiha and Kiope were covered with surf riders when the sea was rough and the surf went all the way up to them. There were two small points on the north side of the sandy landing place, covered with the coarse *'aki'aki* grass, and to the north, a point of pahoehoe. Just a little north of this point were two coral heads which were used to gage the surf. On the inner side of the pahoehoe and on the north of Keikipuipui, was a surfing place for children and for timid men and women.

If the king rode in, he went ashore gracefully on the surf of Huiha; but when it was rough he went right in to Kiope. Sometimes he could hardly reach Kiope because of the narrow entrance. The surf dashed over the point of pahoehoe and washed unobstructed and gently into Kiope. Here the mark that was observed for the rising of this surf was the point of Kaliliki. If the sea sprays rose upward two or three times, that was the number of the waves. If the sea sprays of Kaliliki went upward with force, a high surf was indicated and the timid kept away. The skilled went close to the source of the surf and remained there. As to the king, he was frequently seen leaping from a canoe on this surf. Expert surf riders unused to this surf were tossed about by it and found it was wise to sit still and watch the native sons, who were familiar with it, crouch in the flying sprays. A swimmer daring enough to try to land would be killed.

Many surfs were used in this popular sport. There is a surf on the south side of Huiha. Kiikau is the inner surf; Naohulelua, the outer one. Both run toward the south going shoreward. The surf of Kamakaia at Auhaukeae runs shoreward toward the north. When the sea is rough the surfs there meet with those of Naohulelua.

The surf of Kamoa at Keolonahihi and Puu runs toward the north side of Puu, directly beyond the spring there. The surf of Kaulu in Keauhou is a long one, and similar to the surf of Kamoa. The surf of Kapahukapu is at Napoopoo. There is also a surf at Keei and another on the east side of Kalae in Kau named Kapuuone. Two others are the surfs of Paiahaa at Kaalualu and Kawa in Hilea.

Kanukuokamanu in Waiakea, Hilo, also has a surf; Punahoa has one; and Piihonua has one, named Huia. There is also the surf of Paula at Puueo. The surf of Kapoai is a long one, said to run a distance equal to that of fifteen *ahupuaʻa*, beginning at the Honolii stream. Papaikou has a surf that rolls toward the mouth of the stream. There is also a surf at Laupahoehoe, said to be the surf that Umi and Paiea used. Waipio, in Hamakua, has a surf that runs toward the sand.

The surf of Maliu in Halelua, Kohala, rises on the east side of Kauhola Point and is 3 to 4 chains long, or longer. Kekakau surfed there, and it is said that he was most skilled in surfing. He was a kamaaina of the place, and it was he who led Kaahumanu to the surf of Maliu. Perhaps that was when the chiefs were farming in Kauhola. No one remembers the year, but it is said that Kauhola was cultivated before the two battles of Laupahoehoe.

As the story goes, Kaahumanu and Kekakau swam or went by canoe to the spot where the surf rose. Before they left, Kekakau talked with the king about the nature of the surf and showed Kaahumanu the places to land, which would be signaled by the waving of a white tapa. If the tapa was moved to the right or to the left, she was to go to the side indicated before the sea rose up high and overwhelmed her. If the tapa was spread out, or perhaps wadded into a ball, the signal meant to go in on the middle of the wave. Kekakau told the chiefess to observe the signals on shore while they rode shoreward from the place where the surf rose to the place where the wave rose up high until they landed. Before they started the earth ovens had been lighted for roasting dogs, and by the time they reached shore, the dogs were cooked.

The surf of Kumoho, which is at Naohaku on the left side of Maliu, was not ridden when the sea was rough. The surf of Puakea did not look large, resembling a sea pool, yet it was famous. The surf of Kapuailima is in Kawaihae, and Kahaleula is in Mahaiula. Honokohau has a surf, and there are others in the various districts of the island of Hawaii.

The surf of Puhele is in Hana, Maui; the surfs of Kaleholeho, Kaakaupohaku, and Paukukalo are in Wailuku; Kahahawai and Popoie are in Waihee; and Uhailio and Uo are in Lahaina.

Kapua and Kaihuwaa are surfs on Oahu. Kapuni and Kalehuawehe are at Waikiki, and Ulakua is a surf at Honolulu. Leimoku is a surf that washes up to the sands of Waianae, and Waimea in Koolauloa has a surf that runs toward the mouth of the stream.

The surf of Kamakaiwa is in Kapaa, Kauai, and so is the surf of Kaohala and one that runs to the sand of Wailua. Others are the surfs of Poo, Koalua, and the one that runs to the mouth of the sand-bottomed stream of Waimea, and the surf of Manalau is in Waioli. The surf of Kaununui is in Niihau.

These are the only surfs known. It is up to you to name the remainder.

Here are three kinds of surfboards. The ʻolo is thick in the middle and grows thinner toward the edges. It is a good board for a wave that swells and rushes shoreward but not for a wave that rises up high and curls over. If it is not moved sideways when the wave rises high, it is tossed upward as it moves shoreward. There are rules to be observed when riding on a surf.

The kikoʻo reaches a length of 12 to 18 feet and is good for a surf that breaks roughly. This board is good for surfing, but it is hard to handle. Other surfers are afraid of it because of its length and its great speed on a high wave that is about to curl over. It can ride on all the risings of the waves in its way until they subside and the board reaches shore.

The alaia board, which is 9 feet long, is thin and wide in front, tapering toward the back. On a rough wave, this board vibrates against the rider's abdomen, chest, or hands when they rest flat on it, or when fingers are gripped into a fist at the time of landing. Because it tends to go downward and cut through a wave it does not rise up with the wave as it begins to curl over. Going into a wave is one way to stop its gliding, and going onto the curl is another. Skilled surfers use it frequently, but the unskilled are afraid of this board, choosing rather to sit on a canoe or to surf on even smaller boards.

Body surfers use their shoulders like surfboards. When the surf rises before breaking, it is time to slip onto the wave by kicking hard and working the arms. The contraction in the back of a surfer causes him to be lifted by the wave and carried ashore. The right shoulder becomes the surfboard bearing him to the right, or the left shoulder becomes the board bearing him to the left. Liholiho was most skillful in this sport.

There are many ways to show skill in canoe surfing. The king was especially noted for it, and so was his pupil, Gideon Laanui. They were often seen together gliding on the surf outside of Haleumiumiiole at Kawaihae and at "a handsome young native . . . drove away the flies from him, and from his interesting countenance and becoming behaviour, I should rather have taken him for the king's son" wrote Kotzebue (*A voyage of discovery . . .*, volume 1, London, 1821). A Choris lithograph of Liholiho in "*Voyage pittoresque autour du monde.*"

Kapuni, outside of Kiikiiakoi. They would allow waves to go by until they saw one they wished to glide on, then ride it to the spot where they chose to land. There are ways of selecting waves which will go all the way to shore, and the king and his pupil were unusually skillful at this. Such things were actually taught.

It was said that a person skilled in canoe paddling and estimating waves could overcome obstacles if the wind was from the right direction, and the ability of the participants became something on which to gamble. This custom remains to this day, and it may be so in the future.

Drumming (*ka'eke*) was another skill learned by Liholiho. Usually, five or six people gathered together for this amusement. There was one large drum and several small ones covered with shark skin which was glued in place with kukui gum and laced with sennit cords. Like the young chief, his drumming companions—Daniel Ii, E. Kohia, Keoua, and Kanaina—were experts. These companions were selected for their ability and placed with the young chief for his entertainment and to make his drumming interesting. Liholiho had a large *pahu* drum on his left, and a small *pahu* called a *lapaiki* on his right. At *ka'eke'eke* drumming there were many persons, each with a small drum, except the young chief, who had the large drum. Their drumming was pleasing, indeed, to see and to hear, even to those at a distance and even though it was late at night and awakened the sleepers. Kalaikuahulu was Liholiho's teacher, and the young chief became expert indeed.

In the *hula paipu*, gourd hula drums were moved here and there by the dancers. Their hands gestured forward and back, up and down, in unison with the movement of the drums and to the rhythm of the drum-slapping. The left hand of each performer was beautifully tattooed because that was the hand that held the cord attached to the drum through a hole. The right hand did the gesturing. As this kind of hula was greatly enjoyed, there was much swaying and much chanting of the praises of favorites among the chiefs, favorite children, and native sons. This was kept up from dawn until the sun grew warm. There were but two good times for dancing, morning and evening.

The dancers kept in unison and preserved the pleasing quality of chanting or reciting. Sometimes one would lead and the others would join in; but while he was reciting, the others kept their silence and only gestured with their hands and swayed their drums. At the proper place for the rest to join in, they did so with great vigor. Perhaps there would be two or three dances of that kind, followed by the *hula 'aiha'a*, and so on. The dancers received many gifts, and finally a gift was laid at the opening of the head drummer's instrument.

Liholiho entered the Hale o Keawe in Honaunau during his journeys to the *luakini* heiaus, including Kanoa in Hilo, Wahaula in Puna, and Punaluu in Kau. The journeys began in Kailua, whence he went to Kawaihae, and continued from there around the island to the Hale o Keawe.

The Hale o Keawe at Honaunau. Painting by Paul Rockwood in Hawaii National Park Museum, based on the sketch by William Ellis.

The story of the death of Keawe has been forgotten, but it seems that he died at Honaunau without naming his successor. Perhaps he was succeeded by Alapai, for no chief took precedence over him. We know that Alapai was one of the offspring of Kalanikauleleiaiwi, the sister and wife of Keawe. We have seen the genealogy of Haloa down to these two through their mother, Keakealaniwahine. Their lineage has continued from the time of Alapai to our rulers.

It might have been Alapai and all of the chiefs of Kona who built the Hale o Keawe at Honaunau as a depository for bones. It must have been built either while Keawe was alive or soon after his death. The Hale o Keawe was called Kaikialealea and was a *puʻuhonua,* or place of refuge. Similarly, Kaikiholu and Pakaalana on Hawaii; Kakae in Iao, Maui; Kukaniloko in Wahiawa, Oahu; and Holoholoku in Wailua, Kauai, were places to which one who had killed could run swiftly and be saved. The person whose writing this is often went about them. He has seen the Hale o Keawe, where the bones were deposited, standing majestically on the left side of Akahipapa lava flat. The house stood by the entrance of a wooden enclosure, its door facing inland toward the farming lands of South Kona. The house was good-looking inside and out. Its posts and rafters were of *kauila* wood, which, it is said, was found in the upland of Napuu.

It was well built, with crossed stems of dried ti leaves for thatching. The compact bundles of deified bones were in a row inside the house, beginning with Keawe's bones, near the right side of the door by which one went in and out, and extending to the spot opposite the door.

At the right front corner of the house, heaped up like firewood, were the unwrapped bones of those who had died in war. In that heap were the bones of Nahiolea, father of Mataio Kekuanaoa. Ii saw his own father remove his tapa shoulder covering and place it on a bundle among the other bundles of bones. He must have done this after asking the caretaker about all of them. When Ii saw his father's action he asked, "Have we a near kinsman in this house?" His father assented. There are still some people who have relatives in this house of "life," but perhaps most of them are dead. The ruling chiefs were descended from Haloa, as were their relatives, who served them.

After Liholiho had finished his visit to the house, a pig was cooked and the gathering sat to worship the deified persons there. Then the chief and those who went into the house with him ate together. After the eating was finished, the kapu was removed. When, in 1817, the travelers left the Hale o Keawe and sailed by canoe to Kamakahonu in Kailua, they landed in the evening. There they met Kamehameha.

It is said that because this journey made by Liholiho and other journeys he had made earlier were *maika'i* there was peace among the chiefs and commoners and the people were like those in the time of Keawe. Kamehameha was happy over the success of his heir.

On his return to Kamakahonu, Liholiho saw that the king was lonely without his men, all of whom he had sent to South Kona to cut sandalwood. Only his nephew Kekuaokalani and his men were left to take care of him, and this was their constant cry night after night, "Kaika'owa!"

Liholiho honored those of his presence, who were supplied with war implements, by having them on guard day after day and crying out night after night, as was customary. This was in accordance with the suggestion of Vancouver, the exploring ship's officer of the British kingdom, who taught Kamehameha that the true God is in heaven and also that he should have guards. Vancouver also said, "Do not war against Kaumualii because you have more men and lands, and you know that he has much less, and that would be like murder." Kamehameha heeded all of these suggestions. Guards became customary with him, and that is why the heir was prepared to care for Kamehameha when there were no people around. He had his own guns, bayonets, powder containers, and bullets, all of which he had received from Kamehameha. Thus he cared for the king until all of the men returned from cutting sandalwood, each having obtained the number of pounds of wood required of him.

Although Kamehameha was happy over the deeds of his heir, he was somewhat unhappy over his nephew Kekuaokalani, son of his younger brother,

Keliimaikai, and therefore a "son" of Kamehameha. Liholiho and Kekuaokalani were both regarded as heirs to the kingdom, just as Kiwalao and Kamehameha had been in the days when Kalaniopuu was living, the former to have charge of the land, and the latter to have charge of the god. Liholiho and Kekuaokalani were somewhat unfriendly toward each other. Liholiho was constantly taught by Kamehameha, and he was the one who was supplied with implements of war.

[At this point, John Ii's story of pre-missionary days breaks off. Presumably, had he lived a few months longer, he would have told of the death of Kamehameha and the arrival of the missionaries. Unfortunately, he died before he could write of these momentous events in Hawaiian history, and we must pass over these happenings.

The following chapter contains the actual beginnings of his "fragments of history," which, for the sake of continuity, have been placed in chronological order here.]

CHAPTER XI

FRAGMENTS OF HISTORY, 1819-1832

Kalanimoku and Kaahumanu were in charge of the kingdom under the king, in accordance with the request of Kamehameha I that they serve the *kaikua'ana*, Liholiho (Kamehameha II). Kalanimoku and Kaahumanu, who were raised together as small children, were equals in the presence of Kapoo, the chief who reared them until Kaahumanu became the wife of Kamehameha I. Kalanimoku and Kaahumanu went together to Kamehameha's court, where Kalanimoku was better prepared to serve than any of the other chiefs, hence rose to high positions.

Perhaps some will ask by what right Kalanimoku and Kaahumanu lived together from the time they were little. Why was it? Perhaps it was because of the relationship of their parents. It was Kekaulike who mated with Haalou, to whom were born Namahana, a daughter, and Kekumanoha, a son. Namahana mated with Keeaumoku Papaiahiahi and had Kaahumanu *ma*. Kekumanoha mated with Kamakahukilani; and Kalanimoku, Wahinepio, and Boki were born. Nahiolea, Kekuanaoa's father, was a relative of the same generation as Kekumanoha and Kauhiwaewaeono, according to his genealogy. That was how Kekuanaoa became a *kaikaina* of Kalanimoku and Boki. If so, then it is right that he should be called a "younger brother."

An obscure matter is the question of Kalanimoku's baptism. In "Ka Mo'olelo Hawaii," Samuel Kamakau's history of Hawaii, mention is made of

Sketch by Jacques Arago of the baptism of Kalanimoku reproduced from "Journal de madame Rose de Saulces de Freycinet."

the arrival of a French warship at Kawaihae in 1819 [*l'Uranie*, Captain Louis de Freycinet]. The article states that Olohana, or John Young, told Kalanimoku that a true Christian was on board, and thereby inspired Kalanimoku to be baptized on the ship. If that was so, why did he conceal his intention from Kaahumanu and the many chiefs there with Kamehameha II, who was the king at the time? They had all come in a great company from Kamakahonu after Liholiho became ruler. A ship's officer [Arago] drew a picture of the royal company, a fact which the chiefs knew when they went on board to exchange greetings. Only later did they learn that Kalanimoku had been baptized.

Ioane Luwahine, or John Rives, was probably the person who encouraged Kalanimoku to be baptized, for he was born in the country whose warship it was. Luwahine, who accompanied Liholiho to England, was one of the teachers who afterward set out with the Catholic priests coming to this land [and accompanied them as far as California]. This was the Luwahine who healed Kalanimoku of an ailment from which he almost died.

At the time Liholiho left for England, the chiefs were living along the beach of the harbor of Kou. Kalanimoku lived at the Fort part of the time, but on this occasion he was at his place on the south side of the Fort in his first houses, Papakanene and Mokuaikaua. By this time, the Reverend William Ellis, Daniel Tyerman, and George Bennet had arrived. They were missionaries from England to New Holland and to Tahiti, from whence they proceeded to Hawaii in 1822. Kamehameha II, who was still ruling, granted William Ellis permission to stay in these islands; and he joined the missionaries who had come here earlier because they were of the same faith. He built his house at the corner of King and Punchbowl Streets, on the right side, and Kalanimoku greatly desired to build his stone house nearby. Thus it was that Pohukaina house was built on the north side of Ellis' house, adjoining his yard. It also adjoined the houses of the king, of Kaahumanu, and of other members of royalty. These houses, built in 1824, were surrounded by a very large wooden fence, and the enclosure was called Pohukaina.

New houses were built on the north side of the enclosure, and Kalanimoku called them Halehanaimoa. (This is the place where Kapakuhaili, widow of Kamehameha III, was living at the time of her death.) Kalanimoku lived at Halehanaimoa until the seamen arrived with the coffins of Liholiho and Kamamalu which were left there until the mausoleum just above Pohukaina house was completed. Kalanimoku stayed at Pohukaina with all the chiefs except Boki, who lived in the house he built on Beretania Street which he named Beretania.

While Kalanimoku was lying ill with a swelling at Pohukaina house, he heard a riot at Aikupika between Boki's rum-drinking crowd and Paki *ma*. That was after Lord Byron had departed from Honolulu and about the time Boki began to oppose the peace brought by Kaahumanu and the king to the chiefs and

Engraving after William Ellis, showing Pohukaina house, north of Ellis' house and with the church on the left. Reproduced from Charles S. Stewart's "Journal of a residence in the Sandwich Islands."

144

members of the court, also opposing their plan for education by the first missionaries who came to these islands. Many schools had been established, and those who were being educated rejoiced greatly. Kalanimoku, Kaahumanu, and other chiefs were, by then, members of the church. Those baptized on December 4, 1825, were Elizabeth Kaahumanu, Kalanimoku's infant son Leleiohoku, Lydia Namahana, Deborah Haakulou Kapule, Aaron Keliiahonui, Simeon Kaiu, Gideon Laanui, and Richard Kalaaiaulu. These were the first fruits of the mother church in Honolulu.

When Kalanimoku heard the disturbance created by Boki's drinking crowd he felt sorry for Kaahumanu and their chief Kauikeaouli (Kamehameha III), so he went down in a hand-drawn cart to Aikupika to stop the noise. He then returned to Pohukaina, for he felt that to be the best way to restore peace for themselves and their chief.

It was Boki's privilege to assign work, for he had been governor of the island of Oahu from the time Kamehameha I ordered all the chiefs to Oahu in 1816 to expel the Russians. It was then that the Fort was begun. Kalanimoku was the war leader in charge of the voyage called Kuanolu from Kailua, Kona, Hawaii. Boki left the Fort in charge of Manuia; the men who cultivated sugar cane at Puu Pueo in Manoa under Kekuanaoa; the land of Kemono to Auaia; and the land of Kaeleu to Hinau and Kaleohano *ma*. Boki's actions were seen by Kalanimoku as signs of rebellion. The only thing left was the farmland in Nuuanu; and this too, Kalanimoku felt, would be assigned to one or two of Boki's favorites.

As Kekuanaoa was frequently seen riding on horseback to his work at Puu Pueo, Kalanimoku decided to build a comfortable dwelling near the road, so that he could see him personally. The reason Kalanimoku and his wife had been unable to see this intimate friend of theirs and to tell him the things that others knew is expressed as follows:

Hukia a'e la ka 'alihi wai a ka ua kau iluna,	The water was lifted and placed high above,
Lakou la na holo kahiki,	They, the travelers to foreign lands,
'A'ohe 'ike wale iho ia Malio.	Do not bother to recognize Malio.

Kalanimoku, whose health was not too bad at that time, lived in his "watching house" at Makiki which he named Kilauea. After some time, Kekuanaoa passed below Puu Pueo; and that evening, when he went by again, he was called to come in. He dismounted and entered the house, where he spent the night and discussed all the things that Kalanimoku knew about. It seems that Kekuanaoa had neither heard nor seen those "drops of rain that denote war." Apparently Kalanimoku, the *kaikua'ana*, had told Boki that it was wrong to rebel against Kaahumanu, who had gained prestige for their family. Kalanimoku feared what might happen if he should die, though he knew that no rebel had ever lived to succeed. So it was with Nahiolea, our uncle who deserted Kamehameha to follow Kalanikupule and who was killed at Nuuanu by his *kaikua'ana*, Kekumanoha and Kauhiwaewaeono.

To digress briefly, Nahiolea was struck in the leg by a bullet; and his cousins, who had a grudge against him for rebelling and joining Kalanikupule, followed the trail of blood he left as he entered the hau grove of Kahaukomo, near Kahuailana. When the cousins arrived at Kahuailana, they sat down to eat, knowing that Nahiolea was in the hau grove. They called out, "O Malailua, here we are, your *kaikua'ana*. Here is your favorite, the *'awa*. Come out here." When Nahiolea, who saw there was no way to staunch the flow of blood, heard his cousins' voices he and his wife Inaina came into the presence of his cousins. After they ate and drank together, his cousins killed him as they had planned to do.

After Kalanimoku had talked things over with Kekuanaoa, he left Kilauea house and returned to his stone house at Pohukaina. There his health failed so much that all knew his disease would be fatal. Though skilled doctors sought to help him, he did not improve. Knowing he would never recover, he requested that his cousin Kaahumanu take him to Kamakahonu in Kailua, Hawaii. In January of 1827, Kalanimoku left Honolulu for Kamakahonu, where their lord and benefactor, Kamehameha I, had died. Kalanimoku died there on February 8, 1827. Kaahumanu did not return to Honolulu until the mourning was over.

During the reign of Kamehameha II, or Liholiho, Kekuanaoa was the officer in charge of food-collecting from the *ahupua'a* land sections and the *kupono* lands all over Oahu. Sometimes he took charge of weighing the sandalwood from all the islands, assisted by the foreigners to whom the government was in debt. He was a favorite of Liholiho and accompanied him to Great Britain. He also served the Kamehamehas in other ways.

Kekuanaoa's genealogy is given in *Ke Au Okoa* down to Nahiolea and Inaina. However, according to some, he had two fathers. Remember the dirge of Nakanealoha which went thus:

Ku mai o Kekuanao'a,	Kekuanaoa appears,
Keiki 'oe a Nahiolea,	[You] son of Nahiolea,
O Ki'ilaweau he makua.	Kiilaweau a parent.

These were both the husbands of Inaina. If he was the son of Kiilaweau then he was a younger relative of Ii and of Kanaina. If he was the son of Nahiolea, then Ii is a junior relative of his parents.

Here is another thing: It has been said that before Kekuanaoa went to England he announced to Kalanimoku that he desired to have Pauahi, the daughter of Kaoleioku and a wife of Liholiho, when he returned. The truth of this is debatable, for it was impossible to make such a statement at that time. Such words were never carelessly spoken lest death result, as it did to Haalou while the chief Liholiho reigned as king. And thus it was that Kahalaia was expelled from the king's presence to Lahaina. The older relatives were fearful over his safety, because of his association with Pauahi, and so had him removed to Lahaina, to be their executive officer there.

As to Kekuanaoa taking Pauahi to himself after his return from the foreign land, it was common talk and quite obvious. Perhaps he had had some illicit relations with the wives of the king which had remained hidden and never a breath uttered, but this affair was evident. Because Kekuanaoa was well supplied with tools for farming and fishing, the male and female attendants of Pauahi were eager to have her be his wife. It was said that Kapau also encouraged the chiefess to marry him, for Kapau was a *kaikuahine* relative of Kekuanaoa. She was Kalanimoku's former wife, and they were the foster parents of the chiefess. After the battleship and Lord Byron had returned to England, Kekuanaoa did take Pauahi to be his wife. This was on November 28, 1825. While he was overseer of the sugar-cane growers at Puu Pueo in Manoa, Pauahi became pregnant and bore him a daughter, Keelikolani. She died in childbirth on June 17, 1826.

Kinau, Kamehameha's daughter by Kaheiheimalie, had been widowed April 27, 1826, when her husband Kahalaia died. Kaahumanu then placed Kauikeaouli, the young Kamehameha III, in Boki's care and Boki made Kekuanaoa overseer of all of the military guards of Kauikeaouli. While Kaahumanu was away exhorting the people, Kekuanaoa wooed Kinau and they went with the king to Waoala to hew sandalwood. His position rose to the heights, as is expressed in the following chant:

Ki'eki'e ka lani ke kaulu	High up in the sky, the clouds
Holo nana i ka moku;	Travel and look down on the island;
Kulia kilakila 'ie,	They stand, majestic,
Ke'ehia ku i ka pa'ai;	With the peaks for a footrest;
Papapa luna o Mauna Loa.	They gather thickly on Mauna Loa.

He, in truth, became the seeker of a lord (Kaimihaku) and held government positions until his death.

Perhaps the readers would like to know more of the little details of Kekuanaoa's taking Kinau to wife. This was in 1827, the year that Ii became a member of the Kawaiahao church. He was with the second group that was accepted after Kaahumanu became a member. There were five people in the group who were baptized on December 9, 1827: Lazarus Kamakahiki, Abraham Naoa Ieki, John Ii, Ana Waiakea Kamakahiki, and Abel Wahinealii.

Ii had been made guardian of the king's eating, sleeping, and waking, and as there was no preacher for the king and his companions, he was commanded by Kaahumanu to do the preaching also. It is thought that Ieki was the person she chose to go with the king on his tour with his sister, Nahienaena, to Kilauea, Hawaii, in 1828. Ii stayed with the king until the latter part of 1832, when Kaomi was appointed administrator. Because the king would not heed him, Ii left and went to join the religious chiefesses, Kekauluohi, Kinau, and the others. It is thus that he can explain some of the things concerning Kekuanaoa and his royal wife Kinau.

While Kinau lived in the home of her former husband Kahalaia, Kamehameha III lived in the other half of the house. The royal residence was on the north side, inside the large wall of Pohukaina built by Kalanimoku, close to Haliimaile. Ii, who went there every night, learned something of these things, for he discussed with the chiefess matters of her choosing. Both the king and the chiefess had many people sleeping in their separate parts of the house, and the king had no guard at the time. One evening when Ii entered as usual, he found the place of the chiefs very quiet. He decided to discuss this matter with his friends, and so he went to Kapuukolo. They discussed the subject of guards to watch within the enclosure of the royal residence while the king slept. All agreed that this was a good idea.

The following night they went from Kapuukolo to the royal residence to arrange the mats and other things for sleeping there that night. Later on, as they sat about, the king came out and asked, "Who are these people?"

"Just us," was the answer, and he recognized the voice of the speaker. He asked again about each one until he knew who they all were, and they were H. Hewahewa, N. Kamaunu, John Ii, M. Nawelu, A. Lilinoe, and Sarai Hiwauli.

The king asked, "What do you expect to accomplish by sleeping here?"

They answered, "This place is very lonely at night, so we have come up here to guard your sleep."

"That is a good idea, and my men shall also come here with you," replied the king.

"You should speak of it to your sister Kinau and to your guardian Kaahumanu," he was told. And the king did speak of it to Kinau. He told her all he had heard, and the next day all was told to Kaahumanu.

That night there were enough guards in each of the two enclosures of the house. Later, groups of guards were placed for the king. There were five groups, on guard day and night. The officers over the guards minded the welfare of each one, and the officers of the groups remained inside of the enclosure of the royal residence. Persons were allowed to enter at the will of the king. The guards on duty called out to the officers to let it be known that they were on the alert. Officers of each group preserved the peace of the chiefs dwelling in their residences.

After several months went by, the officers of the guards gathered in answer to a summons. Kaahumanu was there at the meeting, which was held on Ii's broad lanai, just above the enclosure of the royal residence. As the audience listened intently, Kekuanaoa spoke. "O guards, listen this day to the words of the king and of Kaahumanu. She has placed the ruler in the care of her cousin Boki, and he has appointed me to be at the head of all the guards of the king. Because of this, I tell you of the arrangement of the guards. Each officer is to guard the entrance to the royal residence with his guards, and this is for all of the groups. Only the Okaka guards, with an officer over each group, are to watch inside the enclosure of the royal residence."

Some of the officers knew about this matter in advance, for there had been rumors about the new arrangement. When Kekuanaoa sat down, Ii stood up and said, "O chiefess, I have approved of the officer appointed by your cousin, but his refusal to allow the officers of the other groups inside the royal residence they guard does not meet with my approval. Each group of guards loves you and your chief. They have partaken of your food, and your husband Kamehameha I fed them, including the members of the household of this chief of yours, Kauikeaouli, and we who are of the other chief of yours, Liholiho. Therefore, what is the reason for keeping us out?"

Kaahumanu replied, "I thought you had all agreed on this matter." Then she stood up and departed for her house, and the meeting ended. The officer of the guards did not keep Ii and his companions from acting as guards of the royal residence, but the other guards had to remain outside the enclosure. It was believed that this was so because Ii had spoken up.

The first time Kekuanaoa met the chiefess Kinau was when Pauahi was laid away in the royal mausoleum. He was there from evening until almost daylight, when he returned to the royal residence and slept outside of the house. Most of the morning guards saw him do this.

At four o'clock one afternoon Ii entered the gate of the royal residence and sat by the wall to watch the outer guards and to listen to all the commands. The king came out and asked, "Is this your group?"

"Yes," answered Ii.

The king said to him, "We are learning to fence."

"Who is your teacher?" asked Ii.

"Kekuanaoa," replied the king.

"You will be experts in this fine art," said Ii.

"Yes, we shall be, but if the chiefess sits there, Kekuanaoa's skill will be unequaled and the display of his companions, mere child's play. We shall see more of this yet."

Again the gate was guarded, and Ii sat by the gate because it was sheltered by the shadow of the house. Kinau came out to sit with him, and the king joined them. The king said to Ii, "Let the clothing all look alike for me and for your officers of the guards. Have a stripe down the legs of the trousers, and red jackets."

Kinau said to Ii, "I have some red cloth, my share of the allotment at Kawaihae about 1820 from an American merchant ship. A large piece of cloth was given to each of the chiefesses there. I shall find it if I look for it, and you may have all that is left."

Then Ii said, "An idea has suddenly come to me, but perhaps I should not mention it."

The chiefess said, "It should be told."

He replied, "You two should become husband and wife. This is my idea."

Kinau answered, "He may not want me, for I am older than he."

The king said, "I do not think that it should be," and Ii saw that he had not succeeded in his idea concerning the two. It seemed that the king's mind was set on another.

I 'o wale	Away beyond
I 'alo wale laua	Away together
I ke alo Kapo,	In the presence of Kapo,
Wahine a Puanui.	Woman of Puanui.
I nui ko aloha	Great is your love
Makahia iaia la.	That causes sleeplessness.

One night some time after that, when the chiefess saw Ii standing alone outside, she went out and whispered a secret to him, "Kekuanaoa wants me to be his. What do you think of it?"

Ii replied, "I have already told you what I thought and what my suggestion was to you. But it is up to you."

Kinau and Kekuanaoa were anxious to be united, and they were married on September 19, 1827.

I ke kane o Mana	The man of Mana
I ka hao a Limaloa,	Is taken by Limaloa,
I ka li'ula.	By a mirage.
Pau ka li'ula,	The mirage ends,
Maka ka 'ainako,	The cane trash, still fresh,
Pu oia na hale.	Is heaped outside the house.
I Kaunalewa	At Kaunalewa
Hao mai koi,	A gale tears,
A Lolomauna,	The Lolomauna,
Kupu i ke kalio	The familiar gusty breeze
Kalamakopi'i.	Of Kalamakopii.

["A gale tears" refers to Kaahumanu's anger at this marriage, as she desired to have Kauikeaouli and Kinau wed each other.]

Now, Kinau no longer dwelt in the royal residence of Kaahumanu and Kaheiheimalie, but became dependent on the *pu'uko'a* grass [one of lesser rank].

O ka pu'uko'a ka haku i ho'ohaku a i e,	The *pu'uko'a* grass has been made a lord,
I ho'ohaku i na makani o ka lua,	Made a lord over the winds of the pit,
He pu'ulena, he 'awa o Wahinekapu.	The *pu'ulena* and the *'awa* (winds) of Wahinekapu.

One day the king, Kauikeaouli, was missing, and a search hither and thither was in vain until it was learned that he was at Paiaina house. Thus were the *kaikamahine* (nieces) of Kaahumanu disappointed (*hoka*). When Kaahumanu heard of this, she went to her nieces and found them "straining 'awa (hoka

Residence of Kamehameha III at Beretania. Photograph of an original water color, artist and whereabouts of original unknown.

151

ana lakou i ke ahu 'awa)" ["disappointed," a play on the word *hoka*]. She asked them to go and fetch their young king, but the young women merely hung their heads.

When Ii came in Kaahumanu said, "Come. I have told these folks to go and bring their young chief back, but they do not answer. They turn to regard those of worthless blood and neglect the person of worthy blood inherited from their parents. Here they are with bowed heads. Let us go to our chief, for these folks will do nothing."

When the two arrived at Paiaina they found the house crowded with the royal favorites. The king and H. K. Kapakuhaili were lying on the *hikie'e*, and Kaahumanu crept in between them and slept with them from ten o'clock to perhaps two o'clock. The king refused to go home and leave the woman he was sleeping with. It seemed as though he were saying to himself, "Your *kaikamahine* [Kinau] deserted me by not doing as your husband requested, therefore I refuse to heed you." Perhaps that was why the two took the cry of the *nene* with them when they went home: "Inele, Inele" [meaning to fail (*nele*) in their project].

It is well to consider this thing, the trouble that parents have with heedless children. The result is a dwindling of the fine blood strains, in fulfillment of the expression that "one leaves a person of good blood for one who is not," often one who is entirely without it. A blast of wind takes it all. Let us stop, O companions, and discuss Kaahumanu. We have seen how she cherished the chiefs and whom she desired for their *haku*, Kauikeaouli. We know how definitely disobedient Kinau was [in marrying Kekuanaoa instead of Kauikeaouli].

This, perhaps, should be considered. Keopuolani was doubly fathered (*he po'olua 'ia*), by Kamehameha and Kiwalao through Liliha. It seems that that was why Kamehameha set apart Kamehameha II, or Liholiho, and Kamehameha III, or Kauikeaouli, the children of their daughter. He wished the rule to be continued by their grandchildren and considered himself the grandparent of some and the parent of others. Therefore he requested the daughters born to him by his cousins, Kaahumanu and her sisters, to be wives to his "grandsons," his sons by Keopuolani. They were Kamamalu and Kinau, his daughters by Kaahumanu's sister Kaheiheimalie, and were to continue his line. Therefore Kaahumanu directed her talk to her nieces, reminding them that they would be wrong in refusing to heed their father's will. She expressed her approval of Kamamalu, wife of Liholiho, for having heeded. However, there was almost a separation between the nieces and Kaahumanu over the question of whether they should do as they were told in order to continue the family line. Their rank was equal in some respects, and their kapus were equal in some respects and different in others.

It would be well, at this point, to mention a prophecy that came to us about thirteen years ago, perhaps, after the death of Kamehameha III. This prophecy was that the great chiefs of divine descent, whose backs were warmed by the sun (*na'li'i wela kua i ka la Kalaninuiwaiakua*) would cease to be, and so would those who held the *wohi* kapu. The "back warmed by the sun" has been entirely set aside by the right to remain standing.

As we have seen, no chief had the right to rule as king by a mere discussion of these things, and this must be recognized. Perhaps it is thought that through Kekuanaoa's marriage to Kinau his rank was elevated. According to the younger Pakaa, that is not so. In marrying Kekuanaoa, Kinau married a relative of her parents' generation; and he married a relative of a younger generation. Perhaps this is a foolish discussion, so let us stop it.

In December 1826 a decree was passed requiring the members of the court to go and cut sandalwood to repay the debt owed by the government to the haoles of Honolulu. The king, Boki, and the other chiefs—including Kekuanaoa and Kinau—were among those who journeyed to Waoala to cut trees. Kaahumanu arrived there after she had gone around the island exhorting the people, as she did periodically. However, she soon returned to Honolulu.

After Kaahumanu's return, a rumor went abroad that Boki desired to rebel against her. It seems that it was with this in mind that he aided the first teachers sent by the Pope to these islands when they arrived in July of 1827. Boki had by then placed Aua at Waianae and Kanepaiki at Ewa, although Kanepaiki's appointment to remain in Ewa came from Kalanimoku. The lands of the cliffs of Koolaupoko and Koolauloa were excepted.

After the ruler and all the chiefs returned to Honolulu with Boki, a house was built for the king at Beretania, where Boki's dwelling was. This house was lined with the stems of the *uluhe* fern laid horizontally. Later, Boki started a farming project in Nuuanu. It was a huge farm, extending from Luakaha to the gulch of Puwahanui. This was to attract the people, perhaps as Absalom *ma* did.

In the last month of the year 1828 Boki and Kauikeaouli took Nahienaena to Lahaina. Nahienaena *ma* boarded the ship *Paalua*, while the ruler and Boki went by a foreign boat to Lahaina, to Wailuku, and back to Lahaina again. There the ship *Kamehameha* was awaiting the king, having been sent up from Honolulu on January 11, 1829. Kinau, Kekauluohi, and a ship's officer were there, en route to Honolulu from Kailua, Hawaii, where they had left Kaahumanu. They saw the king with Boki before they departed again. The king went on to Kailua and met with Kaahumanu and the other chiefs, who had come from Kaawaloa. The king stayed with Naihe *ma* until he proceeded to Hilo and thence to Lahaina, where Kaahumanu had preceded him. While Boki was there with the king, he heard from someone that Kaahumanu had mentioned the highness in rank of the chiefess Keelikolani. Angered at these words, Boki boarded the ship *Keokoi* and hastened to Honolulu, arriving March 26, 1829. The king remained in Lahaina awhile with Kaahumanu.

Shortly, because of poor health, the king left Kaahumanu and returned to Honolulu. When the ship stopped at Ulakua because a gale blew directly from the upland, Boki boarded her and spoke strongly before the king and Kaukuna

Halekamani, Nahienaena's house at Lahaina as it looked during the tenancy of Solomon D. Gilman, 1851-1861. Drawing in Bishop Museum.

Kahekili, son of Peleuli. The king's men came from the shore while the captain was below and remained aboard for about two weeks.

Before Kaahumanu *ma* returned from Maui Boki bought this kind of clothing and that, this thing and that, and gave them to every person in the household of the king, to relatives, and so on. Manuia was in China at the time, so his share fell to Hinau. Boki continued to behave this way until Kaahumanu returned, when he decided to take the king and his men to hide in Waikiki.

Before they departed for Waikiki, Boki sent secretly for Hinau, Kaleohano, Aua, and Kapalaau and commanded them to gather the people of Kapahu and destroy Kaahumanu. He said, "We will wait at Waikiki and when we hear the report of your guns at Kapahu, we will know that you have carried out the deed." Those who were so commanded were filled with consternation. They discussed the fact that Kaahumanu had no fault, and they refused to carry out the evil deed. They resolved to send Kapalaau to notify Kekuanaoa to inform Kaahumanu of what Boki wanted them to do. Kinau overheard Kapalaau telling Kekuanaoa, and departed tearfully at once to go to Kaahumanu. "What are the tears for?" asked Kaahumanu.

Kinau replied, "Boki plots your death and has commanded Hinau, Kaleohano, Aua, and Kapalaau to kill you. They sent Kapalaau to tell Kekuanaoa because they were sorry for you and refused to carry out Boki's evil plan."

"What matters it if I should die," asked Kaahumanu, "for then I would be a companion in death for my *moʻopuna* David Kamehameha Kekuanaoa."

It was as though Kinau had partaken of cool waters as she told of Boki's jealousy of Kaahumanu, of the things she had heard, and of having seen the wicker-covered remains (*kiʻi kino ʻie*) of Liloa and Lonoikamakahiki in the presence of the king and Kaukuna Kahekili. When Ii came in she asked, "Have I done wrong?"

Ii replied, "You have not done wrong, for you are relatives, one the older, one the younger. Who has a better right to tell each other things than you two?"

When she had finished her report, Kinau went to the house of Kekauluohi, followed by the chiefs, for it was a good place to rest until prayers and eating were finished. Urged on by Boki, Kekuapanio remarked that Keelikolani was a "slave" (*kauwa*). After the meal, when the king arose and departed for Bingham's houses, Ii went with him. On the way, Ii asked the king, "What does the king think of Boki's thoughts about his *kaikuahine?*"

The king replied, "I think nothing of these words." Thus Ii saw that the king's mind was good.

The king rested before returning to the discussion at Kekauluohi's place, and meanwhile Boki had gone home.

Soon after that, Boki took the king to Waikiki. The *"noʻa* pebble" was in Boki's hand, for he was clever. But he had no sooner succeeded in hiding his *"noʻa"* than it was taken by Kekuanaoa's hand. He, too, was clever. Kekuanaoa soon mixed all the *"noʻa* hiding cloths" and ended the game, as he had been ordered to do. Perhaps Boki was embarrassed because he did not succeed in his plan to kill Kaahumanu. The warning in the Holy Scriptures, James 1:15, was yet to be fulfilled:

Ina hapai ke kuko a oʻo,	If desire is carried to maturity,
Alaila hanau mai ka hewa.	Then sin will be born.
Ina oʻo ka hewa,	If the sin matures,
Puka mai ka make.	Death arrives.

Because of the alertness of Kekuanaoa, the king and all of the men were soon ready to go home, except for Boki, who loitered. The king entered a horse carriage and rode in the procession to Pawaa, where Kekuanaoa entered Boki's carriage. The two continued to Honolulu, where they went to Boki's houses. The king went to see Kaahumanu and to tell her how Boki had suggested putting her to death. "I did not agree to his wish because I love you," he said.

Later in that year Captain Finch of the American ship *Vincennes* met with Boki to discuss the debt owed by the government to American merchants. All of

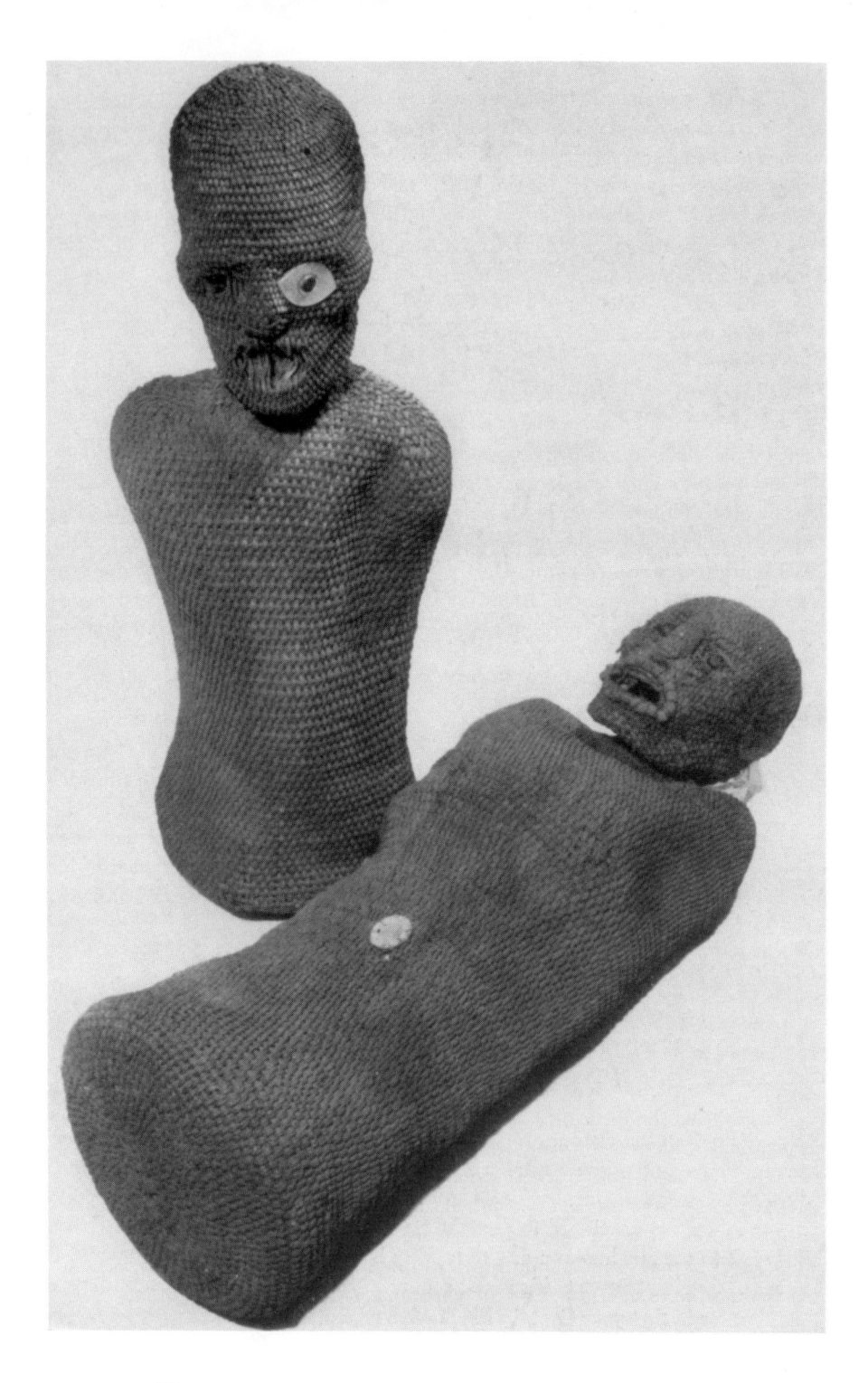

*The woven sennit caskets of Liloa and Lonoikamakahiki
in Bishop Museum.*

Kaahumanu's governors were called to assemble at Honolulu, and they gathered before the captain to ask him to allow the government to pay the debt. When the captain was gone, Kaahumanu asked her *kaikunane* which of them contracted the debt. Most of them denied it, but Boki admitted that he owed much: a debt by one who wished to attract the people! When the chiefs decided at once to gather sandalwood on each island with Aluli as general overseer, Boki gathered the members of his household and his favorites together to go to the mountains of Oahu for his allotment of trees. [Meanwhile a ship arrived with a report that sandalwood was plentiful in the New Hebrides, and Boki decided to go there.]

When Boki was ready to sail, he went aboard ship secretly at night. Kaahumanu was on Kauai at the time. The next day Kekuanaoa was sent to bring his older cousin ashore. Kekuanaoa did not hesitate to board the ship and deliver the king's order to Boki to return, and it is said that there was a long discussion between them. When by afternoon Kekuanaoa had not been heeded, he left Boki and went ashore. Those who were bound for foreign lands sailed away on December 2, 1829, and vanished forever.

The fact that Boki left his birthplace and disappeared, whereas Kekuanaoa remained in his homeland as he was commanded to do, doing many good deeds, is food for thought. His end was different from Boki's because his deeds were right. Boki's end proves the truth of this chant [that a traveler may leave his bones in a land away from home]:

Waiho i Ka'ea	Left at Kaea
Ka iwi o kamahele.	Are the bones of the traveler.
Moe hia'a ke kino,	My body lies sleepless,
Hala'o'a ka maka;	My eyes strain into the distance;
Hala'o'a me he la'au la i ku'u maka,	Straining to see through the "wood" before my eyes,
Me he ka 'ohu hu'i la ka walania,	Like a chilling fog is my bitter grief,
Ka 'eke'eke o ke kanaka i ke aloha.	Making me cringe with woe.
Ka ma'alahia ka 'uhuhua 'ia ia;	There is wailing, moaning, for him;
Ke ku'ina ke aloha wali maoli au e.	The grief that overcomes me makes me weep.

Kaahumanu and her foster son, Kamehameha II, were those who did away with images, *lele* altars for sacrifices, *kuahu* altars for offerings, and heiaus and *luakini* (temples) throughout the six districts of Hawaii and all the islands to Kauai and Niihau. Because they ordered it so, men ate with women out of the same meat dishes and food bowls, and they cast aside all oppressive kapus pertaining to the gods and the images.

Kaahumanu established schools for learning the alphabet and reading in the royal town of Honolulu. These schools were for the old and young among the people of the chiefs' households and were possible through the energetic efforts of the American puritans from Boston, who came as a result of God's having called Henry Opukahaia to America from this kingdom in 1806. Kaahumanu was indeed a mother to all of her people, in that she went around first one island and then another to proclaim the gospel of Jesus Christ. All of her people who followed it were blessed.

Kaahumanu's circuits of the land were always by canoe, for she had learned all about canoeing and surfing from Kamehameha I, her cousin, lord, and husband. On her arrival at Kawaihae, Hawaii, in September 1830, she went up to Waimea for the dedication of the church there. It was named Mahiki because all of the timber in the building was brought from Mahiki. After the dedication, Kaahumanu turned about and descended to Kawaihae on her hand-drawn cart. Upon her arrival at the shore of Kawaihae, she boarded a canoe and sailed to Waipio, while the king and chiefs traveled there over land.

When the canoes arrived outside of Waipio the next day, the waves were very rough and there was no place to land. Therefore, Kaahumanu ordered the paddlers to go out and come in a second time. This time they were close to the back of a wave that rose up directly in front of them, and she encouraged her paddlers to head for it. The canoe came up very close to it and as the wave rose up to a peak and spread out, the craft rode in with the foam to where the prows could be caught by the men on shore. Those on shore remarked to each other how cleverly they were saved, and this became a great topic of conversation.

Another wonderful thing Kaahumanu did was to establish the Lahainaluna School by giving a portion of her uncultivated land at Puunau; and so did the other chiefs who owned uncultivated lands nearby, including the ditch of Auwaiawao. They also gave the fish of Kaipaki on Molokai for the support of the pupils of this school where people went to seek education.

It was wonderful too, how Kaahumanu put out the fires of liquor-making, saloons, and intoxication among her people. Such was the way of a true lover of the chiefs and of the people in general. She slept in peace, even when a strong enemy sought to take her life. The Lord Jesus saved her from the hands of Boki, thus fulfilling the words of Solomon, "The sinful shall be uprooted from the land." Beautiful was the peace of this true worshiper until she fell asleep.

Kaahumanu died on June 5, 1832, at her house with the green shutters in Manoa valley, close to Kawaihoolana. Because of her love for Manoa she went there during her last illness after having been sickly for four or five years. The doctors said that she had intestinal trouble, her intestines having been punctured by a bone. This might have been so. Before her departure from this world, she said to her chief, to her "children," to the friends who came to talk to her, and to her teacher, Bingham, "Hele au la (I am going)." Then she fell asleep. When her body was brought from Manoa to her frame house in the enclosure of Pohukaina, it was accompanied by a great procession. Finally, on the last day of June she was laid in the royal mausoleum there. The Christians greatly regretted losing her, but her Lord knew that it was better to take her.

In July, after the period of mourning was over and Kaahumanu had been laid away, the king sailed to Lahaina to see his relatives and spend about two weeks. He took with him some of his favorites to be enrolled in the Lahainaluna School.

When the king had left on his journey, Kinau gathered the chiefs, the lesser chiefs, members of the court, and the people at Pohukaina and began a proclamation to them, "O you of Hawaii, great island of Keawe; Maui, island of Kama; Oahu, of Kuihewa; and Kauai, of Mano . . . Harken to this, you who are from great Hawaii, land of Keawe, to Kauai, island of Mano. Our royal mother Kaahumanu is dead, she who watched over and cared for us. She has helped in the good work of the Lord among us, and with our king, Kauikeaouli. All of her duties have descended upon me, her successor, and for this reason I desired to have you meet with me and hear these things. Let us look to the administration of the government of our king. . . ."

When Kinau finished speaking, Kekauluohi stood up to speak. "Here am I, of Hawaii a Keawe, of Maui a Kama, of Oahu a Kuihewa, and of Kauai a Mano. I add my approval to the words we have just heard. Our *makua* have gone on their journey, and we have inherited their duties under the guidance of these children of Kamehameha. What she has told us is to look after each other's welfare, and I approve of this."

The multitude expressed their admiration of the two who spoke, for none had ever heard these words before. So did they admire everything else that was said, for the kingdom had been at peace through the administration of Kaahumanu.

When news of these speeches reached Lahaina, the king hastened to Honolulu. He met Kinau, Kekauonohi, Kekauluohi, and Liliha in gladness, for all were united under the king and under the laws made by him and Kaahumanu for the benefit of chiefs and commoners. These laws were for the welfare and prosperity of all Hawaii.

This means of caring for the kingdom is said to have originated with advice often repeated by Kamehameha to Kaahumanu before his death: "When I am gone on my journey away from this world, should the king, Liholiho, fail to regard you, then you, a woman, shall arise in your kingdom. You are well supported by your *kaikunane* from Hawaii to Kauai. If he heeds you, none will rebel against the kingdom." According to her genealogy, Kaahumanu was a chiefess indeed, and it was well that she should rule as had her ancestress Keakealaniwahine.

Keakealaniwahine was once the ruler of all Hawaii, and was succeeded by her son Keawe i Kekahialiiokamoku. Keakealaniwahine was brought up with the *kapu moe*. As there was no other chiefess her equal, she was kept apart, with the chiefs who had the right to the prostrating kapu, and away from places where people were numerous. Her houses, surrounded by a stone wall, stood on an elevation above Keolonahihi in Holualoa, North Kona. She was thought to be a chiefess who would care for the welfare of the people and for the kingdom, and would understand how to benefit it and bring it prosperity.

Later, when she became the ruler, she was in charge of all the heiaus on Hawaii. She offered human sacrifices in the six *luakini* heiaus of the six districts of Hawaii, which were Hikiau in Kona, Punaluu in Kau, Wahaula in Puna, Kanoa in Hilo, Honuaula of Waipio in Hamakua, and Mookini in Kohala. It was said that whenever a ceremony was performed at these heiaus she wore a skirt of *ninikea*, a soft white tapa made by women who were skilled in the art.

Though a woman, Keakealaniwahine was permitted to enter the heiaus to give her offerings and sacrifices. However, she was not allowed to eat any of the offerings and gifts with the priests and the men, who ate by themselves. She participated only in the ceremonies, for men and women continued to eat apart from the time of Wakea, because of Hoohokukalani. [She was his daughter; and to be with her, Wakea established the kapu nights and the eating kapu, in order to have a reason for being absent from his wife Papa.] Thus Keakealaniwahine ate in her own house of the food permitted to women. The only men who ate with the women were those who prepared the food of the chiefess and who had the privilege of serving it to her.

CHAPTER XII

KAMAMALU AND KEKUANAOA

Victoria Kamamalu, the daughter of Kinau and Kekuanaoa, was born on the first of November 1838, at the Honolulu Fort, where Dr. G. P. Judd attended her mother. On the same day, she was placed in the care of the person who relates this history. Though her mother remained with her and nursed her, Ii and his wife carried her and soothed her when she cried.

They became her *kahu* because they were closely associated with her parents. Furthermore, Ii was also Kinau's secretary and she consulted him about the problems of the kingdom while she was the premier, from the time that Kaomi was made a chief and a favorite of Kamehameha III. In July 1837 the chiefess had met alone with Ii and discussed her reason for bearing no more children. During this discussion Ii said, "I did wrong before God, therefore He gave and took away again. So went the other children. But now God has forgiven me for this wrong, and if you have another child, you nurse it and I will be the one to do the carrying around." The chiefess agreed to this.

On the first day of January 1839 the guns were to be fired at the Fort at noon; Kinau with the child Kamamalu, Ii and his wife, and the rest of the household arose early and went to stay at Honokaupu, Kekauluohi's coral stone house at Pohukaina. They did not return to the Fort until after Kinau's death. While they were at Honokaupu house a letter from John Adams Kuakini, who was on

161

The Honolulu Fort and Kalanimoku's houses at Mokuaikaua, a Choris lithograph in *"Voyage pittoresque autour du monde."*

Hawaii, arrived asking for the child to rear. When Kinau told Ii, he asked, "What is Kuakini's thought?"

Kinau replied, "It would be well for us all to go to Hawaii."

"I do not think that is a good idea," Ii answered. G. P. Judd agreed, saying that they should wait until the child had grown before giving her into Kuakini's care. The matter was discussed back and forth, but none knew the best thing to do.

Kamamalu and Pauahi, the daughter Kinau and Kekuanaoa had adopted from Paki and Konia, were both with Kinau at Honokaupu house while she was ill with a dull headache and sore eyes. For this reason, Konia named the daughter she adopted from Keohokalole and Kapaakea, Kamakaeha (Sore Eyes). When Kamakaeha cried for her milk and her wet nurse was away, Kinau would pick the child up, place her in her lap and feed her at the breast. Thus she occasionally nursed two children, Kamakaeha and Kamamalu. Konia, whose regard for the chiefess was high, felt that it was not proper for Kinau to nurse her child, but the chiefess ignored Konia's fussing.

Kamamalu was reared from babyhood according to the covenant her mother and Ii made before God that she was to be the one to nurse her at the breast and that Ii was to be the one on whose lap she would sit and the one who would carry and soothe her. Ii helped to care for the child, fulfilling the covenant. She remained with him, and so the relatives of the husband went without the child, though they had thought that she would be theirs. It was as though Ii was her father and Kinau her mother and wet nurse. Apparently her father, Kekuanaoa, thought that Ii was merely an attendant, but Kekauluohi explained to him, saying, "This man is very closely related to us through Keeaumoku."

Before Kinau left her husband; their children; their *haku*, Kamehameha III; and their relatives, the oldest of her living children, Moses, was taken to Kauai by his foster parent, Kaikioewa. She wanted him to enter an English-speaking school with his younger brother, Lot, and Pauahi. She mentioned an engagement (*'olelo ho'opalau*) between their adopted daughter Pauahi and the second of her sons, Lot, in a statement to Kekauluohi. Kinau also wished Kamamalu to be betrothed (*ho'ohui*) to Kekauluohi's son, Lunalilo, when she was still an infant. Ii was surprised over this thing they talked about, but felt it was their affair. Moses, Lot, and Pauahi were placed in the English-speaking school, as Kinau wished. [Alexander Liholiho, youngest son of Kinau, had been adopted as his heir by Kamehameha III.]

On the last day of February 1839 Honolulu was in the midst of an epidemic of mumps, a disease that is ordinarily not fatal. Ii, who caught it, stayed away from Kinau and Kamamalu, and his wife remained with them. After a few days, when he returned, his wife came down with the disease and was separated from them. In the first week of March Kinau was taken ill, and a few days later Ii's wife returned to her in good health. The chiefess asked, "Are you well,

Sarai?" and Sarai answered that she was. The next day the chiefess said, "Yours was a disease of *manana iki* (small swelling); mine is a disease of *manana nui* (big swelling)."

As her last day approached, it became obvious that her sickness was indeed a *manana nui*. With Kinau in Kekauluohi's house were Kekauluohi, Leleiohoku, Kekuaiwa, Keliiahonui, Kekauonohi, Kalei o Kamehameha, Paki, Keoni Ana (John Young), Haku o Hawaii, Kamakaiouli, and Kalohelani (Kamamalu). They all wept in grief at their loss. Kekuanaoa, gray of hair and of many days, said that he would mourn Kinau until he took his gray head to the grave.

Kekauluohi had been summoned from Lahaina while Kinau was yet alive, and she was able to see their *keiki*, Kekauluohi's son [Lunalilo]. Then the ship *Hooikaika*, which had come in the evening, set forth again; and in the morning the king arrived. By then Kinau was in a coma, and after the king saw her, her breathing ceased.

Kekauluohi and Kekuanaoa left the children in Ii's care during those days, for the older ones were still attending school, including two girls, Pauahi and Loeau, adopted daughter of Kauukualii. When Kinau started on her journey from this world, she left behind much to grow and the affection and tears of her children. The two girl babies, Kamamalu and Kamakaeha, did not understand weeping, however.

When Kinau passed away, on the fourth of April 1839, John Ii and his wife, Sarai Hiwauli, became Kamamalu's foster parents, under the supervision of her father, Kekuanaoa. She was their constant companion night and day; a companion to crouch with in the cold; a child in the damp and cold; a companion snatching away sleep from the eyes when she cried, waking one suddenly when she tossed about. Such was the care given to the child until she walked with her own feet, and much preparation was made for the child to seek knowledge and wisdom.

In conformance with Kinau's wish that the royal children be educated, a consultation was held to decide the best way to build a school for them. It was desirable that they remain together, thereby retaining the harmony among them and discouraging rebellion of one against another. Such things as rebellion and constant wars in the land were known in olden times, because, as William Richards taught, the children of chiefs were reared apart. At the missionary conference in Lahaina in 1838 Richards had been asked by the king and Kinau to teach the chiefs political science, and this request brought about his release by the Hawaiian Missionary Society. The king and Kekauluohi, who succeeded Kinau as premier, agreed on the matter of a school, and G. P. Judd and M. Kekuanaoa were requested to build a school house for the royal children.

During the last months of 1839 the school house was ready and teachers were available. The children gathered there with the king and chiefs for the house

Royal School, a reproduction of a lithograph by Paul Emmert, in Bishop Museum.

warming, after which all of the children remained. The *kahu* of each child supplied his personal needs, and the government took care of most of the needs of the school.

By this time, Ii and Sarai had left Honokaupu house and were living at the Fort with Kamamalu's father. Here she grew and developed with her brothers and her mother's adopted daughter, Pauahi, until the three—Moses, Lot, and Pauahi—were placed in the school. Thus they were separated until Ii and Sarai also went to the school.

We have read in "Ka Moʻolelo Hawaii" about the $20,000.00 taken aboard the *l'Artemise*, whose captain was Laplace, in July 1839. That article stated that the premier, Kekauluohi, and William Richards were the chiefs who carried the money out to the ship. That was only a guess, for the chiefs were Kekuanaoa and Haalilio. The one whose writing this is was left aboard as a hostage for three days, until the money was delivered. When it had been counted and the seals of both governments had been affixed, he was allowed to go ashore. Actually, Mr. Richards was at Lahaina with the king at the time, and they arrived in Honolulu soon after Ii returned to shore. Let us put an end to this, for the *noʻa* stone of the writer of "Ka Moʻolelo Hawaii" has been exposed.

The British Consul, Richard Charlton, said in a speech that W. P. Kalanimoku had leased him the land of Nihoa in Honolulu and declared that J. A. Kuakini had seen the document. This greatly puzzled the chiefs and they questioned the existence of such a lease, for that land belonged to Kaahumanu, who had named it Nihoa in rememberance of the visit that she and Kaumualii had made to that island. When the king and the premier, Kekauluohi, went to Lahaina in January or February of 1840, Ii went along for the purpose of seeking Kuakini and finding out about the alleged lease. After the king reached Lahaina, Ii went on with the premier to Kailua in Kona, Hawaii, where he found Kuakini. He emphatically denied associating with the consul in conjunction with the lease.

When, a few days later, Ii returned to Lahaina, he was delayed there. On the ship's return to Lahaina, a letter from the Royal School was brought by Mr. Richards, asking the chiefs to make Ii the *kahu* of the school. While Ii enjoyed watching the expert surfers, Mr. Richards showed the letter to the premier. Then, Mr. Richards, who was sitting with Kekauluohi, called and beckoned to Ii. The letter was read to Ii, who said that if the chiefs agreed that he bring his child, Kamamalu, he would listen to the will of the chiefs. It was his fondest wish to find a peaceful life for the child, as her mother had wished. Kekauluohi and Richards approved.

When the feast for the king was ready, he called the premier and Ii to go to his residence. It seems that the chiefs had already discussed the matter of Ii's becoming the *kahu* of the children in the school. While they ate and talked of this and that the king asked Ii what he thought of becoming the *kahu*. Ii replied, "My answer to you is the same one I gave to the other two."

Then the king said, "You go there with your child and take my *keiki* with you. If you do not go there, neither will my *keiki*." Because of these words Ii's doubt was like the wind passing by, and he returned to Honolulu with the children. Two days later the king's two nephews entered the school.

Ii, Sarai, and Kamamalu left the Fort and the child's father, Kekuanaoa, to spend a few days at Honokaupu house before going to the school. On the morning of the day that they were to move to the school with the child, Kamamalu's father came early from the Fort to see them. He and Ii met alone, and Kekuanaoa asked that the child be allowed to stay with him and to let Kaluahinenui (Kahamaluihi) take care of her when he went to Lahaina. He was tearful and doubted whether it would be well for the girl to enter the Royal School. He felt that the child should live with him, so that she could take his place when he had to go to Lahaina.

"Can the very weak do heavy work?" Ii asked. "She is a small child and can neither think nor work. Perhaps you think that I am deserting you, or will be careless in taking care of the child. If your wife were living today, then this child would belong to Kuakini. So she told me when she was living. She said that she should go to Hawaii with the child, but I disagreed with her. When she died, Kuakini left the child to succeed you. All the needs of the child are supplied by you, her father, and the person of the child is mine to care for." This answer made Kekuanaoa relinquish the child to Ii.

The routine of the school was established by the teachers so that the work and the supervision might go well. Between breakfast and school was the time for the children to bathe. Some weeks after Ii entered the school he was drawing water at the spring with a bucket and had poured two or three buckets of water into the tub when the child ran and stood beside it. When he went to fetch more water he glanced toward her and saw that she had fallen in headfirst. Perhaps to see her reflection in the rippling water she had bent over too far. Ii ran to her and sucked the water out of her nostrils and soothed her. No one else saw this happen and that trouble passed.

After a month had gone by, there was more trouble; the child's father tried to take her. It was a custom of Sarai to go to the Fort with the wife of Kaluahinenui, Kahanamoku, after the older children were in school, to sew garments for Kamamalu. One night after Sarai returned home, Kaluahinenui arrived with a message from Kekuanaoa, accusing Sarai of having uttered an insulting remark about the king. Ii asked, "If she indeed said that, what will the result be?"

Kaluahinenui said, "I am to come up again with soldiers and take the child away from you."

Ii replied, "Have you the right to do that to us when we have done no wrong, nor opposed you? You two have placed me here to work! It would not be

167

right for you to do such a thing, and if you do, I shall sue you by law for disturbing the peace. I am responsible for all the chiefs living here, and you can do nothing while I live rightly by the power given to me under the rules of this school. If you have greater power and strength than I, then I shall die here on this spot before you take her away. While she is yet a child, she is supervised by me, as a parent."

When they finished speaking, Kaluahinenui turned around and went home and nothing more was heard about this matter.

More trouble occurred some months later. It was customary for the pupils and teachers to go to Kapena Falls on holidays. One day a child was missing when they returned, for he had been detained by Kaiahua and remained at her house, where they had visited before returning to school. At the supper table, one of the children remarked, "Kaliokalani has been detained by Kaiahua." Ii left immediately and went to Kaiahua to ask why the child had been detained. He was told that it was because her *moʻopuna* had been asked to water the plants in the school yard.

Ii replied, "Not only is it asked of your *moʻopuna* but of all the boys, of me, and of their teachers. This strengthens the body like all other kinds of exercise, to the benefit of the child. You have no right in this matter, as the children are placed in my care by the king, and only the personal needs of the child are your affair."

The child was sitting in Kaiahua's lap, and Ii seized the child at once, placing his left foot on Kaiahua's lap as she reached up. They returned to the school with Kapaakea, the boy's father. The children were all glad at the return of the boy. That night, Kaiahua complained to Kekuanaoa about her *moʻopuna* and wanted him brought back to her. But Kekuanaoa said to her, "We have no power to do anything, for I have tried, without success. He has the power from the chiefs, so here we are."

In 1841 a government conference was held at Luaehu, Maui. Accompanying the teachers were all of the older boys and girls of the Royal School and Kamamalu, who was the youngest to attend. The children were comfortably situated at Kuloloia house, in Waihee, on the right side of the churchyard. A swing was made for them on the coconut-leaf lanai outside of the entrance door to Kuloloia house, and whenever Kamamalu swang she sang some of the foreign songs she had learned. Once, while she was swinging, Kauikeaouli *ma* arrived and listened to her merry singing. He remarked, "What a loud-voiced girl. She may have as great a voice as her mother's." She showed no embarrassment whatever, for it seems that she was used to such remarks. When the conference was over, they ended their stay and returned to Honolulu to live until she was about six or seven years old.

In 1843 came a report of a fight in Kau between the Protestants and the adherents of the Pope. The government ordered Ii to go there on the first ship to

Hilo. So, in the first month of the year, Ii left Kamamalu with the teachers. By the time he reached Kau the disturbance was over. The participants in the fight were tried by Ii, and the people there turned to righteousness in our Lord Jesus.

Ii was told that the women of western and eastern Kau planned to journey back and forth every week. He had a pleasant meeting with one company of traveling women and accompanied them to the place where they encamped. They looked at the Bible together and each read a verse. Ii left them all at Kahuku, as they were going home. The women of Kapalilua also gave Ii help until he reached Kahakuwai in Kainaliu, North Kona, where Kuakini raised coffee.

In February 1853 a ship anchored outside of the harbor with a man on board who was very sick with smallpox. The ship was stopped, and those on board were forbidden to come ashore in Honolulu. Some passengers who were local residents landed at Kaluahole in Waikiki, and the sick man was landed at Kahakaaulana in Kalihi. This event caused much excitement. In the month of May the disease appeared in Kapuukolo and death was rife in the section on the Ewa side of Poliahu road. On June 1, after all the members of Ii's household had been vaccinated, they left Mililani house, where they had been living since November 1, 1852, to sail to Hawaii.

They rested at Kawaihae on the Sabbath day, and early Monday morning sailed for Hilo, where Ii and Kamamalu stayed in the home of the Reverend Titus Coan. During their stay with Coan they visited Kilauea, the wonderful earth-devouring fire that the Lord prepared for the Last Day. When they went down into the hollows of the pit and came to the crater proper, which was active, it seemed to Ii that the child's mother and aunts and her cousin Nahienaena were also there, sitting together on the other side where the lava gathered. The lava seemed to be dancing, and from where they stood, the flames appeared to go up and down. When their eyes were satisfied they left the place and went back to the house. The next day they returned to the lowland, where they remained only a few days.

They went next to Kaalualu in Kau and on up to Waiohinu, met with Kini *ma* who were there at the time, and spent the night with them. The ship *Pauahi* left Kaalualu that evening after they started for Waiohinu and sailed to Kalae to wait for them. The next morning they left Waiohinu to return to the ship, but a third person of the group took a different way in order to arrive at Kailikii first.

So Kamamalu and Ii traveled together on horseback over that lonely but peaceful plain. They took the long trail called Puuone which ran along a sand ridge to Kalae, from the shores of Kaalualu and Paiahaa, and to the dust-leaping place of Kaumaea. That was where the Puuone trail met the trail going up the cliff of Molilele and the one leading down to Kailikii. As they proceeded, Kamamalu's fat horse slowed their progress. She asked for a small branch to use as a switch for her horse, but when she whipped the animal's flank it balked and she

Halemaumau Pit in action, a painting by D. Howard Hitchcock in Bishop Museum.

fell to the ground in front of it. Ii dismounted at once, reached for her, kissed her on the cheek and asked, "Are you hurt?"

She answered, "No," with not a sign of anxiety or fear in her eyes and said quickly, "Lift me up on my horse." So they continued until they reached the fork of the trail going straight down to the shore of Kalae, then went on to the ship. They were very hungry and ate rapidly until the discomfort was eased. Then they spent the night there, and the next morning left to spend the second night at Kailikii.

When the third person of the company came aboard with food, they left there and met with night at Kapua. Because it was very calm, daylight found them at Papa, at Kapalilua. Not a breath of wind was stirring there. After breakfast Kamamalu asked to leave the ship and go by rowboat, so she and Kaohe, son of Mahuka, went along close to land until they reached Kolo and Kukuiopae, before the ship did. When the vessel arrived, the residents were ready to supply it with fuel.

They were greeted with the news that smallpox had reached Haleili, about ten *ahupua'a* away from Papa, where death was making havoc. It was said that some people from Oahu had caused the spread of the disease. Ii called out at once, "O Kiheahealani (Heavenly Bloodstain), named for the red blood that issued from the neck, come back now," and Kamamalu returned to the ship. The name Kiheahealani had been given the child by her mother at the time Kauikeaouli had a lump on his neck removed by Dr. G. P. Judd to prevent future trouble. It was the spattering of the blood which caused Kinau to give Kamamalu that name. When Kinau mentioned it to Ii, she said, "Perhaps I did wrong in giving this name to the girl, for the chiefs may object to it."

Ii said, "No, for they know that you are Kamehameha's child and Kauikeaouli is, too."

The ship was becalmed that day, but when evening came, a land breeze, the Kewai, came up. The name Kewai is a Kona term meaning a land breeze mixed with rain. The wind helped the ship until dark, when the dew-laden breeze arose. So they arrived at Napoopoo, outside of Waipunaula and Kiloa, at Kealakekua, for a night of rest. They remained there one day, meeting with the people and helping them build a house for the segregation of the sick, as they had done at Mokuola in Hilo.

Early Monday morning they departed and paused at Keauhou and Kahaluu for food. They moved on comfortably until they arrived at Kailua the same day. After two or three days there, news came that smallpox was now raging at Kawaihae. Several persons, including Puamana, were dead; but those who had been vaccinated were saved.

Early Thursday morning, the ship sailed, pausing at Luahinewai (Kiholo) to bathe and visit that strange water in the lava. After an enjoyable stop at the water with the pretty pebbles, they again sailed. The ship was becalmed outside of Kawaihae; but in the early morning of the following day, a breeze bore it closer to Kohala. At Kapaliiuka they heard the happy voices of the children of that beach of water-worn stones and rocky cliffs crying out to each other, "*Pauahi ka ho—e!* (*Pauahi* ahoy!)" The sun was warm, and the gentle Apaa breeze bore the ship to Kahua and on to Kukaipahu, where the passengers saw a small ship inside of Kapaliokamoa. This was the *Kalaikini*, going to Hana. They left the *Kalaikini* behind, and reached the port of Kapueokahi, Maui, near noon. They looked up at the stronghold of Kauiki, where Kaahumanu was born. It was evening when the smaller ship arrived. As soon as it reached port some of the passengers made haste to go ashore, but their rowboats had not reached the shore when orders came to stay aboard because smallpox had been brought there. As the *Kalaikini* lacked water and food, five bundles of hard poi, ten dried *'awa* fish, and one barrel of water were sent out to the ship.

Ii's ship remained at Kapueokahi until after Sunday, and the passengers associated with the people there. On Monday they left and paused at Ulaino, belonging to John Young II, to bathe in the water at Makapuu, a pool famous in legend. Then they returned with head leis of *palapalai* fern and ginger. In the house where they were received their emptiness became well filled. Then they bade their friends farewell and boarded a boat to return to the ship.

The sails of the lovely one turned hither. Those aboard glanced at the cliffs of Koolau and Hamakua, reaching Halehaku at night, where they paused until day break. Then they moved along, looking at Halehaku and Haiku, seeing the growing koa and kukui trees of Lilikoi and other sights until they reached Kahului. They went ashore there and went to Kaoo's houses at Wailuku and spent two nights there. When they left for Kahului on ox carts, Kamamalu and the others sang. Children, men and women accompanied them until they boarded the boats.

They departed from there, looking up at those lands as far as the cliffs of Kahakuloa, and thought "what a multitude of inhabitants" Kaukini had. Passing Honokohau and Kaanapali, they saw a white flag at Lahaina where people from Oahu were not allowed to land because of the smallpox. They went from the ship to the fort, where they remained apart until the Sabbath and where their prayer meeting was held. They did not know until late that day that most of the congregation at Wainee was eager to have them.

When they boarded the ship on Monday, Keaweiwi joined them to sail to Halawa, Molokai, where he expected to remain a little while. They left Lahaina at two o'clock and paused at Halawa at four o'clock. The ship hoisted its white flag, and a boat came from shore with food and with the information that it was kapu to go ashore. So they returned to Maui, where Keaweiwi went ashore at Mala at six o'clock. The ship entered the harbor of Honolulu the next morning and Ii arrived at Mililani house with Kamamalu in good health.

Mililani, Ii's home in Honolulu where he took residence in 1852. Reproduction of a lithograph by Paul Emmert, in Bishop Museum.

During the epidemic many carts covered with yellowish cloth daily bore away those who had died, and this was a fearful sight. However, at Ii's place there were no deaths. As soon as it was known that the road going up to Kahehuna was good, Kamamalu returned to school. She remained there until February 1855, when she was taken ill at Waikiki.

Kamamalu became a member of the first church in Honolulu, the church to which her mother had belonged and the one in which her grandaunts had pledged to serve the true God. She attended church regularly on Sabbaths unless she was ill. Later she began giving talks to the early-morning gatherings of the women, who were pleased. Sometimes her companions were K. Apani, A. Keomaka, and H. K. Kapakuhaili; but her constant companion was Sarai. Through the influence of this girl some sinners abandoned their ways. She was almost like her grandaunt, Kaahumanu, they declared, and seemed to be following her example. Kamamalu had recognized Jehovah and His laws from childhood because she had been taught about Jehovah and Jesus, His Son. She knew He was her Savior and that He was close to her and to everyone else who possessed a soul. She prayed to Him, in secret sometimes, made speeches at the women's or the men's prayer meetings; and, according to the Word of the Lord, none forbade her to come. It is believed that she became a member of the church in 1854.

Kamamalu's *kaikunane*, Kamehameha III, thought as much of her as he did of Nahienaena. Perhaps he regarded her so highly because they were both descended from generations of rulers over this people. She was more of a favorite than were her brothers, perhaps because they were boys and because her mother died when she was an infant. Her mother had been premier and would have been eligible to ascend the throne should the king be removed. Kamehameha III had two sons who died, leaving only Kinau's sons, whom he hoped would succeed him. He was determined to have Kamamalu as premier to succeed her mother, but as she was too young when her mother died, her aunt, Kekauluohi, was appointed to serve during Kamamalu's childhood.

After Kekauluohi was taken by death in 1845, a letter was written by the king to Kekuanaoa, Kamamalu's father, and Ii telling them of the king's idea of having Keoni Ana (John Young) as premier, because of Kamamalu's youth. The king wanted an opinion and his decision was approved. While Kekauluohi was premier she received from the king all the kahili holders, kahili handles, and feather leis of Nahienaena which the king requested her to keep for Kamamalu's holiday adornment when the time came. After Kekauluohi's death, the king asked what had been done with these things and found they had come into Ii's keeping. The king was the one *kaikunane* among all the others who seemed to think very highly of Kamamalu and who was pleased with all she said.

After the beloved Kamehameha III passed away in 1854, the minister of foreign affairs, R. C. Wyllie, sent for Kamamalu. As she was granted permission to go, but with instructions to not commit herself to anything until Ii had been consulted, she went up and returned in the evening. The next morning after breakfast when they were alone on the upper lanai Ii asked, "What did the minister say to you?"

"He wanted me to live at his place," she replied.

"And what else?"

"That it is not proper for Pauahi and me to stand in the choir on Sundays, because the royalty of England do not. Those were his words to me."

When Ii heard these words he replied, "Child, you know how David, King of Israel, went dancing before God in front of the procession in which the ark of the covenant was borne and laid in a place prepared for it. So I say to you that the time has not come to step over his ways. I think the minister is a man very ignorant in things pertaining to the worship of God, from Whom come all the good for mankind and for you chiefs. They are from Him. So it is mentioned in 1 Samuel 16:12 and 2 Samuel 6:14, 15." Perhaps she understood these things, for she did not associate with Wyllie after that time.

Kamamalu died at 10 o'clock in the morning on May 29, 1866, at Papakanene, Waialae. She was first taken ill in February, at a party for visitors at Haleakala house, the home of Pauahi. She was permitted to leave the party and went to Pihanakalani house. From then on, the illness weighed upon her. It was thought that she would feel better at Pihanakalani, but she wanted to return to Papakanene. When she arrived there paralysis set in, and she was in bed for three weeks before she was taken. On Sunday evenings the members of her two churches pleaded with the Lord, but the trouble was too grave for their petition. The doctors, too, were unable to make her well. The length of her life was twenty-seven years and seven months.

O 'oe ia e ka ohakia manawa'ula,	It is you, O young and rosy bud,
E ke kahuli pua lei kapu o Haona;	O changing, sacred flower for the lei of Haona;
E ka leilei uhu haka o ka po,	The lei, when worn, brings fond memories of the night,
O ka po iki a Ma'akunui, e ku'u hoa.	Of the short night of Ma'akunui, of my companion.
Lu ka ua i ka pua hala o Kanakea,	The rain scatters the hala fruit of Kanakea,
Hele ho'i ha ka mu'o o ka hinalo,	The young bracts of the hala blossom fall too,
Pala maui helo i ka pua na i ke ala,	The overripe fruit, bruised, sends forth a fragrance,
Nu'a aku la i ka 'ae lehua a ka manu e.	The sweetness reaches the lehua blossoms beloved of the birds.
Ua manumanu mohole au i ke aloha,	I am bruised and wounded by grief,
I ka walua 'eha loko o ke kanaka.	I hurt to my innermost depths.
Auhea he wahi 'oko'a ia 'oe ke aloha,	There is none other like you, my dear,
Ku'u keiki! Ku'u keiki e!	My child! My child!

Kekuanaoa, Kamamalu's father, died some two years after her death. On the morning of November 24, 1868, a woman named Rahab came to tell Ii that Kekuanaoa had died the night before. When she was asked from whom she heard this news, she said, "From my husband, who has been to Honolulu."

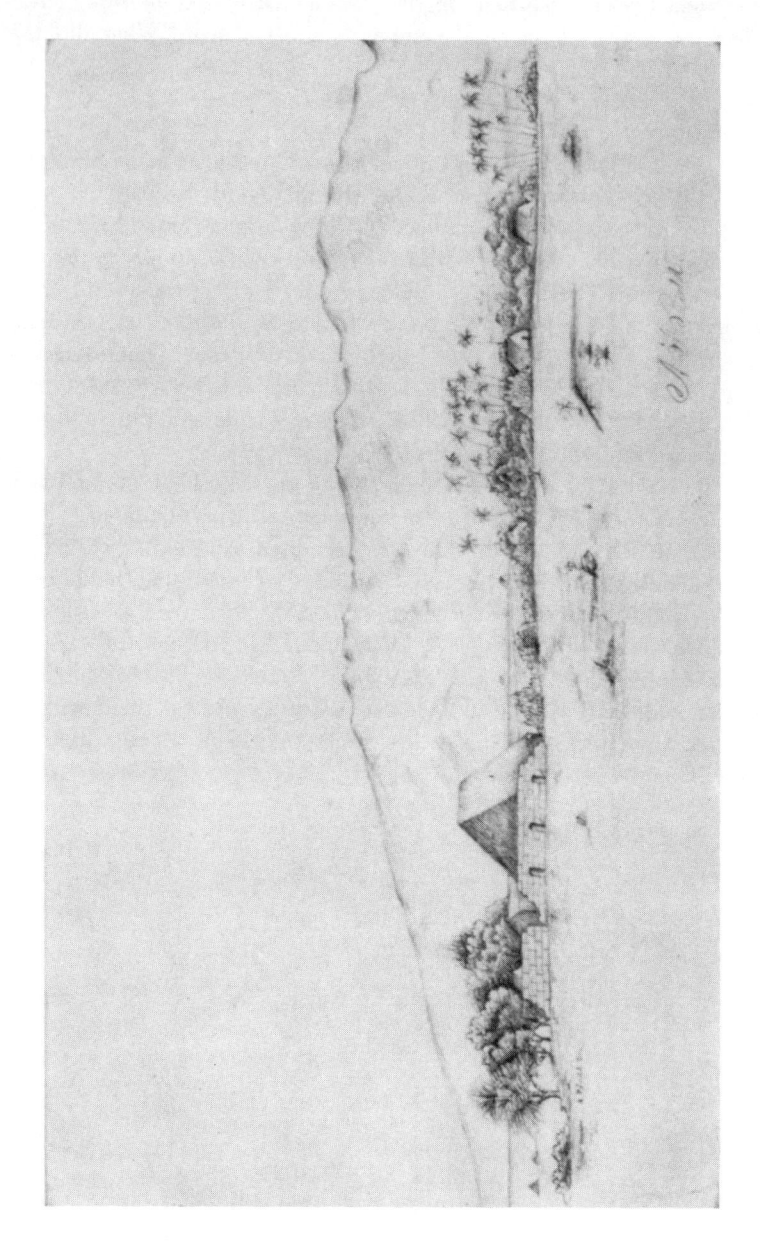

Ii's home in Ewa, where he retired in 1864, from a pencil drawing by A. Francis Judd. Owned by Zadoc W. Brown.

Ii immediately wrote a letter of sympathy to King Kamehameha V and his sister, Keelikolani. These sad voices have come frequently to us, the people, and to the beloved friends among other races who dwell with us. Ii was a companion of Kekuanaoa in the government for many years, from the time Kekuanaoa's royal wife Kinau, the mother of his children, was living. The title of "Imi Haku (Seeker of a lord)" was most appropriate for the deceased.

Kekuanaoa was known to all and was older than some of the elderly people now living. He lived seventy-seven years. Ii, who knew him in youth, found it hard to believe in his death. He was as young as John Meek at the time when Kamehameha I was in Kailua, Kona, Hawaii. They seemed equals physically, but John Meek, who also has gray hair, is still strong.

When John Adams Kuakini left his position as governor of Oahu in 1834 to return to Hawaii, Kekuanaoa had succeeded him to serve the government for more than thirty years; and he was seen in the time of Kamehameha I, when he was sometimes a messenger and a keeper of the king's food. In that capacity he was extremely close-fisted with the things in his care.

When Kekuanaoa was stricken with paralysis of the leg Ii and his wife who were living in Ewa did not fail to visit him as he lay ill. Ii encouraged him to "look to the Lamb of God, who takes away the sins of the world. We are now old men and should be prepared ere we go from this world." They prayed together and it seemed that that was what he wanted. On the night of the fourth of November, Ii went to see him again. Ii found him in the parlor, where he was lying down, and stayed there for three hours. It was only after he had fallen asleep that Ii left him. After twenty days the word came that he was gone.

All truly admired Kekuanaoa and loved him for the many good things he did and for his unlimited kindness. It was through him that Ii held the young Kamamalu in his arms. If he sought the Lord before his departure, then there is a great rejoicing in the eternal kingdom of the Lord who truly loves.

Kilikili hune makani aloha la e,	The gentle zephyr wafts a thought of love,
Aloha 'ini 'u ko aloha o ka makani,	A love mixed with sadness is borne by the breeze,
Ka i 'u ke aloha o ka makani Malana'i, ku a kane,	The Malanai breeze sighs of its love to men,
Pawali me ka malana'i ku wahine.	And whispers of its love to women.
He makani 'alo lau no ha'i	It is a wind that, blowing among the leaves, tells
Eia ke anu me ke ko'eko'e.	That cold and dampness are here.
Ko'eko'e loko i ka wai pi o ka leo,	Chilled is the heart by his inability to speak.
O ka lono ka wai na'e ho'oma'u.	Cold, as though long soaked in water.
O ka welina leo mana'o,	It is the beloved voice that is remembered,
Ho'omana'o wale mai no malaila,	It is recalled as being always there,
Mana'o i ka pua lei he ho—a,	Remembered is the companion as a choice flower to be worn,
Lilo e 'ohi e!	He is gone! Taken away!

Ioane Ii.

Glossary

A

'*aeokahaloa:* a wauke tapa, colored with charcoal, used in religious ceremonies

'*aha:* 1, a cord made of coconut fiber; 2, a sacred cord ('aha kapu) used in religious ceremonies; 3, a service or prayer appealing to the gods for a revelation; 4, an assembly

ahupua'a: a large division of land within a district (moku)

'*aki'aki:* seashore rush grass (Sporobolus virginicus)

ama: outrigger canoe float

'*amama:* the prayer given when offerings were made to the gods; the concluding prayer of a service; concluding words of a prayer

'*ama'u:* all species of an endemic genus of ferns; plural 'ama'uma'u

'*ana'ana:* evil sorcery

anana: length from fingertip to fingertip of outstretched arms; a fathom

anu'u: a scaffold tower covered with tapa used in heiaus

'*apapane:* a Hawaiian honey creeper (Himatione sanguinea)

'*awa:* the kava plant (Piper methysticum); also the drink made from its root

H

haku: lord, master

hala: the pandanus, or screw pine (Pandanus odoratissimus)

halau: a long house

hanai: to raise, feed, nourish, sustain

hanauna: a relative whose relationship was established several generations previously

haole: a white person, American, English, etc.

hau: a lowland tree (Hibiscus tiliaceus)

heiau: a general term for a pre-Christian place of worship

hoahanau: siblings or cousins of the same generation

honi: to press the nose; to kiss (modern)

honi i ka ihu: to touch the sides of the noses

hulu makua: esteemed relative of the parental generation

hunona: a son-in-law or nephew-in-law

I

'iako: boom of outrigger canoe
'ie: aerial root of the 'ie'ie vine, a woody climber (Freycinetia arborea)
'i'iwi: scarlet Hawaiian honeycreeper (Vestiaria coccinea)
'ili (or 'ili 'aina): a land division within an ahupua'a
'ili kupono: a land division paying tribute directly to the king
'iliahi: Hawaiian sandalwood (Santalum)
'ilima: general term for forms of the 'ilima plants (Sida)
imu: underground oven; also spelled umu
'iwa'iwa: general term for maidenhair ferns (Adiantum)
iwilei: length from collar bone to fingertips; a yard

K

kahili: a standard ornamented near the top with feathers
kahu: honored attendant, guardian, nurse, keeper; kahu hanai: guardian or parent of a foster child
kahuna: an expert in any specialized line; usually a priest
kaikaina: younger sibling or cousin of the same sex
kaikamahine: a daughter or niece
kaikua'ana: older sibling or cousin of the same sex; also used as a term of respect for one of higher rank
kaikuahine: sister or female cousin of a male
kaikunane: a brother or male cousin of a female
kalaipahoa: general name for poison gods who originated on Molokai
kalana (okana): a division of land smaller than an entire district
kama'aina: one born in, or well acquainted with, a given place
kapu: sacred, prohibited, forbidden; special privilege or exemption from ordinary tapu
kapu loulou: kapu ceremonies in the luakini heiau for prevention of epidemics, famine, destruction
kapuo: a cry proclaiming a kapu on the approach of a sacred personage or as part of the ceremony; the announcer of such a kapu
keiki: a son or nephew; a child
kepakepa: conversational chant, fast rhythmic chant or recitation
kia'i: guard, watchman, caretaker
koa: native forest tree (Acacia koa)
konane: ancient game resembling checkers
kou: tree (Cordia subcordata)
kuahu: a raised place where offerings were laid

kuili: prayers repeated in unison by several priests
kukui: candlenut tree (Aleurites moluccana), the dried nuts of which were burned for light
kuni: sorcery to retaliate for a death caused by a kahuna 'ana'ana with his own death

L

lama: an endemic hardwood tree (Diospyros, or Maba)
lei: a neck or head wreath; figuratively, a child or loved one of one's own generation
lele: offering stand
lele kawa: to leap into water feet first from a height
lelea: name of the prayer offered while the high chief drank 'awa
loulu: all species of native fan palms (Pritchardia also called lauli'i)
lua: general name for a type of hand-to-hand fighting, that included bonebreaking, quick turns and twists of the spear, noosing, and leaping
luakini: the ruling chief's heiau, where human sacrifices were offered

M

ma: particle following names of persons: and company, and others, and wife, and associates
maika: ancient Hawaiian game suggesting bowling; the stone used in the game
maile: native twining shrub with fragrant leaves (Alyxia olivaeformis)
maka halau: a long house (halau) built to overlook or command a view
makahiki: a year; yearly; in ancient Hawaii, annual tax gathering time, featuring ceremonies and celebrations
makai: in the direction of the sea
makaloa: a perennial sedge (Cyperus laevigatus)
makua: parent; any relative of the parents' generation
makuahine: mother, aunt, other female relative of the parents' generation
makuakane: father, uncle, other male relative of the parents' generation
malo: a loin cloth for men
mamaki: a fiber-yielding plant used in making tapa (Pipturus spp.)
mamo: black Hawaiian honeycreeper (Drepanis pacifica)
mana: supernatural or divine power
manini: the surgeon fish in the adult stage (Acanthurus sandvicensis)
mauka: inland, upland, toward the mountains
maunu: 1, bait used in fishing; 2, objects used in sorcery such as hair, spittle, or parings

moelola: a striped tapa
mo'opuna: grandchild; a relative two generations younger
mua: men's eating house, kapu to women

N

naio: bastard sandalwood (Myoporum sandwicense)
ni'aupi'o: a chiefly rank; the offspring of a union of chiefs who were siblings or first cousins
nene: Hawaiian goose (Branta sandvicensis)
niho palaoa: whale-tooth pendant
no'a: the object hidden in various forms of hiding games; figuratively, secret thoughts or plans
noni: the Indian mulberry (Morinda citrifolia)

O

'ohi'a: a hardwood tree (Metrosideros macropus, M. collina)
'okolehao: liquor distilled from ti root
'oku'u: name given to a disease during the time of Kamehameha I, perhaps cholera
'oloa: a fine white tapa
olona: native shrub (Touchardia latifolia)
'opule: a spotted fish (Anampses curvier)

P

paehumu: a decorated fencing of wood or stone surrounding a kapu enclosure
pala: a fern (Marattia douglasii)
peleleu: large canoe
pia: Polynesian arrowroot (Tacca leontopetaloides)
pili: a grass formerly used for thatching houses (Heteropogon contortus)
pohuehue: beach morning-glory (Ipomoea pes-caprae)
poi: food made from baked taro, mashed and mixed with water
puhenehene: a game: a stone or piece of wood called no'a was hidden on the person of a player, and the other players tried to guess on whom it was hidden; puhene: a variety of puhenehene as described by Ii

T

ti: a woody plant of the lily family (Cordyline terminalis)

U

'ukeke: musical bow played by holding it over the mouth and twanging the strings (other instruments played with the same principle took the name of 'ukeke, that described by Ii being the ni'aukani, or jew's harp)
ulua: certain species of crevalle or jack fish
uluhe: all Hawaiian species of false staghorn fern

W

wiliwili: a Hawaiian leguminous tree (Erythrina sandwicensis)

Index*

A

Adams, Alexander 128
Adams, John (Kuakini) 30, 53, 81, 95, 101, 161-162, 166, 167, 169, 177
'aha services; See *kapu loulu* rites
Ahuena heiau 117, 122-123, 127, 129
Aiea 95
Aienui 85, 91
Aikona 120
Aikupika 143, 145
'*ailolo* 9
Ainahou 30, 82
Aioloolo in Waikele 76
Akahi 61
Akahipapa 13, 138
Akalele 131-132
akua hana 124
akua hanai 124
akua hulu (feather gods) 39, 41
akua loa (Lono) 70, 72, 73, 75
akua pa'ani 70, 71
akua panauea 41
akua poko 75-76
Alahonua wind 122
Alanaio pond 119
Alapai (Alapainui) 3-6, 19, 53, 138
Alapai Maloiki 53
Alawai pool 59
Albatross (*Makanimoku*) 88, 106
Alexander, a haole 85
Alexander Liholiho; See Kamehameha IV
Aliipalapala 70; See also Kamehameha I, children
altars
  kuahu 72, 75, 123, 157
  lele 35, 39, 45, 56, 157
Aluli 157
Amamalua 9
'*amama* prayer 35, 37, 38, 44, 45
amusements; See games and sports
  loku 63-64
Anahulu river 98
Anana, Mr. 127
anchors, making of 103, 104
anu'u tower 35, 38, 44, 56, 123
'*aoa* shrine 26
Apaa breeze 172
Apani, K. 174

Apuakehau 108-109
Apuakehau stream 17, 92
Arago 143
[*Argentina*]** a man-of-war 128-129
Argentinian (Spanish) ships 128-129
Armetise, l' 166
Aua 153-155
Auaia 145
Auhaukeae 110, 134
'*aulima* (fire lighting) 26
'*aunaki* (fire lighting) 26
Auwaiawao ditch 158
Awa, Waiawa, Ewa 85
Awalua, Hawaii 110
Awalua, Oahu 82
Awili in Kaawaloa 121, 132

B

Battles
  Iao 15, 70, 100
  Keoneula 100
  Koapapaa 79
  Laupahoehoe 37, 134
  Mokuohai 15, 49, 70
  Nuuanu 15, 20, 69
  Puana 15, 18, 92
  sham 7, 10, 76
Bennet, George 143
Beretania 143, 153
Beretania house 143
betting 67-68, 137
Bingham, Rev. Hiram 155, 158
Boki Kamauleule 19, 145, 147-148, 153, 157
  ancestry 53, 141
  house 143, 153
  as a medical kahuna 47, 48
  plots against Kaahumanu 154-155
  quest for sandalwood 157
boxing 73-74, 76
Byrd, Lelia; See Keoua
Byron, Lord 143, 147

C

canoe(s)
  description 129-130
  paddling of 130-133
  parts of 129-131
  righting of 130-131

---
*For financial assistance in the preparation of this index, grateful acknowledgment is made to the University of Hawaii Committee for the Preservation and Study of Hawaiian Language, Art and Culture.

**Words within square brackets [] have been inserted for additional clarity: they do not necessarily appear in the text.

canoes, names of
  Halemanu 83
  Humuuloa 41
  Noiku 13, 41
cession of Kauai 79-83
chanting 63-64, 108
chants, texts of 18, 29, 39, 42, 43, 45, 50, 73, 98, 101, 108, 145, 146, 147, 150, 157, 175, 177; *See also* prayers
Charlton, Richard 166
Chinese 94
Coan, Rev. Titus 169
council of chiefs 81, 123
courthouse (Hale Hookolokolo) 56
custom house 94, 120

D

dance(s) (ing) 11, 18, 63, 137
  hula 'aiha'a 137
  hula kala'au (stick hula) 70, 94
  hula paipu 137
Davis, George Isaac [Hueu] 95
Davis, Isaac 70, 79, 83
Davis, William Heath 88, 106
Diamond Head; *See* Leahi
drum(s) (ing) 35, 38, 137

E

Eeka 86
Eeka breeze 110, 121
Ellis, Rev. William 143
Elou trail, Oahu 97
Enepalai (Isabella) 88, 106-107
epidemics; *See also 'oku'u*
  mumps 163-164
  smallpox 169, 174

F

farming 68, 69, 145, 153
feather gods (*akua hulu*) 39, 41
Finch, Captain 155
fire lighting 26
fishing 69, 109
foot racing 67
Forester (Kaahumanu) 126
Fort, Honolulu 143, 145, 161, 166-167
Fourth of July celebration 88
Freycinet, Capt. Louis de 143
fur trade 87

G

gambling 67-68, 137
games and sports 63-64, 66-68, 70
  card 127
genealogies 19-20, 50, 52-53
god houses 58, 91
gods
  akua hulu (feather gods) 39, 41
  akua panauea 41
  kalaipahoa 124
    akua hana 124
    akua hanai 124
    ke 'kua hana 124
  makahiki 70, 72, 73, 75, 76, 115, 121
    akua loa (Lono) 70, 72, 73, 75
    akua pa'ani 70, 71
    akua poko 75-76
    Lono (*akua loa*) 70, 72, 73, 75
  of medicine 45-46, 60
  ololupe 123
Gods, names of
  Haumea 44
  Hiiaka 18
  Kaalaenui a Hina 47
  Kahoalii, the man-god 41
  Kahuilaokalani 47
  Kaili (Kukailimoku) 58, 95, 101, 104-105
  Kalaipahoa 18, 91
    images 124
  Kalamainuu (Kihawahine) 44
  Kamehaikana (Haumea) 44
  Kaneikaulanaula 18, 47
  Kaneikoleamoku 45
  Kapo 18, 47
  Kihawahine 44, 91
  Koleamoku 123
  Kukailimoku (Kaili) 58, 95, 101, 104-105
  Lono 72, 73, 75
  Lonomakua 60
  Lonopuha 45
  Ololupe 124
  Pua (Puanui) 18, 47, 150
  Puanui (Pua) 18, 47, 150
  Walinuu 44
Great Mahele 50
guards 88, 139, 148-149
guns(s)
  drilling with 54
  sites for gun drilling 66, 91
  training in use of 69

H

Haae 53
Haalelea 100
Haalilio 127, 166
Haalou, daughter of Kalelemauli and Haae 17, 18, 141
Haalou, son of Wanaoa and Kamahauluae 19, 146
Hahakea 68
Haiha 110, 133
[Haiha]; *See* Naihe
Haiku, Maui 172
[Hakaleleponi, wife of Kamehameha III]; *See* Kapakuhaili, H. K.
Hakau 129
Haku o Hawaii, epithet of Lot [Kapuaiwa] 164; *See also* Kamehameha V
haku 'ohi'a; *See kapu loulu* rites
Halakika 91
Halaulani 33, 76
Halawa, Ewa, Oahu 20, 70, 95
Halawa, Kohala, Hawaii 13
Halawa, Molokai 83, 172
hale 'aina (women's houses) 64, 66, 119, 120, 121
Haleakala House 175
Haleauau 97
Halehaku, Maui 172
Halehanaimoa 143
Hale Hookolokolo (courthouse) 56
Hale Hui 58, 64
halehui 'ilimai'a 123
Haleili 171
Haleino 123
Halelau 59-61
Halelua, Kohala 134
Hale Mahoe (Swan and Clifford Building) 64
Hale Mana 35, 43
Halemano land and stream 98
Halemanu, canoe 83
hale mua (men's houses) 46, 58, 64, 75, 111, 119, 121
hale nana mahina 'ai 117, 119, 122, 123
Haleohiu, Hawaii 110
Hale o Kaili 58
Hale o Keawe (Kaikialealea) 13, 58, 137-139
Hale o Lono 56-58, 59, 110, 123
Hale o Papa 39, 44, 45

Hale Pahu 33
Haleumiumiiole at Kawaihae 135
Hale Umu 35
Hale Waiea 35, 39
Haliimaile 148
Haloa 19, 52, 138, 139
Hamohamo 70
Hana 135, 172
Hanaiakamalama House 69
Hanaki 120
Hanaloa fishpond 20, 24
Hanapi 15
Hanauma Bay 104
Hapuu 68
Harbottle, Capt. J. M. 105
Hauiki in Mokuohai 14
Haumea 44
Haupuu 97
heiau(s) 157
  ceremonies 72, 75, 123; *See also kapu loulu* rites
  luakini 35, 45, 70, 72, 75-76, 157, 160
  medical 45-46, 59-61, 89
heiaus, names of
  Ahuena heiau 117, 122-123, 129
  Hale o Keawe (Kaikialealea) 13, 58, 137-139
  Hikiau heiau 115, 123, 160
  Honuaula heiau, Waipio, Hamakua 160
  Kaikialealea (Hale o Keawe) 13, 58, 137-139
  Kanoa heiau in Hilo 137, 160
  Keikipuipui heiau 110, 117, 133
  Mailekini heiau 17
  Mookini heiau 160
  Papaenaena heiau 33
  Punaluu heiau in Kau 137, 160
  Puukohola heiau 15, 17
  Wahaula heiau in Puna 137, 160
Helemano; *See* Halemano
Helumoa 17, 69, 92
Hewahewa 39, 91
Hewahewa, H. 148
Hiiaka 18
Hiiakanoholae [Kamano] Point 110
Hika 120
Hikiau heiau 115, 123, 160
Hilea 134
Hinau 101, 145, 154-155

187

Hiwauli, Sarai, wife of John Papa Ii 148, 161, 163-164, 166, 167
Hoaeae 95
[Hoapiliwahine]; See Kaheiheimalie
Holoholoku puʻuhonua 138
Holomaialuhe 19
Holualoa 6
Honalo 132
Honaunau 4, 13, 14, 137, 138
hono; See kapu loulu rites
Honokaupu in Honolulu 91, 92, 95, 114
Honokaupu House 161, 163, 166, 167
Honokohau, Honolulu 110, 135
Honokohau, Maui 172
Honolii stream 134
Honolulu (Note: The following references direct attention to Honolulu as the locale of action or incident but do not include every mention of the name: 29-30, 45, 50, 51, 53, 63-64, 66, 68-69, 70, 79, 86, 88.)
trails of 89-92, 94-95, 120, 143, 157
Honouliuli 32
Honuakaha 89, 91, 92, 101
Honuaula heiau, Waipio, Hamakua 160
Honuaula land, spring, and cave 110-111, 119, 133
Hoohokukalani 160
Hooikaika 164
Hookalo 85
Hookena in South Kona 115
Hookio 48
Hookuku 59, 89, 121
Hoolua wind 122
Hoomakau; See Hoomakaukau Keawekolohe
Hoomakaukau Keawekolohe (Hoomakau) 18, 107-109, 111, 116
Hoona, Hawaii 110
Hoowilimoo, ʻaha of; See kapu loulu rites
Houses 110, 111, 119-122, 143
of Boki 143
of Ellis 143
foundations for, 117
god, 58, 91
of Kaahumanu
in Honolulu 59, 66, 143, 158
in Kamakahonu 119
of Kalanimoku
in Honolulu 143, 145
in Kailua, Kona 128
of Kamehameha I
in Honolulu 64, 66, 91
at Kalakee, Kona 110
in Kamakahonu 117-121
in Nuuanu 69
in Waikiki 17, 69
of Kamehameha III 148, 153
of Keakealaniwahine 6, 159
of Liholiho
in Honolulu 58, 89
in Kona 110, 121
men's (hale mua) 46, 58, 64, 75, 111, 119, 121
stone 120
for tribute 129
women's (hale ʻaina) 64, 66, 119, 120, 121
houses, names of
Beretania 143
Haleakala 175
Halehanaimoa 143
Hanaiakamalama 69
Honokaupu 161, 163, 166, 167
Hookuku 59, 89, 121
Kapapoko 59, 66
Kauwalua 95
Kawaluna 121
Kekuaokalani (Kuihelani) 69
Kilauea 145, 146
Kualalua 59
Kuihelani (Kekuaokalani) 69
Kuloloia 168
Mililani 169, 172
Paiaina 150, 151
Paliiki 92
Papa 59, 110
Papakanene 143
Pihanakalani 175
Pohukaina 143, 145, 146, 148, 158, 159, 161
Hudson's Bay Company 127
[Hueu], Davis, George Isaac 95
Huia 79
Hulahula, ʻaha of; See kapu loulu rites
hulas; See dance(s)(ing)
Hulihee Palace 110
Humuuloa, canoe 41

I

Iao 99, 138
battles 15, 70, 100

188

Ieki, Abraham Naoa 147
Ihiihilauakea 104, 109
Ii, Daniel Papa; See Papa Ii, Daniel
Ii, John Papa 17, 88, 146, 149-150, 152, 155, 161-177
   ancestry 19
   attendant and guard of Kamehameha III 147-152
   baptized 147
   birth 20
   childhood training and experiences 20, 22-24, 26-30, 32, 45, 46, 48, 53-56
   enters court 55-56, 58
   experiences in court, Honolulu 59-61, 68
   experiences in Kona 113-115, 123, 129, 130
   goes to Hawaii 104-111
   at Hale o Keawe 138-139
   homes 91, 148, 175
   hostage aboard *l'Armetise* 166
   imitates *makahiki* gods and games 76
   intoxicated 85, 107
   kahu and foster parent of Victoria Kamamalu 161 *ff*.
   kahu of Royal School 166-168
   learns English 86, 128
   as personal attendant of Liholiho 58-59, 104, 113, 114, 123, 129
   takes Kamamalu to Hawaii 169, 171-172
   wife Maraea [mother of Irene Kahalelaukoa Ii] 177
   wife Sarai Hiwauli 148, 161, 163-164, 166, 167
Ii, Papa 9, 17, 18, 20, 22, 23, 24, 33, 45-46, 53, 55, 58, 76-77, 82-83, 86, 106, 111
   ancestry 19
   death 115-116
'*iliahi*; See sandalwood
Ilipeahi 19
Imaikalani 20
"Imi Haku (Seeker of a lord)"; See Kaimihaku
Inaina, *kaikunane* of Kaneikapolei 6, 8
Inaina, mother of Nahiolea 146
intoxicants
   abolition of 158
   brewing of 85
   drinking of 85-86, 101, 107-108
   '*okolehao* 107, 128
   rum 120, 128

Iolani [Liholiho] 41; See *also* Liholiho
Isabella (*Enepalai*) 88, 106-107
Iwikauikaua 6, 52

J

Judd, Dr. G. P. 161, 163, 164, 171

K

Kaaawa 70
Kaahulue 92
Kaahumanu (Elizabeth) 14, 15, 17, 18, 26, 33, 48, 70, 83, 86-87, 88, 106, 120, 141, 146, 155, 157-159, 166, 174
   affair with Kanihonui 50-51
   ancestry 53, 151
   baptized 145
   birthplace 172
   Boki plots against 153-155
   death 158
   guardian of Kamehameha III 141, 147-150, 152
   houses 59, 119, 153, 158
   surfing exploits 133-134, 158
Kaahumanu (*Forester*) 128
Kaaihee in Makiki 92
Kaailipoa 108-109
Kaaipaai 67, 68
Kaaipu 92
Kaaipuhi spring 111
Kaakeke, Molokai 106
Kaala 56, 97, 98
Kaalaenui a Hina 47
Kaalawai 94, 105
Kaaloa 94
Kaaloaapii 53
Kaaloakaulani 94
Kaalualu in Kau 134, 169
Kaananiau 92
Kaanapali, Maui 172
Kaapuiki 76
Kaawa 117
Kaawaloa 115-116, 117, 120, 132, 153
Kaeamamao [Kalaninuiiamamao] 52
ka'eke 137
ka'eke'eke 137
Kaelehuluhulu, Hawaii 109
Kaeleu 145
Kaena 98
Kaeo 15, 95

189

Kahahana 15, 17
Kahaiki 98
Kahakaaulana in Kalihi 169
Kahakuhaakoi (Wahinepio, Kamoonohu) 19, 49-50, 53, 141
Kahakuloa, Maui 172
Kahakuwai in Kainaliu 169
Kahala 94
Kahalaia 50, 147-148
Kaha lands 109
Kahalapalaoa 109
Kahalepoai 99
Kahalii 15
Kahalio 53
Kahalo 99
Kahaluu, Hawaii 113-115, 132, 171
Kahamaluihi (Kaluahinenui) 167-168
Kahanahaiki (Kahaiki) 98
Kahanamoku 167
Kahanaumaikai 92, 105
Kahanui; See Keeaumokuopio
Kahapaakai 32
Kahauiki 95
Kahaukomo in Nuuanu 146
Kahauloa 4, 134
Kahee 83
Kahehuna, Honolulu 174
Kaheiheimalie (Kalakua) [Hoapiliwahine, Kaniu] 18, 33, 50, 53, 70, 87, 120, 147, 150, 152
[Kahekili Keeaumoku]; See Keeaumokuopio
Kahekili, king of Maui 8-11, 15, 17, 18, 53, 100
Kahekili, son of Kaumualii 82
Kahekili, son of Peleuli; See Kaukuna Kahekili
Kahiki 47
Kahiko 101
kahili, bearers of chiefs', 11, 23, 113
Kahilipa 124
Kahina 27
Kahoa 87
Kahoalii, the man-god 41
Kahohonu 95
Kahoikekanaka 68
Kahoiwai 92
Kaholoakeahole 86, 91
Kahoolawe 128
Kahoopahee Point 132

Kahoowaha 50
Kahua 172
kahua; See sites
Kahuaiki, Waipio, Ewa 50
Kahuawai 20
Kahuawailana in Nuuanu 146
Kahuewai 95
Kahuhuki 70
Kahuilaokani 47
Kahuku, Kau 169
Kahului 11, 172
kahuna 'ana'ana 124
kahuna ka'i malo 44
kahuna kapapa ulua 43
kahuna kuni 124
kahunas, medical 33, 46-48
Kaia 116
Kaiahua, a chief of Kauai 81
Kaiahua [*makuahine* of Kapaakea] 168
Kaiaka River 98
Kaiakekua 110, 119, 121
Kaiaulu breeze 98
Kaihikapu pond 92
Kaikialealea (Hale o Keawe) 13, 58, 137-139
Kaikioewa 29, 81, 163
Kaiko [son of Peleuli] 59, 95, 101
Kaili (Kukailimoku) 58, 95, 101, 104, 105
Kailikii 11, 169, 171
Kailio 46
Kailipono 110
Kailua, Kona 13, 107, 114, 116, 117-121, 127-129, 130, 132, 145, 146, 153, 166, 171, 177
Kailua, Koolaupoko, Oahu 30, 32, 76
Kaimihaku (Imi Haku), epithet of Kekuanaoa 147, 177; See also Kekuanaoa, Mataio
Kaimihau 30, 77
Kaimuki 94, 104
Kaina 92
Kainaliu, North Kona 169
Kaioea 123
Kaipaki, Molokai 158
Kaipu o Lono 50
Kaiu, Simeon 145
Kaiwikokoole 91, 114-115
Kaiwiopele 35
Kaiwiula 95
Kakaako 55, 88, 91

Kakae pu'uhonua 138
Kakanilua 8, 10, 52
Kalaaumaloo 19
Kalae in Kau 134, 169-171
Kalaemano at Kaawaloa 132
Kalaeokailio 10
Kalaepohaku in Kapalama 70
Kalahu 92
Kalaikane, *kaikunane* of Wanaoa 115
Kalaikane, mother of Daniel Papa Ii, 22, 23
Kalaikane, mother of John Papa Ii; *See* Wanaoa
Kalaikini 172
Kalaikoa 95
Kalaikuahulu 81, 123, 137
Kalaimamahu 6, 7, 14, 33, 49-50, 53, 70, 91
Kalaimoku, Capt. William P. 107
Kalaipahoa 18, 91
　images 124
Kalakee 110, 117
Kalakoa 99
Kalakua; *See* Kaheiheimalie
[Kalama, wife of Kamehameha III]; *See* Kapakuhaili, H. K.
Kalamainuu (Kihawahine) 44
Kalamaku 47
Kalamanamana 113
Kalanakamaa 3
Kalani 68
Kalaniakua 91, 99-100
Kalanikahua 92
Kalanikauleleiaiwi 52-53, 99, 138
Kalanikupule 15, 95, 100, 146
Kalanimoku 29, 48, 49, 51, 76-77, 81, 83, 86, 91, 108, 141, 143, 145-148, 153, 166
　ancestry 19, 53
　baptized 141-143
　death 146
　houses 128, 143, 145
Kalaniopuu 3-4, 6-11, 13-14, 19, 52, 70, 129, 140
Kalanipuu 92
[Kalaniuniiamamao] Kaeamamao 52
Kalaoa in Hilo Paliku 15
Kalaoa lands, Hawaii 110
Kalapauahiole 18
Kalauao 20
Kaleiheana 51, 55-56, 105, 111, 112, 114-116
Kaleimakalii, ancestress in Luluka family 22

Kaleimakalii, daughter of Kalaikane of Kukuilolo 22
Kaleinakauhane [Leilono] 95
Kalei o Kamehameha, epithet of Alexander Liholiho 164; *See also* Kamehameha IV
Kalelealuaka 99
Kalelemauli 53
Kalena 97
Kaleohano 145, 154
Kalepolepo 3
Kalia 49, 89, 92
Kalihi 45, 95
Kalilikauoha 86
Kaliliki 110, 122, 133-134, 169-171
Kaliokalani 168
Kaloa 6, 9, 11, 52-53, 99, 100
Kalohelani, epithet of Victoria Kamamalu 164; *See also* Kamamalu, Victoria
Kaloko 110
Kalua 82
Kaluahinenui (Kahamaluihi) 167-168
Kaluahole 92, 169
Kaluakoi 47
Kaluaokau 70
Kaluhiapawa 48
Kama 46, 47
Kamaalaea 10, 107, 109
Kamahauluae 7-9, 19
Kamaholelani 79, 82
Kamaile 97
Kamakaeha [Liliuokalani] 163-164
Kamakaeheikuli 6, 53
Kamakaeheikuli, *kaikuahine* of Papa, 110, 115
Kamakahelei 15
Kamakahiki 54
Kamakahiki, Ana Waiakea 147
Kamakahiki, Lazarus 147
Kamakahonu 110, 116, 139, 143, 146
　Kamehameha's residence at 117-123
Kamakahukilani 19, 53, 141
Kamakaimoku 6, 52-53
Kamakaiouli 164
Kamakanuiahailono 47
Kamakau, Samuel 105, 141
Kamalalawalu 100, 129
Kamalo 9, 17, 19
Kamaloo 19
Kamamalu 53, 59, 70, 143, 152

191

Kamamalu, Victoria (Kalohelani, Kiheahealani) 161 ff.
  birth and infancy 161-164
  death 175
  named Kiheahealani 171
  in Royal School 167-168
  trip to Hawaii 169-172
  trip to Maui 168
Kamananui 98
Kamanawa 11, 69, 92
Kamani 98
Kamano 111
[Kamano] Hiiakanoholae Point 110
Kamanuwai 68, 92
Kamaua 115
Kamauawahine 53
Kamauleule (Boki Kamauleule) 19, 145, 147-148, 153, 157
Kamaunu, N. 148
Kameeiamoku 11, 69, 70
Kamehaikana (Haumea) 44
Kamehameha 153
Kamehameha (or Lunalilo), son of Kamehameha I; *See* Kekuaiwa
Kamehameha I (Note: The following references directly concern Kamehameha but do not include every mention of him: 3, 4, 6, 7-10, 18, 33, 49-50, 66, 88, 152, 159)
  acquires Kauai 79-83
  activities in Honolulu 68-70
  affair with Kaneikapolei 7, 49
  ancestry 53, 99
  breach with Kau chiefs 13-15
  canoeing 13, 131-133
  children 15, 33, 53, 70, 147
  council in Honolulu 81
  council at Kamakahonu 123
  farm at Kuahewa 114
  has *kapu noho* 59
  houses: Honolulu 64, 66, 69, 91
    Kalakee 110
    Kamakahonu 117-121
    Waikiki 17
  incidents in Kona 127-129, 139-140
  inherits *kapu wohi* 52-53
  at *kapu loulu* ceremonies 33, 35, 37-38
  returns to Hawaii 103-107
  surfing 8, 133-134, 135, 137
  synopsis of rise to power 15-16

Kamehameha II; *See* Liholiho
Kamehameha III (Kauikeaouli) 42, 50, 127, 143-159, 161-168, 171, 174
Kamehameha IV (Alexander Liholiho) 42, 69, 163, 164
Kamehameha V (Lot Kapuaiwa Kamehameha) 69, 163, 164, 177
Kamehamehanui 53, 95, 100
Kamehameha's return to Hawaii 103-107
Kamoakupa 70; *See also* Kamehameha I, children
Kamoiliili 92, 94
Kamokupanee 91
Kamokupanee, epithet of Kamehameha I 55; *See also* Kamehameha I
"Ka Moʻolelo Hawaii" 141, 166
Kamoonohu; *See* Kahakuhaakoi
Kanahoahoa 18
Kanaina 137, 146
kanaka no mau haʻalelea 42
Kanalu, kahuna class of 39
Kanaueue Point 132
Kaneiakama 26, 29
Kaneiakama, name given to John Papa Ii, 26-27
Kaneikaheilani 53
Kaneikapolei 6-8, 49
Kaneikauaiwilani 52
Kaneikaulanaula 18, 47
Kaneikoleamoku 45
Kanekoa 66
Kanelaau 120
Kaneloa in Waikiki 69
Kaneohe 76
Kanepaiki 66, 101, 153
Kanepililua 19
Kanepuniu 23
Kanewai 70
Kaniakapueo 30
Kanihonui 50-51, 88
[Kaniu]; *See* Kaheiheimalie
Kaniukahi 53, 86
Kanoa heiau in Hilo 137, 160
Kaoaopa in Honolulu 23, 29, 53, 58, 59, 82, 86, 89, 91, 104
Kaohe 171
Kaoleioku 7, 59, 66, 81, 92, 124, 146
Kaomi 147
Kaoo, medical kahuna 48
Kaoo of Wailuku, Maui 172

192

Kaoo, wife of Kuihelani 100
Kaopua 18, 107
Kapaa 135
Kapaakea (person) 163, 166
Kapaakea (place) 94
Kapaehala 69
Kapahu 154
Kapakai, Kokoiki 3
Kapakuhaili, H. K. [Hakaleleponi, Kalama] 105, 143, 152, 174
Kapalaau 154-155
Kapalama 68, 69, 75, 95
Kapalauauai 99
Kapaliiuka 172
Kapalilua in Kona 13, 110, 168, 171
Kapaliokamoa 172
Kapapakolea 95
kapapa ulua; See *kapu loulu* rites
Kapapoko 59, 66
Kapau 147
Kapauhi 88, 92
Kapaulapulu 105
Kapena Falls 168
Kapo 47, 81
Kapohakukikeke 94
Kapohonau 110
Kapoo 141
Kapoukahi 17
Kapua, Hawaii 169, 171
Kapua in Waikiki 51
[Kapuaiwa]; See Haku o Hawaii *and* Kamehameha V
Kapueokahi, Hana 172
kapu hoʻomahanahana; See *kapu loulu* rites
Kapukaki 95
Kapule, Deborah Haakulou [Kekaihaakulou] 145
Kapulena 92
Kapulikoliko [daughter of Peleuli], foster child of Piipii 59
kapu loulu rites 33, 35-45
 ʻ*aha* of Hoowilimoo 39, 43
 ʻ*aha* of Hulahula 39, 43
 haku ʻohiʻa 42-43
 hono 43-44
 kaʻi malo 44-45
 kapapa ulua 43
 kapu hoʻomahanahana 45
 kauila nui 35-38, 39, 41-42
 kuili 43

kapu moe 11, 51-52, 95, 159
Kapuna 32
Kapunahou 70
Kapuni 92
kapu noho 28, 59
kapu ʻohiʻa 77
kapu sticks 11, 41, 58-59, 89, 91
kapu wohi 51-53, 153
kapuo stick; See kapu sticks
kapus, chiefs' 22, 51-52, 58, 59
 observance of 11, 28, 51-52, 89
 prophecy of overthrow of 152-153
kapus, gods'
 ending of 157
 observance of 95, 104, 160
kapus, violations and punishments 22, 23, 35, 43, 59-61, 101
Kapuukolo 94, 148, 169
Kauakahiakuaanaauakane 52
Kauanonoula 64
Kauaua a Mahi 19, 53
Kauhiakama 120, 129
Kauhiwaewaeono 141, 146
Kauhola 134
Kauikeaouli; See Kamehameha III
Kauiki (person) 120
Kauiki (place) 172
Kauila 108
kauila nui ceremony; See *kapu loulu* rites
Kaukaha in Napali, Kauai 81
Kaukaopua, the sea of Ewa 98
Kaukini 172
Kaukuna Kahekili, son of Peleuli and foster child of Piipii 59, 95, 153-155
Kaulainamoku 23
Kaulana fishpond 132
Kaulapohu 83
Kaulunae 53
Kauluwai 4
Kauluwela kapu 72
Kaumaea, Kau 169
Kaumakapili 92
Kaumakapili Church 92
Kaumalumalu 115
Kaumualii 15, 16, 79-83, 139, 166
Kaunakakai, Capt. 107
Kaupe 107, 111, 113
Kauukualii 164
Kauwalua 95
Kauwamoa 95

193

Kawa 87
Kawaiahao 54, 92
Kawaiahao Church 147
Kawaihae 4, 17, 19, 59, 70, 109, 131, 132, 135, 143, 149, 158, 169, 171-172
Kawaihapai 98
Kawaihoa at Maunalua 108-109, 113
Kawaihoolana in Manoa 158
Kawailoa 98
Kawaimomona 132
Kawaiolaloa 68
Kawaluna 121
Kawehewehe 17, 92
Kawelo 76-77
Kawiwi 97
Kawiwi stronghold [pu'u kaua] 97
Keaa 8
Keaau, Hawaii 14
Keaau, Oahu 98
Keahia 94
Keahumoa 97
Keakaakipoo 19
Keaka a Mulehu 7, 19
Keakamahana 6, 19, 52
Keaka, wife of Alapai and of Luluka 3-9, 17, 19
Keakealanikane 19, 22
Keakealaniwahine 4, 6, 19, 45, 52, 129, 138
 as ruler of Hawaii 159-160
Kealaehu trail 120
Kealakehe 110
Kealakekua 4, 46, 171
Keauhou 132, 134, 171
Keauhulihuli 64
Keawakaheka 132
Keawaula 98
Keawawahie 98
Keawe (Keawe i Kekahialiiokamoku) 52, 99, 138, 159
Keawe a Heulu 7, 8, 11, 70, 117
Keawe a Mahi 117
Keaweamauhili 7, 13
Keawe i Kekahialiiokamoku (Keawe) 52, 99, 138, 159
Keaweiwi 172
Keawekolohe; See Hoomakaukau Keawekolohe
Keawekuikekaai 22
Keaweopala 4
Keaweopu 81, 123

Keawepoepoe 19, 53
Keeaumoku, brother of Kaahumanu ma; See Keeaumokuopio
Keeaumoku, father of Kaahumanu ma; See Keeaumoku Papaiahiahi
Keeaumokunui (Keeaumoku) 52-53, 99
Keeaumokuopio (Kahanui, Keeaumoku) [Kahekili Keeaumoku] 53, 106
Keeaumoku Papaiahiahi (Keeaumoku) 14, 19, 33, 37, 38, 51, 53, 70, 100, 141, 163
Keei 4, 13, 134
Keelikolani 147, 153, 155, 177
Kehualele 99
Keikipuipui heiau 110, 117, 133
Keimolaaupalau a Keeaumoku 19
Keinohoomanawanui 99
Kekaha, Hawaii 122, 132
Kekaha, Kauai 53
[Kekaihaakulou] Kapule, Deborah Haakulou 145
Kekakau 134
Kekaulike 53, 100, 141
Kekauluohi 119
Kekauluohi (person); See Kekauluohi o Mano
Kekauluohi o Mano 50, 53, 120, 148, 153, 155, 159, 161-166, 174
Kekauonohi 50, 89, 99, 100, 159, 164
Kekela, a man 81
Kekela, a woman 50
Kekelaokalani 52-53, 99
Kekoena 22
ke 'kua hana 124
Kekuaipiia; See Namahana, Lydia
Kekuaiwa; See Moses Kekuaiwa
Kekuaiwa (or Lunalilo) Kamehameha, son of Kamehameha I, 33, 59, 69, 70, 91, 106, 164
Kekuanaoa, David Kamehameha 155
Kekuanaoa, Mataio 47, 69, 91, 139, 145-149, 153, 154-157, 161-168, 174, 177
 death 175, 177
 takes Kinau to wife 47, 150, 193
 takes Pauahi to wife 146-147
Kekuaokalani 18, 59, 82, 92, 124, 139-140
Kekuaokalani (Kuihelani) 69
Kekuapanio 155
Kekuapoi [Kekuapoiula] 17, 18
[Kekuapoiula] Kekuapoi 17, 18
Kekuhaupio 9, 10, 13, 66

Kekuiapoiwa (Kekuiapoiwanui) 4, 52-53, 99
Kekuiapoiwa II 4, 6, 53, 99
[Kekuiapoiwa, mother of Keopuolani]; See Liliha Kekuiapoiwa
Kekuiapoiwanui (Kekuiapoiwa) 4, 52-53, 99
Kekumanoha 53, 61, 91, 100, 141, 146
Kekuolelo 99
Keliiahonui, Aaron 145, 164
Keliialaalahoolaawai pool 59
Keliimaikai 33, 59, 70, 81, 92, 94, 124, 140
Kemono 145
Keohokalole 8, 163
Keokoi 153
Keolonahihi 6, 134
Keomaka, A. 174
Keoneula 69, 95
Keoni Ana (John Young II) 164, 172, 174
Keopu 114
Keopuka 132
Keopuolani 15, 33, 35, 51, 52, 59, 89, 152
Keoua 137
Keoua, father of Kamehameha I; See Keoua Kupuapaikalani
Keoua (Keoua Lelepali, Lelia Byrd) 66, 85, 103-107, 113, 120, 128
Keoua Kuahuula 14, 15, 37
Keoua Kupuapaikalani 3-6, 53
Keoua Lelepali; See Keoua
Kepaalani 132
Kepulu 4
Kewai breeze 171
Kewalo 85
Kiha a Piilani 99
Kihawahine 44, 91
Kiheahealani, epithet of Victoria Kamamalu 171; See also Kamamalu, Victoria
Kihei 81
Kiholo 120; See also Luahinewai
ki'i kino 'ie, wicker-covered remains of Liloa and Lonoikamakahiki 155
Kiilaweau 146
Kikaha 92
Kikihale 91-92, 94, 95
Kilauea 145, 146
Kilauea crater 147, 169
Kiloa at Kealakekua 171
Kinau, daughter of Kamehameha I; See Kinauwahine

Kinau [Kahoanoku Kinau], son of Kamehameha I 33, 37, 49-50, 89
Kinauwahine (Kinau) 53, 59, 69, 70, 148-155, 161-163, 171, 174, 177
  becomes premier 159
  becomes wife of Kekuanaoa 147, 150
  death 163, 164
  illnesses 163-164
Kini 169
Kinopu 49, 51
Kiope 110, 133
Kipapa 28, 99
Kiwalao 6, 7, 9, 11, 13, 14, 15, 52, 140, 152
Kiwalao, Ii's attendant 20
Koapapaa in Hamakua 79
Kohanaiki 110
Kohia 137
Kohokoho 95
Koholaloa 63
ko'ie'ie 63
Koihala 129
Koiuiu 95
Koko 94
Kokoiki 3
Koleamoku 123
Kolekole 27, 97, 99
Kolo 171
Kolowalu 92
konane 63, 67
Konia 163
ko'oko'o prayer 60
Kou 53, 54, 104, 105, 107, 143
Kuaana 19, 22
Kuaena (Malamaekeeke) 19, 83, 111, 113-115, 139
Kuahewa 114, 117
kuahu altars 72, 75, 123, 157
Kuaikua stream 99
Kuakini; See Kuakini, John Adams
Kuakini, John Adams 30, 53, 81, 95, 101, 161-162, 166, 167, 177
Kuakuaka 92
Kualalua 59
Kualii, a chief of Oahu 95
Kualii, a paddler 132
Kuamookane 104
Kuanolu voyage 145
kuapala 52, 58
Kuapola 72
Kuaua 46, 47

195

Kuekaunahi stream 92
Kuhia 123
Kuhonua wind 122
Kuihelani 18, 94-95, 101, 105
Kuihelani (Kekuaokalani) 69
Kuike 111
kuili; See *kapu loulu* rites
Kukailimoku (Kaili) 58, 95, 101, 104-105
Kukaipahu 172
Kukaniloko 53, 98, 99
   puʻuhonua 138
Kukehi stream 97
Kukiiahu 95
Kukuihaele 47
Kukuilolo 22, 23, 24
Kukuiopae 171
Kukuipuka 32
Kukuluaeo 82, 89
Kulailua company 69, 91, 101
Kuloloia 168
Kuloloia (person) 100
Kuloloia (place) 59, 100
Kumaaiku 53
Kumaipo trail, Oahu 97
Kumelewai 20, 23, 28, 45, 85
Kunia 23, 97
Kuokoa 98
Kupahu 76
Kupapaulau at Waikele 76
Kupikipikio 105
kuʻula shrines 26
Kuwahine 29

L

Laanui, Gideon 135-136, 145
Ladd, W. N. 120
Laeahi; See Leahi
Lahaina 17, 81, 106, 107, 109, 121, 122, 135, 147, 153, 158, 164, 166, 172; See also Lele
Lahainaluna School 158, 159
Laie, Koolauloa 50, 70
Lalaione 35
lands, apportioning of
   Hawaii 13-14, 70
   Maui 70
   Oahu 20, 26, 69-70
Lanihau 128
lapaiki drum 137
Laplace, Capt. 166

lauʻauʻa, gamblers 68
Laupahoehoe 134
Leahi 33, 35, 51, 55, 70, 92, 104
Leepoko Point [Puaena Point] 98
Lehua 111
[Leilono] Kaleinakauhane 95
lei o mano 14
Lele 106, 109; See also Lahaina
Leleahana 91
lele altars 35, 39, 45, 56, 157
lelea prayer 58-59
Leleiohoku 145, 164
lele kawa 14
Leleo 95
Lelepali; See *Keoua*
Lelepua 99
Lelia Byrd; See *Keoua*
lemu hao; See *ʻokolehao*
Lepekaholo 92
Liberty Hall; See Lepekaholo
Liholiho, Alexander; See Kamehameha IV
Liholiho (Kamehameha II) (Note: The following references directly concern Liholiho but do not include every mention of him: 23, 29-30, 45, 51, 53-56, 58-59, 70, 86-87, 99, 113, 123, 127-128, 139-140, 152, 157)
   birth and infancy 15
   instructed in government 129
      in *kapu loulu* ceremonies 37-38
   learns drumming (*kaʻeke, kaʻekeʻeke*) 137
   learns English 86, 128
   religious duties 123, 129, 137-139
   returns to Hawaii 104-107
Lihue, Oahu 53
Liliha Kekuiapoiwa (Liliha, Kekuiapoiwa Liliha) 15, 52-53, 91, 99-100, 152
Liliha, mother of Keopuolani; See Liliha Kekuiapoiwa
Liliha, wife of Boki 159
Lilikoi 172
Lilinoe, A. 148
[Liliuokalani] Kamakaeha 163-164
Liloa 47
Liloa, wicker-covered remains of 155
Loeau 164
Lokoea pond 98
loku 63-64, 91, 92
Lolokui 101
Lolomauna wind 152

Lono 72, 73, 75
Lonoakai 105
Lonoapii 99
Lonohiwa 67
Lonoikahaupu 53
Lonoikamakahiki, wicker-covered remains of 155
Lonomaaikanaka 52
Lonomakua 60
Lonopuha 45
Lot [Kapuaiwa], son of Kinau and Kekuanaoa; See Kamehameha V
Luaehu, Maui 168
lua fighting, schools for 68-69, 101
Luahine 19
Luahinewai (Kiholo) 171
Luakaha 32, 153
luakini 35, 39, 45, 70, 72, 75-76, 157, 160
Lualewa, epithet of Liholiho 55; See also Liholiho (Kamehameha II)
Lualualei 23
Luheluhe 120
Luia 81
Luluka 4, 6, 7, 9, 17, 19
Luluka family 18, 19, 22, 23, 51, 94
Lunalilo [King] 50, 163, 164
Lunalilo, son of Kamehameha I; See Kekuaiwa
Luwahine, Ioane (John Rives) 86-87, 128, 143
Luwahine [Luahine], epithet of Kaahumanu 86; See also Kaahumanu (Elizabeth)

M

Maaa breeze 109, 121
[Maalaea] Kamaalaea 10, 107, 109
Maeaea 98
Mahaiula, Hawaii 110, 135
Mahiki 158
Mahiki Church 158
Mahu 97
Mahuka 171
maika
  rolling 63, 66-67
  sites 66, 91, 97, 99, 106
  stone 66
Maikuli, Mr. 127
Mailekini heiau 17
Makaha 97, 98
maka halau 121

Makahauka 97
Makahiki; See also Gods, *makahiki* ceremonies and activities 70-76
  restrictions 72, 75, 115
  taxes 121
Makaho 63, 85
Makamakaole 64
Makanimoku (Albatross) 88, 106
Makapala in Kohala, Hawaii 50
Makapuu, Oahu 94
Makapuu pool, Maui 172
Makaula 132
Makea (Punaaikoae) 44
Makiki 92, 145
Makua 98
Mala 172
Malailua, epithet of Nahiolea 146; See also Nahiolea
Malamaekeeke; See Kuaena
Malamanui 97, 98
Malanai wind 177
Maliu 134
Maloi 66
malo of bird feathers 28
Mamala 82, 88, 105
Manana 97
Manoa 68, 92, 158
Manuia 53, 86, 104, 111, 145, 154
Maoloha 19, 22, 59, 85
Marin, Paula 94, 95, 120
Marshall 128
mat, bearers of chiefs' 11, 23
Maunaloa 47
Maunalua 94, 108
Maunauna 97
maunu 8, 124
mausoleum at Pohukaina 143, 158
Mauumae 94
medical kahunas 33, 46-48
medical training 46-47
medical treatment 47-48, 115
Meek, John 92, 177
meeting of Kamehameha and Kaumalii 81-83
Mela 20
men's houses (*hale mua*) 46, 58, 64, 75, 111, 119, 121
Miela 120
Miki 33
Mililani 169, 172

197

Milu 47
Moae breeze 98
Moanalua 70
model ships (*moku hoʻoholoholo*) 29-30
Moehonua 49
Moiliili Kamoiliili 92, 94
Mokaulele 4
Mokuaikaua 143, 175
Mokuaikaua (place) 100
Mokualoha, epithet of Kaahumanu 20; *See also* Kaahumanu (Elizabeth)
Mokuhinia 109
moku hoʻoholoholo (model ships) 29-30
Mokuleia 97, 98
Mokuohai 14, 15
Mokuola in Hilo 171
mole hao; See ʻokolehao
Molokini 109
Moluhi 48
months, names of Hawaiian 72
Moo 37
Mookini heiau 160
Moo Ku order of kahunas 39, 42
Moo Lono order of kahunas 39
Moses Kekuaiwa 163, 164, 166
mua; See men's houses
mumps 163-164; *See also* epidemics
Mumuku wind 107

N

Naahu 91
Naaimakolu 124
Naeole 3
Nahienaena 147, 153, 169, 174
Nahikilalo 97
Nahili 53, 111, 116, 123
Nahiolea 19, 139, 141
  death of 146
"na hono o Piilani" 109
Nahoounauna 107, 111, 113
Nahuina 32, 100
Naihe [Haiha], son of Keawe a Heulu 81, 83, 117, 153
Naihe, son of Lonohiwa 67, 68
Naihekukui 10
naio; See sandalwood
Naipuawa 115
Nakaiwahine 53
Namahana 91
Namahana, Lydia (Piia, Kekuaipiia) 53, 141, 145

Namahana, mother of Kaahumanu *ma* 53, 91, 100
Namahana, mother of Kahekili Kaumualii 82
Namahoe 69
Namakaeha 61
Namakaimi 68
Namakeha 15, 16
Nanakuli 29
Nanamake 87
Nanaulu 70; *See also* Kamehameha I, children
Naoa, a haole 87
Naohaku 134
Napali, Kauai 81
Napeha 20, 95
Napuauki 68
Napuu 138
Nawaakoali 101
Nawaawaa 132
Nawelu, M. 148
net making, Molokai 106
Niauloa 30
niʻaupiʻo chiefs 73, 75
Nihoa in Honolulu 64, 166
niho palaoa 14
Niihau 135
Niolopa 68
Niu 109
Niuhelewai 68
Niumalu, Kona 110
noʻa
  used figuratively 101, 155, 166
  used in game 64
Noiku, canoe 13, 41
Northwest people 127
Nounou 83
Nuuanu 30, 68, 69, 92, 145, 146, 153
"Nuuanu" (card game) 127
Nuuanu Pali 32, 50, 92

O

Oahunui 99
Oana 87
O'Cain (*Ogena*) 88, 106-107
Ogena; See O'Cain
[Ohikilolo] Nahikilalo 97
Okaka guards 149; *See also* guards
ʻokolehao (*lemu hao, mole hao*) 107, 128
ʻokuʻu 16, 33, 46, 51; *See also* epidemics

Olaa 14, 83
Olohana (John Young) 70, 143
['*olohe*] robbers 97
Ololupe 124
ololupe god 123
'*olopu* adz 42
Olowalu 109
Ooma 109, 110
Opaeula stream 98
Opukahaia, Henry 15, 46, 157
Opunui 83
opu tower 56
Oulu 11
Oven House (Hale Umu) 35

P

Paaiea fishpond 132
Paakonia 26
Paalaa land and stream 98
Paalua 153
Pahia 14
Pahoa (person) 26
Pahoa (place) 70
Pahoauka 27
Pahoehoe in Kaumalumalu 115
pahu drum 137
Pahulemu; *See* Wanaoa
pahu pulo'ulo'u 58
Paia (person) 19
Paia (place) 11
Paiahaa, Kau 169
Paiaina house 150, 151
Paiea 134
Paieie 3
Pakaalana *pu'uhonua* 138
Pakaka 82, 88, 91
Pakaka, Kimo (James Robinson) 91
Paka stream 99
Paki 143, 163-164
palaoa, niho 14
Palena 19
Paliiki 92
Paliiki in Punahoa, Hilo 92
Palolo 94
Pa o Umi 13, 110, 117, 121
Papa (house) 59, 110
Papa at Kapalilua 171
Papaenaena heiau 33
Papa Ii; *See* Ii, Papa
Papa Ii, Daniel 22, 23, 24, 137

Papa Ii, John; *See* Ii, John Papa
Papa's ship 108-110
Papaikou 134
Papakanene 143
Papakanene, Mokuaikaua 175
[Papakolea] Kapapakolea 95
Papalima 101
Papaula in Honuaula 114, 121
Papawai 109
Pau 70
Pauahi 169, 172
Pauahi [Bernice] 163-166, 174
  home 175
Pauahi, daughter of Kaoleioku 146-147
Pauoa stream 92
Paupalai 99
Paupauwela 97
Pawaa 19, 92, 94, 155
Peapea 95
Pelekane 109
peleleu fleet 15, 17, 70, 92, 105, 124
Peleula in Honolulu 46, 68, 120
Peleuli 33, 154
Pihanakalani 175
Piia; *See* Namahana, Lydia
Piianio 92
Piihonua 134
Piikea 99
Piilaniwahine 99
Piipii 59
Piliamoo 99
Piopio 89
Poaeaewahine 19
[Poamoho] Poo a Moho stream 98
Pohakea 23, 27, 97
[Pohakukikeke] Kapohakukikeke 94
Pohukaina house and enclosure 143, 145,
  146, 148, 158, 159, 161
Pokai 97, 98
Polelewa 92
Poo a Moho stream 98
Poopoo 92
prayers, texts of 37, 42, 123; *See also*
  chants
  '*amama* prayer 35, 37, 38, 44, 45
  ko'oko'o prayer 60
  lelea prayer 58, 59
Pua (Puanui) 18, 47, 150
Puaa, North Kona 133
Puaaiki 82

199

Puaaliilii 17, 69, 92
Puaaloa 3
Puaauka 114
[Puaena Point] Leepoko Point 98
Pualoalo at Peleula 92, 120
Puamana 171
Puanui (Pua); See Pua
Puehuehu 63
Pueohulunui 97, 99
puhene 64, 67
puhenehene 63, 67
Pulee 98
Punaaikoae (Makea) 44
Punahoa, Hilo 92, 134
Punakou, Molokai 109
Punaluu heiau in Kau 137, 160
Punaluu in Koolauloa 70
Punaluu, Waipio, Oahu 99
Puueo 134
puʻuhonua 138
Puu in Holualoa 6, 134
[*puʻu kaua*] Kawiwi stronghold 97
Puukohola heiau 15, 17
Puuloa 76, 97
Puunahawale 99
Puunau, Maui 158
Puu o Kaloa 120
Puu o Kapolei 27, 29, 97
Puuolai, Maui 109
Puu o Manoa 92
Puuone trail, Hawaii 169
Puuopae 24
Puupueo in Manoa 69, 92, 145, 147
Puupuu 30
Puuwaawaa 132
Puwahanui gulch in Nuuanu 153

R

Rahab 175
Richards, William 127, 164, 166
Rives, John (Ioane Luwahine) 86-87, 128, 143
robbers [*ʻolohe*] 97
Robinson, James (Pakaka, Kimo) 91
rope making 68
Royal School 164-168
rum 120, 128; See also intoxicants
Russians in Hawaii 79, 145

S

sandalwood (*ʻiliahi, naio*) 87-88, 94, 106, 113, 128, 139, 146, 147, 153, 157
[*Santa Rosa*]; See ships, Argentinian (Spanish) ships
ship building 64, 101, 113
ship models 29-30
ships
  Albatross (*Makanimoku*) 88, 106
  Apuakehau 108-109
  [*Argentina*] a man-of-war 128-129
  Argentinian (Spanish) ships 128-129
  Armetise, l' 166
  Enepalai (*Isabella*) 88, 106-107
  Forester (*Kaahumanu*) 128
  Hooikaika 164
  Isabella (*Enepalai*) 88, 106-107
  Kaahumanu (*Forester*) 128
  Kaailipoa 108-109
  Kaaloa 94
  Kalaikini 172
  Kamehameha 153
  Kekauluohi 119
  Keokoi 153
  Keoua (*Keoua Lelepali, Lelia Byrd*) 66, 85, 103-107, 113, 120, 128
  Keoua Lelepali; See *Keoua*
  Lelia Byrd; See *Keoua*
  Makanimoku (*Albatross*) 88, 106
  Marshall 128
  Namahana 91
  O'Cain (*Ogena*) 88, 106-107
  Ogena (*O'Cain*) 88, 106-107
  Paalua 153
  Papa's ship 108-110
  Pauahi 169, 172
  [*Santa Rosa*]; See ships, Argentinian (Spanish) ships
  Uranie, l' 143
  Vincennes 155
shrines (*Kuʻula*) 26
sites, 64, 66-68, 91-92, 97, 106
  for braiding rope 68
  for foot races 67, 91, 92
  for gun drilling 66, 91
  for indoor amusements (*loku*) 64, 91, 92
  for *maika* rolling 66, 91, 97, 99, 106
  for spear throwing 66, 91
smallpox 169, 174; See also epidemics
Solomon, Mr. 109
sorcery 8, 124-125
Spanish (Argentinian) ships 128-129

spears
 training in use of 54-55, 66
 use of 10, 13, 20, 69
spitoon, bearers of chiefs' 11, 18, 23, 113
Stangenwald, Dr. "Not-a-Minute-Lost" 66
stone slinging 11
stone throwing 14, 76
sugar cane growing 145, 147
Sumner, W. 108
surfing 109, 166; See also surfs
 board 20, 63, 133-134
 body 135
 canoe 63, 82, 133, 135-136
 lele waʻa 133, 134
 surfboard 135
surfs 51, 63, 82, 110, 133-135; See also surfing
Swan and Clifford Building (Hale Mahoe) 64

T

tattoo 9, 137
trails
 of Hawaii 111, 114, 117, 119-120, 121, 128, 169-170
 of Oahu 27, 29, 89-99, 120, 143, 157
Tyerman, Daniel 143

U

Ualakaa 68, 69
ʻukeke 55
Ukoa pond 98
Ukumehame 107
Ulaino, Maui 172
Ulakoheo 66
Ulakua 63, 82, 88, 153
Uluhaha 18
Uluhua 87
Ulukou 92
Ululani 7, 8
Ulumaheihei [son of Kameeiamoku] 81
uma 63, 67
Umi 20, 114, 134
Umukanaka pond 89
Uo 109
Uranie, l' 143

V

vaccinations for smallpox 169, 171
Vancouver 106, 139
Vincennes 155

W

Waaakekupua 92
Wahaula heiau in Puna 137, 160
Wahiawa, Oahu 97, 100, 138
Wahinealii, Abel 91, 147
Wahinepio; See Kahakuhaakoi
Waiakaaiea 98
Waiakea, Hilo 14, 134
Waiakemi 92
Waiakoae 44
Waialae land and stream 70, 92, 94
Waialee in Koolauloa 23, 24, 108
Waialua 97, 98, 99, 100
Waianae 23, 26, 27, 97, 108, 135, 153
Waianaeuka 97
Waiau 97
Waiaula 92
Waiawa, Ewa 85, 97
Waiea 4
Waihee, Maui 135, 168
Waihoikaea 83
 used figuratively in chants 157
waiiki treatment 47-48
Waikahalulu 63, 81, 83
Waikakalaua stream 99
Waikele 32, 33, 76-77
Waikiki 17, 49, 51, 55, 63, 68, 69, 70, 91-92, 104, 105, 135, 154-155, 174
Wailua, Kauai 83, 135, 138
Wailua, Maui 47
Wailuku 135, 153
Waimalu 20, 33, 95
Waimanalo, Ewa, Oahu 29, 97, 98
Waimano 97
Waimea, Hawaii 158
Waimea, Kauai 129, 135
Waimea in Koolauloa, Oahu 135
Wainee, Maui 172
Waioahukini in Kau 11, 70
Waiohinu, Kau 169
Waiolama 3
Waioli 135
Waipa 105
Waipio, Ewa, Oahu 19, 23, 28, 33, 76-77, 83
Waipio in Hamakua 47, 134, 158
Waipunaula at Kealakekua 171
Waipunauliki in Napoopoo 116
Wakea 39, 160
Walinuu 44
Wanaoa (Kalaikane, Pahulemu) 19, 20, 22, 23

Waoala 147, 153
Wawae 9, 17, 19
winds
  Alahonua 122
  Apaa 172
  Eka 110, 121
  Hoolua 122
  Kaiaulu 98
  Kewai 171
  Kuhonua 122
  Lolomauna 152
  Maaa 109, 121
  Malanai 177
  Moae 98
  Mumuku 107
Winship, Jonathan 88
Winship, Nathan 81, 88
women's houses (*hale 'aina*) 64, 66, 119, 120, 121
Wyllie, R. C. 174-175

Y

yam garden, Kamehameha's 88, 92
Young, John (Olohana) 70, 143
Young, John II (Keoni Ana) 164, 172, 174